The Image of the Poet
in Ovid's *Metamorphoses*

Publication of this volume has been made possible, in part, through the generous support and enduring vision of WARREN G. MOON.

The Image of the Poet
in Ovid's *Metamorphoses*

Barbara Pavlock

THE UNIVERSITY OF WISCONSIN PRESS

The University of Wisconsin Press
1930 Monroe Street, 3rd Floor
Madison, Wisconsin 53711-2059

www.wisc.edu/wisconsinpress/
3 Henrietta Street
London WC2E 8LU, England

5   4   3   2   1

Library of Congress Cataloging-in-Publication Data
Pavlock, Barbara.
  The image of the poet in Ovid's Metamorphoses / Barbara Pavlock.
      p.   cm.—(Wisconsin studies in classics)
  Includes bibliographical references and index.
  ISBN 978-0-299-23140-8 (hardcover: alk. paper)
    1. Ovid, 43 B.C.–17 or 18 A.D.—Criticism and interpretation.   2. Ovid,
43 B.C.–17 or 18 A.D. Metamorphoses.   I. Title.   II. Series.
PA6519.M9P385   2009
873´.01—dc22
2008040710

In memory of my father and mother,
  AUGUST and ESTHER PAVLOCK,
and my brother
  MARK

Contents

Acknowledgments

Ovid's *Metamorphoses* has played a major role in my intellectual life for more than a decade, sustaining me in painful as well as pleasant times. My understanding of this protean work has been deepened not only by many fine recent—and older—critical studies but also by conversations on Ovid with numerous fellow classicists. This book, however, has taken longer to complete than it ideally should have, in part because of events that were beyond my control. If I fail to express my thanks to everyone to whom I owe some debt of gratitude, I regret any such omission.

The late Charles Segal encouraged me to begin this book through his enthusiastic and discerning remarks about an article that I wrote on the Tereus episode. A portion of an early version of chapter 5, which began as an exploration of Ovid's exploitation of etymological plays in the Ulysses episode, was presented as a paper at the Cambridge Conference on Ancient Etymology in England in 2000. I am grateful to Francis Cairns, Robert Coleman, and Andreas Michalopoulos for their insightful remarks and to co-organizer Christos Nifadopoulos for his editorial comments on my paper for the published conference proceedings. The following scholars gave important help in oral discussions or in written comments on my manuscript at various stages of composition: Alessandro Barchiesi, Denis Feeney, Stephen Harrison, Niklas Holzberg, Frank Romer, and Marilyn Skinner. I owe Frank Romer a special debt of gratitude for generously offering advice and for obtaining from the library of the University of North Carolina at Chapel Hill a scan of the Lemire image of Ovid used for the cover of this book.

I also happily acknowledge other forms of assistance that helped bring this book to publication. My Lehigh colleague Scott Gordon and computing consultant Sandy Edmiston were unstintingly generous with their expertise in word processing matters. I also thank the staff of the library of the American Academy in Rome and of the Institute for Classical Studies at the University of London for making it easier to complete my research on Ovid. My thanks go as well to my editor Raphael Kadushin for supporting my work and to Adam Mehring for seeing it through the copyediting process to the printed page. Finally, I am grateful to Lehigh University for a Faculty Research Grant that enabled me to finish some work on Narcissus in Italy and for a Provost's Travel Grant that supported my trip to the Cambridge Conference on Ancient Etymology.

A portion of chapter 3 appeared as "Daedalus in the Labyrinth of Ovid's *Metamorphoses*," *Classical World* 92.2 (1998), 141–57.

A portion of chapter 5 appeared as "Ulysses' Exploitation of Etymological Puns in *Metamorphoses* 13," in *Etymologia: Studies in Ancient Etymology*, ed. Christos Nifadopoulos (Munster: Nodus Publikationen, 2003), 143–51.

A small section of chapter 5 entitled "Ulysses' Wounds in the Contest over the Arms of Achilles" is forthcoming in *Classical World* 102.2 (2009).

The text of the *Metamorphoses* used, unless otherwise noted, is W. S. Anderson, *Ovidius: Metamorphoses* (Leipzig: Teubner, 1977). The translations are my own. The text of the *Aeneid* used is R. A. B. Mynors, *P. Vergili Maronis Opera* (Oxford: Clarendon Press, 1985 [1969]). The translations are my own.

The Image of the Poet
in Ovid's *Metamorphoses*

Introduction

Ovid begins the *Metamorphoses* by explicitly stating his theme of transformation: "In nova fert animus mutatas dicere formas / corpora" ("My spirit impels me to speak about forms changed into new bodies" [1.1-2]). The governing principle of change is manifested most obviously in the metamorphoses of human bodies to lower forms of life.[1] But it also applies to "forms" in almost every sense in this inventive poem that sweeps widely from cosmogony to the supremacy of Rome under the rule of Augustus. Furthermore, as he announces the almost impossible scope of his project, Ovid implies a major paradoxical aspect of his poem: it is simultaneously lengthy (*perpetuum*) and polished (*deductum*).[2]

Major studies of Ovid have recently illuminated the importance of paradox in the *Metamorphoses*. On the level of style, Ovid employs paradox, along with puns and syllepsis, as a microcosmic version of the constant flux that is the very subject of the poem.[3] On the ontological level, the poet creates a dynamic of absent presence, especially in episodes where a character is motivated by a futile desire for a loved one.[4] Ovid even plays with the paradox of the poet as both bard who is delivering an oral performance to his "narratorial audience" and implied author who is clearly producing a text for a sophisticated readership.[5]

On the level of character, considerable critical attention has been paid to the particularly paradoxical figure of the weaver Arachne who in book 6 challenges Minerva to a contest and, incurring the goddess's anger, is transformed into a spider. Arachne shows that talent is not tied to class yet proves to be obtuse at interpreting the significance of the goddess's tapestry. On the one hand, this young woman of low social status, the daughter of a dyer, produces a work of the highest elegance

3

and refinement; on the other, she ignores the clear message in her divine opponent's weaving that mortals pay a heavy price for offending the gods.

This episode illustrates a tension between a "centripetal" pull toward a moral point of view consistent with epic as a high, "official" genre and a "centrifugal" pull toward empathy with the young woman as an artist and a victim of divine anger.[6] In spite of her hubris, Ovid to some extent identifies with Arachne whose weaving, as many scholars have observed, has strong affinities with his poem. My purpose here is to point out how Arachne may serve as a paradigm for other highly flawed characters who also, in paradoxical ways, function as surrogates for the poet.

In her behavior with Minerva, Arachne exhibits a surprising intransigence. Having angrily rebuffed the goddess in disguise as an old woman, she refuses to yield even when Minerva reveals herself (24–51). She makes no effort to spare the goddess's feelings when she weaves into her tapestry an allusion to a desecration of Minerva's own temple.[7] Vergil's brief but compelling account of the foolish Misenus in *Aeneid* 6 is but one of numerous examples in epic of the importance of observing the distinction between divine and human and of deferring to the gods. Playing on his conch, the trumpeter calls the gods to a contest and then pays for his hubris, for he is said to have been drowned by the sea god Triton (156–78). Vergil does not explain why Misenus challenged the gods to a musical contest but characterizes him as mad (*demens* [172]) to do so. Here, Arachne's impiety is bound up with a hubristic belief that her talent is, in effect, self-generated.[8] When Minerva transforms her into a spider, Arachne's fate is ironically apropos: the spider seems to weave from nothing but itself.[9]

Ovid's ekphrasis of Arachne's tapestry, however, shifts the focus away from moral criticism of a flawed individual. The aesthetic appeal of Arachne's work seems clear: its erotic subject matter of gods who adopt disguises in order to rape women is rendered through free-flowing scenes, with the settings sketched out in some detail and the characters marked by individualized features. The poet indeed exclaims that Envy could find no fault with her work ("non illud carpere Livor / possit opus" [129–30]).[10] As critics have observed, her tapestry is a graphic analogue of Ovid's loosely structured narrative emphasizing amorous subjects.[11] Arachne's weaving manifests a sophisticated aesthetic analogous to a Callimachean *carmen deductum*.[12] The human weaver thus shares Ovid's own preference for the refinement of the Hellenistic poet Callimachus.[13] Her tapestry, then, is a *mise en abyme* of the *Metamorphoses*, a "miniature model" mirroring much of the poem's content and illuminating ways by which the narrative operates.[14]

The poet, I believe, reinforces his affinity with Arachne by implying a literary analogue for Minerva's work as well. The material of the goddess's tapestry is arranged in a formal and balanced way. Its central scene represents her victory over Neptune in the contest for patronage of Athens, in the presence of all the Olympians, and each of the four corners contains a myth depicting the punishment of human impiety through metamorphosis into nonhuman form (70–102). Though clearly elegant, Minerva's weaving reflects a stylistic classicism and emanates with a sense of power and privilege that the poet of the *Metamorphoses* does not espouse. Both the aesthetics and the ideology represented by Minerva, however, are in accord with the *Aeneid*, as manifested in miniature form by the shield of Aeneas in book 8.

In Vergil's ekphrasis, the center scene depicting the battle of Actium and its aftermath (675–728) highlights Octavian, aided by Apollo, Neptune, Venus, and Minerva, against Marc Antony and Cleopatra, supported by the dog-headed god Anubis. Traditional, Olympian order validates Octavian and the Romans and brings down Cleopatra and her eastern forces. Surrounding scenes on the periphery reinforce the values embodied in the central panel. Like the punishments on Minerva's tapestry, they are represented in what appears to be a highly structured manner (though the shield, of course, has no corners), with the rescue of the Capitoline from attack by the Gauls on the top, the punishment of the conspirator Catiline, who is contrasted with the lawgiver Cato, in the underworld on the bottom, and exemplary scenes from the kingship and republican history on the facing sides.[15] Ovid thus suggests that Minerva's and Arachne's tapestries are microcosmic versions of two very different epic poems. By setting these two tapestries in opposition to each other here, the poet implies that the *Metamorphoses* unfolds in a dynamic tension with the *Aeneid*.

Even in her metamorphosed state Arachne embodies paradox. On the one hand, the spider endlessly weaves webs that are the product of automatic, mechanical impulses.[16] The spider's work, furthermore, elicits none of the individual acclaim awarded to the woman herself.[17] On the other hand, although Ovid states nothing specific about the nature of the spider's web here, earlier in the poem, the internal narrator Leuconoe compared the fineness of the net by which Vulcan caught Venus and Mars in adultery to the most delicate threads and to the spider's web (*aranea*) hanging from a wooden beam (4.178–79).[18]

To some extent, the image of the spider's web conveys the Hellenistic stylistic refinement that in general characterizes the tales of the daughters of Minyas in book 4.[19] Furthermore, although the woman pays the price for her hubris, Ovid suggests that even in her transformed state as a lowly spider she retains a symbolic defiance. For, by harking back to Leuconoe's narrative, the poet associates the spider's web not only with the artful cunning of Vulcan's trap but also with the story as narrated by a female who does not share Homer's emphasis in *Odyssey* 8 on the punishment that even a god must pay for adultery.[20] The spider's web in this poem is thus a paradoxical symbol, representing harmony through its symmetry but closely connected to females who represent centrifugal forces undermining traditional social norms.

By aligning himself with Arachne as artist and distancing himself from Minerva, Ovid raises questions about the fate of the poet and of his work as well. It does not appear that Arachne uses her weaving skills specifically in order to criticize the gods for assuming disguises to rape women. Whereas the goddess's tapestry conveys a strong message, the human weaver's does not. The brilliance of its design and the beauty of its execution appear to predominate over any moral underlying its content.[21] Yet Minerva not only transforms Arachne; she also destroys her tapestry.

Ovid's poem itself contains numerous amorous narratives likewise involving the gods (and their human equivalents) and potentially exposing them to ridicule. The poet in this episode thus implicitly situates himself in the position of Arachne vis-à-vis authoritarian powers and suggests that his own work is subject to such forces. However, in his epilogue at the end of book 15, Ovid boasts that his poem will be invulnerable to the "anger of Jupiter" ("Iovis ira" [871]). The *Metamorphoses*, of course, was spared the fate of Arachne's tapestry. But the poet himself did not escape the wrath of a "god" when he received the order of *relegatio* from Augustus, banishing him from Rome for the rest of his life.

In the five chapters that follow, I explore major characters who supplement Arachne's function as a surrogate for the poet. Although only Orpheus among them is a bard, the others in various ways perform activities that have analogues in the poetic sphere. They engage in a lament (Narcissus), deliver a powerful monologue (Medea), act as a dramatic storyteller (Achelous and Orpheus through his own surrogate narrator Venus), deliver a persuasive speech in competition (Ulysses), and, in the manner of Arachne, produce a material work that has a close affinity with the design of Ovid's epic (Daedalus).

Ovid connects each of these characters with social customs or institutions that represent the centripetal movement of epic in validating traditional mores and values. But the poet also moves in a centrifugal direction, for these characters blur boundaries, often hubristically, by undermining operative social norms and traditional antitheses between feminine and masculine, weak and strong, fluid and stable. Ovid further destabilizes central epic values through the ways by which these surrogates are connected to his poetics; he enacts problems related to the status of the image, the generation of plots, the matter of repetition, the opposition between refined and inflated epic style, the reliability of the narrative voice, and the relation between rhetoric and high epic style. Although he often appears to espouse a Hellenistic aesthetic, Ovid reveals through these surrogates a poetics governed by tensions, not least between traditional epic and the low genre of elegy. Ultimately, the principle of instability affects his poetics as well as his vision of the universe.

By limiting my analyses to these particular characters, I do not imply their exclusivity as representatives of the poet. Other prominent characters, to be sure, have programmatic significance. But they are not transgressive to the same degree through boundary violations that resonate on moral and ethical levels as well as in the aesthetic sphere. The Muse Calliope in book 5, for instance, produces a "miniature *carmen perpetuum*" on the rape of Proserpina, reflecting in particular Ovid's own tendency to employ embedded tales of metamorphosis and to explore the success or failure of communication.[22] Incorporating a variety of stories about metamorphosis, the Muse even appears to lend divine authority to the myths recounted by Ovid's own persona.[23]

Calliope, however, is in an important way an antithesis of Ovid as poet: along with her unnamed sister who dismissively summarizes the Pierides' story about the Giants' attempt to overthrow the gods, she is firmly on the side of Olympian authority. She acts in concert with her sister, who in the framing narrative with Minerva expresses outrage at the Pierides' challenge to the Muses (5.300–317) and then describes their metamorphosis into bats as punishment (664–78). Calliope's song incorporates similar punitive transformations: even a young child is turned into a newt, silenced for laughing at Ceres when the goddess was quenching her thirst (446–61). The Muses' transformation of the

Pierides aligns them primarily with Minerva against Arachne in book 6 rather than with Ovid. Although the poet incorporates stories about the powers of the gods to exact punishment, he by no means serves as their mouthpiece.

Pythagoras in book 15 also functions to some extent as a surrogate for the poet. Fundamentally, his speech provides a quasi-philosophical underpinning for Ovid's stories of transformation through his doctrine of metempsychosis. It does so, moreover, in a manner recalling major literary precedents for Ovid's poem: Ennius's Pythagorean dream of Homer explaining his metempsychosis in the *Annales*, Lucretius's recollection of that same vision in *De rerum natura 1*, and Vergil's account of the soul through Anchises' lecture to his son in the underworld passage of *Aeneid 6*.[24] Ovid employs Pythagoras in part as a means of suggesting his own place in the tradition of philosophic-political poetry, analogous to the position of Rome in the world.[25] But he does not engage in a deep exploration of this character so as to suggest a complex association between surrogate and poet.[26]

By its particular focus on the constructed author in the *Metamorphoses*, this study aims to complement recent criticism focusing on the role of fictional audiences in the poem and of the reader and, more generally, to contribute to the body of contemporary scholarship illuminating the ways by which Ovid destabilizes traditional epic narrative. My method involves close attention to the text, including lexical details and tropes by which the poet simultaneously problematizes his surrogates and reflects his own radical position vis-à-vis the values and the perspectives of his predecessors in epic.

On the semantic level, I examine Ovid's plays with diction, especially his incorporation of heavily charged language in unexpected contexts, as a register of style and genre. An important element of my analysis of language is Ovid's manipulation of etymological puns at critical moments as markers of his deviation from conventional epic. Among the major tropes employed by the poet, I discuss his radical use of extended similes for a variety of subversive purposes, for instance, by drawing attention to the problematic nature of images and by evoking tensions between epic and other genres, such as elegy and tragedy. In the hands of Ovid, even the classical rhetorical device of *repetitio* becomes something altogether new, as repetition not only is a key feature of the poem's structure but also serves the thematic function of distancing the poet's major surrogates from their earlier incarnations in epic and tragedy.

The first chapter examines Narcissus's fixation on his own image in book 3. Ovid aligns his story of Narcissus with traditional epic values by connecting it closely to Tiresias's rise to authority as the prophet of Thebes. But by incorporating language and tropes drawn from the low genre of elegy, the poet not only underlines the paradoxical nature of his character but also creates a tension within the language of Tiresias's prophecy itself.

Examining Ovid's exploitation of elegiac conventions in the Narcissus episode, this chapter follows on recent scholarly work exploring the poet's clever play with the underlying assumptions of elegy in the *Metamorphoses*.[27] My focus is on specific ways by which Ovid incorporates elegy so as to expose the paradoxes of that genre's obsession with images. I begin by discussing Ovid's allusions to the physical attributes of the poet-lover's mistress Corinna in the *Amores*, such as her skin, hair, and eyes, suggesting Narcissus's essence as an elegiac image. The chapter goes on to show that, by evoking the voice of the *praeceptor* of the *Ars amatoria*, Ovid calls attention to the importance of images in his didactic elegy, where the pupil is persistently reminded of the need to create illusions so as to deceive the object of desire. I then discuss the youth himself as he adopts the persona of an elegist, recalling the poet-lover Propertius lamenting in a deserted landscape. Narcissus thus paradoxically assumes the dual roles of the elegiac object of desire and the masculine voice of the elegist constructing images of the beloved.

Although Narcissus cleverly refashions conventional tropes used by the elegiac poet, he also reveals the ludicrousness of his bizarre situation through etymological play, even with the term "elegy" itself, and numerous rhetorical excesses. Finally, I discuss Narcissus's demise and apparent metamorphosis by analysis of extended similes and descriptions that draw attention to the instability of images. In particular, an allusion to the image of ripening grapes in Horace, *Odes* 2.5, reinforces the absurdity of Narcissus's state as a frustrated elegiac lover by evoking the inherent instability of the poet-speaker's desire for the beloved.

The second chapter focuses on Medea, who dominates the action of book 7, betraying her father out of love for Jason, murdering King Pelias, and attempting to poison the hero Theseus. Ovid to some extent adopts the traditional view in Greek epic and tragedy about the dangerous nature of this female but also represents Medea's cunning in ways that associate her with the poet himself. I begin with Medea's monologue on her quandary over helping Jason win the Golden Fleece.

Although she reflects on the underlying moral issues and voices her dilemma in an apparently sympathetic manner, Ovid has Medea subtly assimilate a male voice. Allusions to Euripides' *Medea* and Apollonius's *Argonautica* reveal that this character assumes a dominant role at an earlier stage in her involvement with the hero than implied in the two major Greek versions of the myth. Ovid himself manifests a similar paradox vis-à-vis his Greek predecessors, making himself appear the forerunner of those very poets.

After considering her relationship with Jason, the chapter discusses Medea's deception of Pelias's daughters, who unwittingly kill, rather than rejuvenate, their father and her flight from the kingdom. Ovid significantly plays on the etymology of Medea's name in connection with cunning plots. The narrative then takes the form of a geographical tour that, by alluding to Hellenistic-based myths on the themes of intrafamilial strife and unhappy love, serves as a kind of blueprint for the recherché material in the second half of the *Metamorphoses*. The focal myth concerning a proud youth named Cycnus is a quintessentially Ovidian narrative in its treatment of erotic and heroic material and in its clever use of etymological play with the name of the youth's mother Hyrie. The extended account of Medea's adventures in book 7, however, implies the paradoxical nature of Ovid's poetics: the commitment to Callimachean principles is reinforced ironically in an episode that threatens to expand beyond proper limits.

The third chapter begins by discussing Daedalus, the architect of the Cretan labyrinth and the inventor of wings for human flight. I explore the paradoxical nature of Daedalus both as artisan and as father, in particular against the background of Vergil's use of this mythical figure as a poignant symbol of humanity in *Aeneid* 6. Reflecting Ovid's rejection of his predecessor's vision of the archetypal artisan, this core episode illustrates the importance of the *Aeneid* as the "exemplary model" for the *Metamorphoses*.[28]

I first discuss the labyrinth as an image of the shifting, circuitous nature of Ovid's poem by pointing out the etymological play which the poet employs to contrast his poem with Vergil's: whereas the *Aeneid* is a highly articulated work in which a series of difficult wanderings and labors moves toward an end sanctioned by fate, the *Metamorphoses* has a loose structure emphasizing the process by which the poet often surprises and sometimes misleads the reader. Ovid extends the implications of the labyrinth by exploring father-son relations in Daedalus's story. First, filling in a gap in Vergil's ekphrasis of Daedalus's artwork, he recounts Daedalus's invention of wings, the flight with his son, and Icarus's disastrous fall. Then, by shifting the narrative chronologically back to Daedalus's murderous act against his nephew and protégé Perdix, Ovid reveals how Daedalus displays a negative form of repetition through his failure in the paternal sphere.

The chapter then considers book 8 as a microcosm of the *Metamorphoses* in its myriad narrative shifts that work against Vergil's view of the redemptive value of heroic labor. I examine labyrinthine patterns in the Meleager episode: the repetitive nature of the heroes' futile displays of prowess in the hunt for the Calydonian boar and structural and rhetorical forms of repetition conveying the tortuous inner conflict experienced by the hero's mother over her opposing loyalties after Meleager has killed her two brothers.

The final section discusses multiple forms of repetition in the poet's account of the river god Achelous as both host and narrator. Relating the tale of Erysichthon's violation of a grove sacred to Ceres, a story harking back to Callimachus's *Hymn to Demeter*, the river god depicts the man's impiety in a manner replete not only with rhetorical excesses but also with distorted allusions to Vergil's narrative of the fall of Troy and its aftermath. Ovid paradoxically juxtaposes Achelous's story with Lelex's tale of Baucis and Philemon's reception of Jupiter and Mercury, in which the gods respond favorably to the old couple's humble fare and the narrative simultaneously remains faithful to the spirit of the model in Callimachus's *Hecale*.

Finally, I discuss Achelous's labyrinthine narrative style continuing into book 9, where he recounts his contest with Hercules over Deianira largely through misplaced allusions to Aeneas's struggle with Turnus in the last books of the *Aeneid*. Throughout his tale of the river god, Ovid's clever play with the motif of consumption calls Achelous's hospitality as well as his narrative style into question. Achelous is a parody of Ovid by representing pitfalls that the poet, for the most part, avoids as he engages with his major Augustan predecessor.

The fourth chapter examines the archetypal bard Orpheus, who assumes the role of narrator for most of book 10. Orpheus himself includes an extended inset tale told by the goddess Venus to her beloved Adonis, thus drawing attention to the complex function of internal narrators.[29] By explaining the origin of the Adonia, this episode appears to offer the possibility of consolation for loss by a symbolic recovery of the dead but in fact exposes the instability of the bases on which the ritual was founded.

My discussion first considers the self-centeredness underlying Venus's cautionary tale about the metamorphosis of Hippomenes and Atalanta into lions. Moreover, driven by an undercurrent of desire conveyed in part through deployment of language related to valor, her narrative appeals to its immediate audience for the wrong reasons, spurring the aggressive behavior that she presumably wishes to deter. I then turn to the problem of role changing, which suggests the complex nature of the goddess's desire for the handsome youth, and discuss the undertones of incest implied in allusions to the problematic heroine Phaedra, as represented both in Greek tragedy and in Ovid's own earlier epistolary poetry. Ultimately, the manner of Adonis's death and Venus's response to the loss reflect the goddess's self-absorption. An extended simile in an unexpectedly low register and etymological play on the name of the flower that the goddess creates from the youth's blood reinforce the insubstantiality of her efforts to preserve him in a meaningful way.

In giving voice to Venus and then recounting Adonis's disastrous fate, Orpheus seems blind to the narcissistic underpinnings of this tale. The goddess's story evokes the bard's personal experience: the heroic efforts of Hippomenes to win Atalanta in the race have a counterpart in Orpheus's bold descent to the underworld to retrieve his bride Eurydice. By memorializing the youth through the ritual of the Adonia, the goddess shows a self-absorption analogous to Orpheus's ambivalent attempt to preserve Eurydice's memory by his songs in book 10. Ovid, furthermore, implies that the desires of the principal narrator may not in essence be different from those of the flawed characters who fill this poem, and his stance of authority is left open to question.

The fifth chapter examines Ulysses' contest with Ajax over the arms of Achilles. The poet appears to take a point of view in accord with a conservative Roman tradition by suggesting at the end of the episode that eloquence triumphed unfairly over valor. But, through the speech that he attributes to the Homeric hero, Ovid challenges the authority of the great poet of the Trojan War and the values that underlie the heroic world.

First, I examine how the devious Greek hero undermines the stability of the concepts of paternity and lineage, which were essential to traditional heroic identity. Ulysses suggests the superiority of his own family line over that of Ajax by calling attention to his descent from Mercury but suppresses his relation to the archetypal thief Autolycus. As he reveals himself to be a true scion of Mercury, Ulysses mirrors the poet, who himself identifies closely with this stealthy god in the *Metamorphoses*. I then consider how Ulysses manipulates events familiar to the reader from Homer. The Greek cleverly magnifies his role in the night raid that resulted in the death of the Trojan spy Dolon and the newly arrived ally Rhesus, whose valuable horses the Greeks take as booty. He adapts for his own advantage Homer's description of the warriors vanquished by Odysseus on the battlefield, and he views the significance of a warrior's wounds in contradictory ways so as to privilege himself and devalue Ajax.

To reinforce his claim to be the legitimate heir to Achilles' arms, Ulysses even creates a symbolic kinship with the great hero, especially through clever etymological play, central to Ovid's own technique throughout the poem. Showing a mastery of the epic device of ekphrasis, Ulysses implies a comprehensive understanding of the designs on Achilles' shield by etymological play with the word *caelum*. The hero even appropriates a feat traditionally attributed to Ajax, the rescue of Achilles' body from the battlefield.

Like Ulysses who subverts traditional accounts of the Trojan War, Ovid persistently challenges the privileged status of Homer and Vergil. The poet implies that his own authority may only be as reliable as the Trojan War hero's ability to convince the Greek leaders to award the arms of Achilles to him rather than to Ajax. As the controlling poet, however, Ovid creates a text that provides the means for understanding the problems at its core, enabling the reader to emerge from his encounter with the poem better equipped to assess the reliability of inherited traditions in literary, social, and political spheres.

1

Narcissus and Elegy

Narcissus in *Metamorphoses* 3 stands out among the plethora of Ovidian characters who in various ways transgress boundaries, for unable to distinguish self from other, he makes his own image the object of desire. Having refused intimacy with all others, including the nymph Echo, Narcissus is cursed by an embittered male suitor and punished by Nemesis with a futile desire for himself. Unable to stop gazing at his own reflection in a pool and frustrated in his effort to possess it, he wastes away until his body disappears and only a flower is found in its place (339–512).

It is surprising that this bizarre love story occurs at the center of a book focused on the city of Thebes, beginning with its foundation by Cadmus and ending with the horrible death of the young king Pentheus.[1] Within this context of the disturbing myths underlying the origins of Thebes, Ovid connects his tale of Narcissus closely to the ancient institution of prophecy. The story begins when Narcissus's mother Liriope inquires of Tiresias if her infant child will have a long life and receives this ambivalent response from the Theban prophet: "si se non noverit" ("if he does not know himself" [348]). At the end of the episode, the poet remarks that when the story of Narcissus's disaster spread through Greece, it greatly increased Tiresias's reputation as a prophet ("nomenque erat auguris ingens" [512]). Ovid thus appears to validate the authority of prophecy as the voice of divine truth for the individual and the community.[2] But he complicates this issue by the discourse that pervades Narcissus's story itself.

It is well known that as he finds himself unable to possess the beautiful reflection in the pool, Narcissus vents his frustration in the language of elegy and reflects the symptoms of the suffering elegiac lover.[3]

But the youth staring at his image is paradoxically both subject and object, lover and beloved. Scholars have been less attentive to the relation of Narcissus to this other side of the elegiac equation, the object of desire.[4] I believe that, by giving Narcissus the double status of a desirable elegiac image and a lamenting elegiac lover, Ovid exploits the circumscribed nature of that genre. He exposes an underlying, if suppressed, truth of elegy: the elegist, in rendering the beloved an object and in obsessively gazing on and pursuing the image of his own making, reveals his inherent narcissism.[5]

This chapter argues that Narcissus's obsession with his own reflection is more fully connected to the discourse of elegiac poetry than scholars generally acknowledge. In particular, I examine how Ovid associates Narcissus with pictorial images by which the poet-lover in the *Amores* envisions his mistress Corinna. Then I discuss how the poet exploits rhetorical elements of the *Ars amatoria* that emphasize the importance of manipulating appearances. By alluding to the concept of self-knowledge as expressed in his didactic elegy, he ironically connects erotic and prophetic language.

The chapter then moves on to consider Narcissus as an elegiac poet. As a poet-lover lamenting the elusiveness of his beloved, the youth produces a clever array of elegiac tropes but ultimately becomes undone as he literalizes metaphors intrinsic to that genre, including the *servitium amoris*. In the final section, I suggest how Narcissus's story shows Ovid in the *Metamorphoses* distancing himself from the limitations of elegy, in particular, its obsession with the image.[6] In his depiction of Narcissus's demise, Ovid undermines the youth's fixation on the image through pictorial analogues emphasizing fluidity and instability. An allusion to Horace, in particular, provides an ironic comment on the paradox of Narcissus as elegiac poet-lover by revealing the transient nature of the lyric poet's fixation on his own object of desire.

Narcissus and the Elegiac Image

Ovid thus describes Narcissus on the threshold of adulthood as an object of both young male and female desire:

multi illum iuvenes, multae cupiere puellae;
sed (fuit in tenera tam dura superbia forma)
nulli illum iuvenes, nullae tetigere puellae. (353–55)

[Many youths and many girls desired him, but there was such a harsh pride in the delicate beauty. No youths and no girls touched him.]

   This brief passage conveys the paradox of Narcissus through complex forms of imaging. The two echoing lines in this passage are themselves an echo of Catullus 62, a well known wedding poem in which a chorus of young women responds to a group of young men about the desirability of marriage.[7] The two verses replicate their model verbatim, except that the verbs *cupiere* and *tetigere* substitute for *optavere* (42 and 44).[8] The word *illum* in Catullus's poem refers to a flower, which the girls conceive as the symbol of their own virginal state.[9] In the epithalamium, the females repeat the verse in a negative form ("nulli illum pueri, nullae optavere puellae" [44]), driving home their point that once plucked, the flower withers away (*defloruit* [43]). Expressing their sense of loss in marriage, they delicately detail the growth of the flower in a sheltered garden, undisturbed by shepherd or plow (39–41).
   Allusively evoked, Catullus's flower image resonates in Ovid's episode. Philip Hardie points to an ironic implication of the flower allusion for Narcissus: whereas the bride in the epithalamium is soon to be deflowered by her husband, the flower that bears the name of the self-involved youth can be casually plucked by anyone.[10] By conjuring up Catullus's delicate flower through the word *illum* but applying it to the character himself, the poet suggests Narcissus's very essence as an *image* of beauty. He reinforces this departure from his model by enclosing within his two Catullan echoes a verse that contrasts Narcissus's beauty (*forma*) with his pride (*superbia*). In doing so, he hints that Narcissus is not only an inversion of the bride in the epithalamium but also another type of feminized literary image. As Gregson Davis observes, Ovid's description of Narcissus here draws on a typically elegiac contrast between delicate and harsh (*tener* and *durus*).[11] By adding the discourse of elegy to his epithalamial allusion, Ovid suggests that Narcissus is the epitome of the cold-hearted object of desire, the elegiac *dura puella*.
   Ovid cleverly employs semantic paradoxes as he conveys the process by which the youth becomes both the lover and the beloved of elegy. The very pool in which Narcissus discovers his reflection, suggestively described in terms of a mirror, is the scene of a double thirst:[12] "dumque sitim sedare cupit, sitis altera crevit" ("And while he desired to satisfy his thirst, another thirst increased" [415]). Frederick Ahl comments on the cleverness of the word *sitis* here: the repetition of the word creates a verbal echo, and the nominative form is a palindrome reinforcing the

effect of a reflected image.[13] The language of paradox quickly becomes more clearly elegiac. Here, the poet concisely couches Narcissus's dilemma in the language of elegy: "dumque petit, petitur pariterque accendit et ardet" ("And while he seeks, he is sought, and he simultaneously lights the flame and burns" [426]).[14]

Descriptive images in this passage subtly suggest a specific elegiac identity for the youth. Ovid compares Narcissus gazing at his reflection to a statue made of Parian marble ("ut e Pario formatum marmore signum" [419]). The luminous quality of Parian marble made it especially favored for statues.[15] It also served as a symbol of sublime beauty.[16] Here, the static nature of the image is emphasized as Narcissus is fixed in place in amazement at his reflected beauty.[17] The passage recalls *Amores* 1.7, where the poet similarly conveys the exquisite beauty of his mistress Corinna as she is caught in a moment of stasis: "caeduntur Pariis qualia saxa iugis" ("such stones are cut from Parian ridges" [52]).[18] Ovid even sustains the analogue of a statue by describing Narcissus's neck as ivory ("eburnea colla" [422]), a material commonly used for sculpture. Although not applying the term to his mistress's neck in the *Amores*, the poet refers to the delicate beauty of her arms with the same epithet: "illa quidem nostro subiecit eburnea collo / bracchia, Sithonia candidiora nive" ("She indeed threw her ivory arms, whiter than Sithonian snow, around my neck" [3.7.7–8]).

Ovid further connects Narcissus with the object of desire in his elegy by using color terminology to depict his complexion. The youth's face has a delicate mix of pink and white tones: "in niveo mixtum candore ruborem" ("a blush mingled with a snowy whiteness" [423]). The poet in the *Amores* created a similar pictorial image of Corinna's coloration, which he says is preserved in spite of her breach of faith with him: "candida, candorem roseo suffusa rubore, / ante fuit: niveo lucet in ore rubor" ("Fair she was before, with a rosy blush spreading over her fair skin; the blush still glows on her snow-white face" [3.3.5–6]). The repetition of three specific words conveying color from *Amores* 3.3 (*candor*, *rubor*, and *niveus*) thus connects Narcissus to Corinna through the delicacy of his looks.

Other aspects of Narcissus's beauty also have a background in Ovid's own elegiac poetry. The youth's hair, for instance, recalls the unshorn locks of the gods Bacchus and Apollo: "et dignos Baccho, dignos et Apolline crines" ("His hair is worthy of Bacchus and worthy of Apollo" [421]). In *Amores* 1.14, the poet similarly draws on artistic representations of youthful divinities with flowing hair, though for an ironic purpose. He specifically claims that Corinna's hair was even superior to the locks of Bacchus and Apollo before she caused it to fall out by dyeing it too much:

formosae periere comae, quas vellet Apollo,
 .quas vellet capiti Bacchus inesse suo. (31–32)

[The lovely hair, which Apollo would desire, which Bacchus would desire on his own head, has been lost.]

An emphasis on the brilliance of Narcissus's eyes also has close parallels in the *Amores*. Here, Ovid describes the youth gazing at his own eyes reflected in the pool: "spectat humi positus geminum, sua lumina, sidus" ("Positioned on the ground, he looks at a double constellation, his own eyes" [420]). In *Amores* 3.3, purporting to be amazed that Corinna's beauty remains intact in spite of her treachery, the poet-lover singles out his beloved's eyes among her physical assets, both because they shine like stars ("radiant ut sidus ocelli" [9]) and because Corinna swore her oath by them (10–14). An even closer parallel occurs in *Amores* 2.16. Lamenting his separation from his mistress, Ovid again refers to the beauty of Corinna's eyes, similarly in the context of an oath that she has made to him:

at mihi te comitem iuraras usque futuram—
 per me perque oculos, sidera nostra, tuos! (43–44)

[But you had sworn to me that you would be my companion forever, through me and through your eyes, my stars!]

The poet's description of Narcissus not only shares the stellar analogy with the two passages in the *Amores* but also imitates the use of the elegant construction of "neoteric apposition" in 2.16.[19] In *Metamorphoses* 3, moreover, Ovid adapts this device of enclosing a metaphor within the words for its referent by inverting the terms; the metaphor now provides the frame for the object which it describes. Ovid's rhetoric heightens the impression of Narcissus's exemplary beauty: in this unexpected reversal, the metaphor instead of its referent has become the direct object of the verb, and even the term for "eye," *lumen* (light), is itself a metaphor, used instead of *oculus,* the standard word for "eye," or the affective diminutive *ocellus.* Among Narcissus's exquisite features evoking Corinna, his eyes in particular are the essence of beauty.

In his depiction of the youth's initial encounter with his reflection, then, Ovid employs the language and conventions of elegy to imply Narcissus's status as an image. By incorporating elegiac diction into his allusion to Catullus 62, Ovid subverts the symbolic association of the flower with marriage and at the same time suggests that Narcissus is a feminized elegiac object of desire. Ovid makes the youth with his luxuriant hair, delicate complexion, and brilliant eyes a kind of hyper-elegiac image modeled on Corinna in the *Amores*. By constructing Narcissus as a beautiful elegiac object through allusions to Corinna, Ovid exposes the narcissism of elegy. From the *Monobiblos* of Propertius on, it is clear that the real subject of elegy is the man, not the woman.[20] But Ovid went much further by *inventing* his mistress Corinna, whose very existence was questioned even in the poet's own day.[21] She is in essence a fiction, a figure of his imagination. By fixating on his mistress Corinna, Ovid in fact adores his own creativity.

Ovid's Apostrophe to Narcissus and the *Ars amatoria*

A long apostrophe by the narrator to Narcissus as he is unable to grasp the real nature of the *puer* in the water has a close parallel in elegiac poetry. As the youth becomes fascinated with his reflection and cannot tear himself away from it, the narrator admonishes Narcissus on his misunderstanding in a highly animated break in the narrative:

credule, quid frustra simulacra fugacia captas?
quod petis, est nusquam; quod amas, avertere, perdes.
ista repercussae, quam cernis, imaginis umbra est:
nil habet ista sui: tecum venitque manetque,
tecum discedet, si tu discedere possis. (432–36)

[Foolish one, why do you grasp in vain at fleeting images? What you seek is nowhere: turn away; you will lose that which you love. It is the shadow of a reflected image at which you gaze. It has nothing of its own: it both comes and remains with you; it will depart with you, if you should be able to depart.]

In both its length and its tone, this surprising apostrophe by Ovid's narrator is without precedent in Greek or Latin epic. Vergil's address to Dido in *Aeneid* 4 (408–11) differs significantly because of the pathos of the narrative voice whose engagement in the plight of the doomed queen reflects a sympathy modulated by the moral issues at stake.[22] In the critical discussion generated by this rupture in the narrative, scholars have debated whether the poet is too caught up in his own narrative. Hermann Fränkel, for instance, finds the poet responding in the manner of an excited child.[23] Kenneth Knoespel similarly perceives

Ovid's abrupt break in the fiction as analogous to Narcissus's own
delusion.[24] Louise Vinge and Gianpiero Rosati, by contrast, suggest that
the poet consciously breaks the illusion of the fiction, thereby ironically
detaching himself from the narrative.[25] My own view is somewhere be-
tween that of Fränkel and Knoespel, on the one hand, and Vinge and
Rosati, on the other. I examine the surprising gesture of the narrator
here as a particular literary strategy utilizing didactic elegy that enables
Ovid to project an impassioned, yet authoritative, voice attuned to the
problematic nature of images.

As he attempts to dissuade the youth from a foolish infatuation, the
narrator here resembles the *praeceptor* of the *Ars amatoria*. The didactic
tone in an amorous context recalls the master image maker who offers
numerous examples of erotic folly so that his student may not stray from
the path to victory in the game of love. In an excursus on females ac-
tively pursuing their objects of desire, the *praeceptor* mentions a number
of aggressive women from myth, including Byblis, Myrrha, Pasiphae,
Scylla, and Medea. Expanding on the story of Pasiphae, he interrupts
his account of her strange passion with a lengthy apostrophe similar to
the narrator's here in *Metamorphoses* 3:

quo tibi, Pasiphae, pretiosas sumere vestes?
　　ille tuus nullas sentit adulter opes.
quid tibi cum speculo, montana armenta petenti?
　　quid totiens positas fingis, inepta, comas?
crede tamen speculo, quod te negat esse iuvencam.
　　quam cuperes fronti cornua nata tuae!
sive placet Minos, nullus quaeratur adulter:
　　sive virum mavis fallere, falle viro! (1.303–10)

[What purpose do you have in putting on costly garments, Pasiphae? That
adulterer of yours comprehends no riches. What good is a mirror to you as you
seek the herds in the mountains? Why, foolish one, do you so often arrange
your hair? Trust, however, in the mirror, which denies that you are a heifer.
How you would wish for horns on your forehead from birth! If Minos pleases,
let no adulterer be sought; or if you prefer to deceive your husband, deceive
him with a man!]

Within a general discussion of women's inclination to sex, Ovid's
poetic persona offers "proof" of their willingness to be seduced through
the glaring example of one who actually sought out a bull. The didactic
impulse of the *praeceptor* is so strong that it has in fact spilled over even
to a mythical character who is addressed instead of the pupil.[26]

The *praeceptor's* address to Pasiphae shares not only its impassioned tone with the narrator's to Narcissus but also a number of specific elements. Both admonish with strong imperatives: *crede* and *falle* in the one and *avertere* in the other. The character in each case is addressed with a vocative adjective denoting foolishness (*inepta, credule*). Furthermore, the narrator's reproach to Narcissus for his misperception of the image in the reflecting surface of the pool is analogous to the *praeceptor's* rebuke to Pasiphae for her obsession with looking at herself in the mirror (*speculo* [305 and 307]).[27] Concerned about improving her appearance for the bull, Pasiphae madly scrutinizes her image in a mirror, which would be an appropriate gesture if she were trying to attract a human. Like the obsessed Pasiphae, Narcissus has failed to grasp a tenet essential to the world of the *Ars:* an understanding of one's self and the object of desire is required in order to exploit images most effectively and thus to secure one's goal. Self-deception is fatal to the enterprise.

The *Ars* is a poem about consciously manipulating images, about creating a self-image in order to deceive and ultimately to control the object of one's desire.[28] But going beyond his persona in the *Ars*, the poet probes more deeply into the nature of images in *Metamorphoses* 3. To that end, he follows his reflection on Narcissus himself with the long, complex tale of Pentheus's intransigent rejection of the power of the images created by Bacchus (511–733).[29]

The narrator's gesture here complements Tiresias's prophecy at the beginning of the episode that Narcissus will live a long life only if he does not know himself. The background of this prophecy is suggestively ambivalent. Scholars have generally perceived an ironic reference to the inscription "gnôthi seauton" on the temple of Apollo at Delphi, which is fulfilled when Narcissus recognizes that the *puer* in the water is in fact himself ("iste ego sum! sensi"; "I am that one, I realize it" [463]).[30] To emphasize the pathological aspects of Narcissus's story from its very beginning, Peter Knox observes that the prophecy also evokes the erotic meaning of the verb *nosco* and its compound form *cognosco*, which Catullus exploits to powerful effect in a bitter elegiac poem to Lesbia (Catullus 72).[31]

The reader familiar with the *Ars*, moreover, would find additional literary resonance in Tiresias's words. The poet represents the prophet in a context resonant of the milieu of the *Ars*. First, he explains why Tiresias is chosen to settle a dispute between Jupiter and Juno. This *vates* of Apollo acquired his oracular skills because of the uniqueness of his sexual experience. When he once saw two snakes copulating and then separated the pair with his staff, he was transformed into a female; after seven years, on seeing the snakes together again, he repeated the act and was then changed back into a male (324-31). Since he has lived as both a man and a woman, Jupiter and Juno choose him to arbitrate their disagreement about whether the male or the female receives more pleasure in sex.

Although Ovid did not invent the basic facts of this myth, his concise version is particularly suitable as an introduction to the story of Narcissus, for it has significant connections to the elegiac tradition of both the *Amores* and the *Ars*. The poet emphasizes that the dispute between the king and the queen of the gods was part of an evening's entertainment: Tiresias is summoned as an *arbiter* (332) of one of a series of merry jokes ("remissos . . . iocos" [319-20], "de lite iocosa" [332]) that have taken place during a setting of convivial drinking ("forte Iovem memorant diffusum nectare curas / seposuisse graves"; "they say that by chance Jupiter, relaxed with nectar, put aside his heavy cares" [318-19]). By stating that they were pleased (*placuit* [322]) to summon Tiresias to resolve the matter, the narrator implies that the two gods take the issue in the amicable spirit of sympotic festivities, though Jupiter's affair with Semele (3.259-315) may continue to weigh heavily on Juno's mind, if not on her husband's.

Although *iocus* occurs only here in the *Metamorphoses*, it belongs to elegiac discourse and is operative in the milieu of the *Ars*.[32] Ovid has the *praeceptor* play up the advantages of such *ioci* to his pupil in his approaches to a mistress, actual or potential. As he warns against quarrels in a convivial context, for instance, the *praeceptor* in book 1 recommends levity: "aptior est dulci mensa merumque ioco" ("Banquets and wine are more suitable to pleasant jesting" [594]). He advocates any kind of *iocus* for which the pupil has ability, including singing and dancing, so as to please the woman (595-96). He even urges the pupil to appear a bit drunk so that inappropriate actions or words may later be attributed to the wine (598-600). Here in *Metamorphoses* 3, however, the *iocus* goes awry. Although the goddess at first engages wholeheartedly in the jest, she reacts excessively ("gravius . . . iusto" [333]) to losing, totally out of proportion to the frivolous subject ("pro materia" [334]). When Tiresias takes Jupiter's side and affirms that women experience the greater pleasure, Juno is incensed and blinds him. Powerless to undo Juno's act, Jupiter provides compensation by endowing Tiresias with prophetic powers (332-38).

The prophecy which Tiresias delivers about Narcissus echoes Apollo's injunction about self-knowledge in *Ars* 2. In an epiphany, the divine prophet admonishes the *praeceptor* to take his pupils to the Delphic temple in order to contemplate its famous inscription:

is mihi "Lascivi" dixit "praeceptor Amoris,
 duc, age, discipulos ad mea templa tuos,
est ubi diversum fama celebrata per orbem
 littera, cognosci quae sibi quemque iubet.
qui sibi notus erit, solus sapienter amabit,
 atque opus ad vires exigit omne suas.
cui faciem natura dedit, spectetur ab illa:
 cui color est, umero saepe patente cubet:
qui sermone placet, taciturna silentia vitet:
 qui canit arte, canat; qui bibit arte, bibat.
sed neque declament medio sermone diserti,
 nec sua non sanus scripta poeta legat!" (497–508)

[He said to me, "Teacher of wanton love, come, lead your pupils to my temple, where there is a phrase, celebrated in fame through the various regions of the world, which orders that each man be known to himself. He who knows himself will alone love wisely and will complete every task according to his own resources. Let the one to whom nature has given a comely face be looked at for that; let the one whose skin has a warm glow often lie with shoulder exposed; let him who is pleasing in conversation avoid dead silence; let him who sings skillfully sing; let him who drinks skillfully drink; but neither let eloquent men declaim in the midst of conversation, nor let the mad poet read his own writings!"]

The famous dictum is emphatically phrased twice in this passage ("cognosci quae sibi quemque iubet"; "qui sibi notus erit") and given concrete applications. But, inscribed in an elegiac context, Apollo's words cynically misapply the lofty philosophical concept of self-knowledge, as the god advises the *praeceptor* to see to it that his students are properly instructed in the art of manipulation and deception.[33] Here, "knowing oneself" entails presenting one's best asset effectively and exploiting it to the maximum.[34] In his list of qualities conducive to success in love, Apollo places good looks first: a man endowed with a handsome face (*faciem*) should be looked at (*spectetur*) specifically for it. As Apollo's prophet, Tiresias in *Metamorphoses* 3 assimilates this elegiac dimension of "self-knowledge" espoused by the god in the *Ars*. Elegy has in effect contaminated prophetic discourse. The seer thus has the foreknowledge that Narcissus will indeed "know himself" in the elegiac sense: putting his looks on display will be a disaster for him because he will not be able to control the object of desire, his own self-image, but instead will be controlled by it.

Narcissus as an Elegiac Poet

As he laments his failure to possess his object of desire, Narcissus himself assumes the voice of an elegiac poet. His outpouring of frustration is virtually a distillation of the discourse and themes of that genre. Ovid's distraught youth begins his lament by crying out to the woods:

"ecquis, io silvae, crudelius" inquit "amavit?
scitis enim et multis latebra opportuna fuistis." (442–43)

["Oh woods," he said, "has anyone loved more cruelly? For you know, and you have been a convenient retreat for many."]

Narcissus's lament in a wooded setting owes a debt, I believe, to Propertius 1.18, an elegy in which the poet-lover has retired to a forest setting with fountains and rocks to lament his mistress's change of heart.[35] By connecting this section to the Augustan predecessor whom he so greatly admired, Ovid makes Narcissus's complaint virtually a formal elegy.[36] A clever variation on the *exclusus amator* theme, Propertius 1.18 imaginatively explores the problem of separation from the beloved. From the very first lines of the elegy, the self-absorption of the poet-lover is thinly disguised. Although the lover claims that the isolation of the place will keep his complaints secret (1–4), the poet of course makes his lament a public event for his own glory.

Like Narcissus, the elegist directly invokes the trees: they will be the witnesses ("vos eritis testes" [19]) of his devotion to Cynthia. Attributing amorous experience to the beech and the pine in their past existence, he specifically alludes to Pan's love for Pitys ("Arcadio pinus amica deo" [20]). He conveys the experience of loss and longing for his mistress through the motif of an echo resonating in the woods. Here, he affirms both the oral and the written signs of his devotion to Cynthia:

a quotiens teneras resonant mea verba sub umbras,
    scribitur et vestris Cynthia corticibus! (21–22)

[Ah, how often my words resound in the delicate shade, and Cynthia is written on your bark!]

The poet-lover not only refers directly to echoing with the word *resonant* but also creates an inscribed echo by repeating the name Cynthia here from an earlier line in the same position metrically, at the beginning of the second half of the pentameter: "quod mihi das flendi, Cynthia, principium?" ("What first cause do you give me for weeping, Cynthia?" [6]).

As the final component of an elegant ring composition, the last distich succinctly and effectively brings the motif of echoing to a climax in this elegy:

sed qualiscumque es resonent mihi "Cynthia" silvae,
    nec deserta tuo nomine saxa vacent. (31–32)

[But whatever you are like, let the woods echo "Cynthia" to me, and let the rocks not be devoid of your name.]

The poet-lover here reiterates his wish that his mistress's name be echoed, here by both the trees and the rocks. The concluding lines, moreover, inscribe echoes of the beginning of the poem.[37] There is a repetition of two key words, *deserta* from the first line and *saxa* from the fourth, and a reiteration of the name "Cynthia" in the same metrical position as in the first mention of her name: "unde tuos primum repetam, mea Cynthia, fastus?" ("From what source should I first trace your disdain, my Cynthia?" [5]). As he repeatedly addresses Cynthia, questioning her as if she were able to hear him and respond, the poet-lover in a sense negates the absence of his object of desire.[38] But the absent mistress is the essence of cold pride. The poet's repetition of the name "Cynthia" has further implications: since the word is the title of the *Monobiblos*, the gesture is also self-referential: Propertius thus reaffirms his commitment to elegiac poetry as much as to his mistress per se.[39]

Narcissus, like Propertius, addresses the forest at the beginning of his lament. In a similarly impassioned manner ("io, silvae" [442]), acknowledging their propriety as the place for his lament, he emphasizes that the trees are well acquainted with lovers' dilemmas ("multis opportuna latebra fuistis" [443]). In the end, the woods also respond to him: "totidemque remisit / verba locus" ("The place returned just as many words" [500–501]). Unlike Propertius, however, Ovid informs the reader about the specific reasons for Narcissus's punishment. Although not providing any details about the youth who uttered a cry of revenge when rebuffed by Narcissus, the poet fully reveals his callous behavior in his encounter with Echo. In his lament, Narcissus from the first assumes that his suffering is unique, which is ironic in light of his behavior with the oread.[40] When the youth asks the woods if anyone has ever loved more cruelly ("'ecquis, io silvae, crudelius' inquit 'amavit?'"

[442]), Ovid's reader would, of course, think immediately of Echo. For after Narcissus coldly rejects her, Echo lives alone in caves, unable to bear her shame and grief, and her body wastes away to mere bones (394–98).

The elaborate echoing effects of Propertius 1.18 may in part have prompted Ovid to include the story of Echo within the framework of Narcissus's self-love. Ovid indeed appears to have been the first to interweave the stories of Echo and Narcissus.[41] Critics have long been fascinated by this interplay, beginning with Fränkel, who discusses the opposition of character, total absorption in the self versus total lack of self.[42] Hardie has proposed that Ovid's interweaving of these two myths serves as a critique of Lucretius's account of auditory and visual reflections in *De rerum natura* 4.[43] On the rhetorical level, Ovid's inclusion of the encounter of Echo and Narcissus motivates a variety of echoing effects: direct repetition of particular words from the end of Narcissus's speech; chiastic word order suggesting the forward and backward movement of a return (e.g., "dixerat 'ecquis adest?', et 'adest' responderat Echo" [380]); repetition of the same verb in different forms (e.g., "vocat illa vocantem" [382]); and placement of repeated words in the same metrical position in sequential lines (as with "sit tibi copia nostri" in 391 and 392).

In Narcissus's lament, Ovid's use of replication not only signals a connection to Propertian elegy but also links the myths of Echo and Narcissus by associating verbal and visual images. Narcissus expresses his initial confusion about the nature of the image by reduplicating a pair of verbs in a chiastic arrangement: "et placet et video, sed, quod videoque placetque, / non tamen invenio" ("He both pleases and I look, but I nevertheless do not find that which I look at and which pleases" [446–47]). The verbal echoing here creates a visual effect; the order of the words in reverse in the return functions as a kind of mirror image. In a list of the gestures made by the *puer*, including stretching out his arms and smiling back to him, Narcissus mentions the tears that his object of desire sheds in response to his own: "lacrimas quoque saepe notavi / me lacrimante tuas" (459–60). The very structure of the verse highlights Narcissus's absorption in the beautiful boy in the pool: the words referring to the tears of the beloved serve as a framing device enclosing the phrase for the youth's own weeping, and the participle for weeping (*lacrimante*) echoes the noun for tears (*lacrimas*).

Narcissus evokes his earlier dialogue with the unfortunate Echo in a way that reinforces his self-entrapment through the language of elegy.

He thus conveys the paradox of his situation: "inopem me copia fecit" ("My abundance has made me poor" [466]). The word *copia* has elegiac associations, especially in Propertius.[44] The word ironically emphasizes Narcissus's self-absorption, for having insisted to Echo that he would die before giving her an opportunity to enjoy intimacy with him ("copia nostri" [391]), he now experiences a *copia* that makes him destitute. As A. A. R. Henderson notes, the phrase "inopem me copia fecit" is a "very clever oxymoron."[45] Ovid reinforces the power of that poetic figure here by providing an etymological play that points to the inherent self-reflexiveness of the character himself. For he implies that the word *copia* is derived from *cum* plus *ops* ("power" or "aid"; pl., "wealth"), the noun on which the adjective *inops* is based: the descriptive thus merely reduplicates the noun.[46] Narcissus's adeptness with the paradoxes common to elegy reflects the problematic nature of his character: in this case, a clever aphorism parallels his own fixation on turning back to himself.

The youth persists in employing the language and tropes of erotic elegy even though he has come to realize that his object of desire is simply his own reflection. He has in fact articulated this awareness strongly, in a kind of tragic anagnorisis: "iste ego sum! sensi; nec me mea fallit imago" ("I am that one! I realize it, and my image does not deceive me" [463]). Yet he continues to speak as if the image were alive. Narcissus gives way to expectations of death as an elegiac lover: acknowledging that grief has robbed him of his strength, he proclaims through the metaphor of fire that he is extinguished (*extinguor* [470]) in early youth.

Narcissus further echoes traditional elegiac discourse by asserting, "hic, qui diligitur, vellem, diuturnior esset!" ("I would wish that he who is loved might live longer!" [472]). Ovid himself has his persona in the *Amores* utter such a sentiment when Corinna is in danger of death after having had an abortion (2.13.14–15). But Narcissus's wish to have his beloved survive him is particularly strange after he has identified the *puer* as his own image. Since he himself has become fixated on death, his odd request points to what may be an intolerable truth: that his own perfect looks will not last forever. In the static world of elegy, the physical appearance of the object of desire does not in essence change. Even Corinna's loss of hair ends as a subject for jest with Ovid, since he asserts that it will grow back (1.14.55–56). Here, Narcissus is perhaps wishing that his physical beauty, which is by nature temporal, could remain constant.

Resuming his lament after his tears disturb the reflection, Narcissus responds as the poet-lover of elegy so often does with his harsh mistress, endowing his image even more than before with a will of its own and pleading for its return. First, he calls it cruel and begs it not to desert its lover ("nec me, crudelis, amantem / desere!" [477]). Then, he asks the image only to permit him to look at (*aspicere*) that which he cannot touch and to, provide sustenance for his pitiful madness ("misero praebere alimenta furori" [479]). But, even as Narcissus expresses his thoughts in an elegiac mode, Ovid destabilizes the language of elegy: paradoxically, the "food" that the youth seeks in his madness causes him literally to waste away and to lose the alluring image of his own beauty.

As the youth falls into utter despair, the poet hints further at the problematic nature of the elegiac-based image. After Narcissus strikes his chest and sees his reddened reflection in the water, Ovid comments succinctly: "non tulit ulterius" (487). Is the wretched young man unable to bear the suffering because of his frustrated passion or because of the change in the beautiful image?[47] As the poet proceeds to describe the alteration of Narcissus's appearance, with the loss of color in his complexion and of strength and vitality in general (491–93), the youth's final cry of despair (*eheu* [495]) would seem to be doubly motivated. On the one hand, Narcissus cannot possess his beloved, and, on the other, the image itself has not remained static as a thing of perfect beauty.

With Narcissus's last exclamations of despair, Ovid reinforces the youth's connection to the elegiac tradition through echoes involving etymological play. Here, the poet conveys Narcissus's repeated exclamation of grief:

... quotiensque puer miserabilis "eheu"
dixerat, haec resonis iterabat vocibus "eheu." (495–96)

[And as often as the wretched boy had said, "Alas," she repeated "alas" with her resonant voice.]

The phrase "puer miserabilis 'eheu' / dixerat" encapsulates the elegiac lover's state of misery. The word *miserabilis*, for instance, is the term used by Horace to summarize the plaintive poems of Albius (presumably the elegist Tibullus), whom he thus teases in *Odes* 1.33: "neu miserabilis / decantes elegos" ("Nor may you keep singing pitiful elegies" [2–3]). With the words "'eheu' / dixerat," Ovid recalls the supposed derivation of the Greek word for "elegy" (*elegos*) from the expression "'ê ê' legein" ("to say 'alas'").[48]

Although the genre of elegy in Latin emphasizes lament as the expression of erotic suffering, it also incorporates lament as mourning for the dead. In *Amores* 3.9, Ovid evokes lament in referring to the death of the poet Tibullus:

flebilis indignos, Elegia, solve capillos:
  a, nimis ex vero nunc tibi nomen erit! (3–4)

[Loosen your hair, tearful Elegy, undeserving of suffering; ah, now will your name be too true!]

In the process of expressing grief for the dead poet, *Amores* 3.9 recalls the full spectrum of Tibullus's love poetry, incorporating the characteristics of piety, gentleness, physical frailty, and thoughts of death that defined his relations with his first love Delia and her successor Nemesis.[49]

Here in *Metamorphoses* 3, Ovid's allusion to the dual nature of elegy reveals a contrast between Narcissus's final laments and Echo's response to him. On the one hand, Ovid seems to unmask his own fiction about Echo as a person when he states that in response to the youth's cry of "heu frustra dilecte puer!" (500), the place (*locus* [501]) returned the words. But he also recalls Narcissus's initial cry to the woods, which in true elegiac fashion respond to him now. The trees have listened, but in contrast to Propertius 1.18, their response comes late and without solace for the youth. More important, whereas Narcissus merely exudes self-pity, Echo represents elegy as real dirge. Ovid indicates that the nymph grieves in spite of her anger: "quae tamen ut vidit, quamvis irata memorque / indoluit" ("Nevertheless, when she saw him, although angry and unable to forget, she lamented" [494–95]).

When she repeats Narcissus's cry of *eheu* (496), which conveys his frustrated desire, Echo laments his imminent death.[50] With this resonating cry, Ovid shows that the spurned lover Echo rises above the self-absorption exhibited by Narcissus with a gesture of pity toward him. There is a poignancy in the very brevity of the oread's echo of the single word *eheu*. Furthermore, the poet implies that it is repeated over and over, for the plural of *vox* in the phrase "resonis iterabat vocibus" suggests Echo's expression of sympathy at each outburst of Narcissus's self-pity. Sound effects contribute to the pathos of Echo's reply to Narcissus in response to the youth's farewell to his image: "dictoque vale 'vale' inquit et Echo" (501). In addition to assonance, the hiatus after the second *vale*, which necessitates a shortened final vowel, lends the effect of a lingering, slowly fading, sound.[51]

Ovid employs a final allusion to the discourse of elegy so as to show

how even in the moment of death Narcissus remains completely mastered by his visual reflection. The poet here describes the youth's end in the language of enslavement: "lumina mors clausit domini mirantia formam" ("Death closed the eyes marveling at the image of the master" [503]). The word *dominus* here appropriately alludes to the elegiac convention of referring to the mistress as the poet-lover's *domina*.[52] If Propertius maintains an impression of Cynthia's powerful effect on him through the course of their relationship, her death breaks that hold, and the poet-lover moves on to other interests, in particular the aetiological poems of book 4.[53] In Ovid's *Amores*, Corinna is a *domina* principally because convention requires her to assume that role: his poetic persona needs her as material for his verse, but that persona consistently undermines the reader's expectations of a deep passion overcoming the inevitable obstacles faced by a poet-lover.[54] Although the *dominus* for Narcissus is only an insubstantial image of the self, it completely controls the lover. The rhetorical fiction by which the elegist traditionally represents himself as the slave to a mistress here assumes a grotesquely literal form in which the bondage of servitude is taken to the extreme end of death.

Elegy and the Lament for Narcissus

In the scene following Narcissus's death, Ovid uses verbal echoing to contrast nature's response with the youth's own self-absorption. Paying a touching tribute to the beautiful youth whom they all loved, the nymphs emerge in full force to lament his death. The poet includes all three major groups of nymphs in mourning for the beautiful youth:

. . . planxere sorores
naides et sectos fratri posuere capillos,
planxerunt dryades: plangentibus adsonat Echo. (505–7)

[His naiad sisters lamented and put down the locks of hair which they had cut off for their brother; the dryads lamented; Echo resounds in response to them as they lament.]

The poet moves further away from traditional erotic elegy in emphasizing the presence of the nymphs here and may be recalling a powerful example of elegy as lament in the genre of pastoral. In Theocritus's first *Idyll*, Thyrsis begins his lament for Daphnis by asking the nymphs where they were when the cowherd-singer died: whereas even animals, wild and domesticated, responded in grief, the nymphs were not at his side or in their usual haunts (66–75). Among the three divinities who approach the youth, Aphrodite is overtly sarcastic and revels in the triumph that she has won over him by his approaching death (95–98).

Daphnis's response to the goddess is in kind: he taunts her by referring to her affair with the mortal Anchises, her loss of the beautiful young Adonis, and Diomedes' humiliation of her on the battlefield at Troy even as he affirms that he will remain hostile to Eros all the way to Hades (100–113). Like Narcissus, he represents an extreme case of erotic suffering and literally wastes away to the point of liquefaction. Although it is not clear why the nymphs avoided the cowherd in the throes of death, Daphnis was suffering at Aphrodite's hands because he had for some reason rejected love.[55] In that context, the nymphs may have remained absent from the scene of Daphnis's death in resentment of his adamant and, at the end, vocal hostility to love, but they had clearly esteemed this compelling bucolic singer ("ou numphaisin apechthê"; "not hateful to the nymphs" [141]) for his talent.

Whereas the landscape for Daphnis is highly animated, the setting for Narcissus in his lament is sterile, with no presence of herds or flocks. As Charles Segal has observed, the forest setting mirrors Narcissus in its unnaturally pristine state.[56] On the other hand, the active role of the nymphs after his death here contrasts with their notable absence in Theocritus's poem. The anaphora with the verb *plango* calls attention to the grief of three different types of nymphs. Ovid employs familial terms (*sorores, fratri*) that reinforce the compassion of the nymphs: viewing the dead Narcissus as a brother, the nymphs come to perform the funeral rites owed to a family member. This social behavior of the nymphs, including the oread Echo, offers a striking contrast to the solipsistic attitude of Narcissus himself. The present tense ("plangentibus adsonat") that the poet uses to describe the oread Echo, in contrast to two perfect tense verbs applied to the naiads and dryads (*planxere, planxerunt*), has an affective function, as if the oread continues to express her grief. Integrated in the natural landscape, the nymphs here represent a communal gesture of sympathy and, as such, connect elegy with lament in the true pastoral spirit. Narcissus, by contrast, remains constrained within the bounds of erotic elegy. Encompassed by the beauty of the image which he cannot bear to lose, he echoes the conventions of that genre to the very end.

Ovid may have had another model in the background of the lament for Narcissus, nature's response to Gallus in *Eclogue* 10.[57] Vergil closely recalls *Idyll* 1 in the section of his poem in which the trees and mountains weep for Gallus and three divinities as well as rustics come to console him (9–30).[58] Gallus in *Eclogue* 10, like Narcissus here, is clearly pining away because of unrequited love ("indigno cum Gallus amore peribat" [10]). As scholars have shown, Vergil's fictionalized Gallus laments in language that echoes the real Gallus's own elegiac poetry.[59] Ovid may allude to *Eclogue* 10 for another important reason: that poem is Vergil's farewell to the light genre of pastoral. With Narcissus's demise, Ovid in a sense moves away from elegy.

The Final Images of Narcissus

An unusually dense cluster of extended similes, two sets of double analogies within eight lines, marks the final stages of the youth's *furor,* after he persists in the role of pursuer in spite of his realization that the *puer* is only an image of himself. On the surface, these comparisons seem close to the visual images for the beloved in the *Amores,* which take the form of similes drawn from nature.[60] But, along with the flower that remains after the youth disappears, these visual analogues for Narcissus call attention to the very instability of the image.

The first of the extended similes in this section occurs after Narcissus tears open his garment in order to beat his chest. Ovid calls attention to that act through the formal harmony of a golden line: "nudaque marmoreis percussit pectora palmis" ("He struck his naked chest with his marblelike hands" [481]). He then elaborates on the youth's condition through a double simile:

pectora traxerunt roseum percussa ruborem,
non aliter quam poma solent, quae candida parte,
parte rubent, aut ut variis solet uva racemis
ducere purpureum nondum matura colorem. (482–85)

[His chest after being struck took on a rose-colored redness, just as apples, which are white in part and in part grow red, or as grapes, not yet mature, are accustomed to acquire a purple color on the variegated clusters.]

The rosy hue on the fair skin recalls the earlier description of Narcissus looking at his reflection in the pool for the first time: "in niveo mixtum candore ruborem" ("a blush mingled with a snowy whiteness" [423]), where as we observed, the poet recalled Corinna's complexion in the *Amores.*[61] Here, however, Narcissus has inflicted an injury on himself and suffers the redness of bruised skin as the first stage of his physical demise.

The specific images of apples and grapes, furthermore, add to the irony through their traditional associations with desirability.[62] In one elegant fragment (105a Campbell), apparently describing a young girl, Sappho uses the analogy of a red apple to portray the girl as a quintessentially desirable object that has been unattainable because it is too high up in a tree or that has simply gone unnoticed. Sappho's greatest admirer among Roman poets also plays on the erotic associations of this fruit. In Catullus 65, an apple, presumably sent as a love gift, suggests sexual passion: when her mother enters the room and disrupts a young woman's reverie, the fruit falls from the fold of her dress and brings on a guilty blush ("conscius rubor" [24]).[63]

The ripening grapes acquire a special resonance as an ironic image of desire through an allusion to Horace. In *Odes* 2.5, the lyric poet employs an extended metaphor from viticulture in advising his addressee to wait for his young object of desire to mature:

> Tolle cupidinem
> immitis uvae: iam tibi lividos
>   distinguet Autumnus racemos
>   purpureo varius colore. (9–12)

[Cast aside your desire for unripe grapes. Soon Autumn of many colors will adorn the pale clusters with a purple hue.]

The similarity of the language in book 3 to the image of unripe grapes here suggests that Ovid had Horace's passage in mind.[64] The lyric poet himself has cleverly adapted an image with a long poetic history by contextualizing it in a manner relevant to Ovid's passage.[65] As the ode begins, the poet admonishes his addressee to be patient, for the desirable Lalage is too young. In this strophe, he paints a vivid picture of the change to come by using the seasonal metaphor of ripening: the personified Autumn, as if an artist of nature, will perform his work of "adorning" (*distinguet*) the fruit with a purple coloration. Sexual fulfillment will come, the poet promises, as relentless time rushes on: Lalage will in fact soon seek a husband (13–16).

It is significant that Horace in *Odes* 2.5 does not name his addressee: the anonymous individual is most likely the persona of the poet himself.[66] The slippery erotic poet thus masks his own identity and intentions. Extensive animal imagery in the first four strophes intensifies the underlying frustration of Horace's desire for the young Lalage.[67] Yet, after assuring himself that Lalage will soon take the initiative in love, Horace abruptly shifts gears. The lyric poet places his obsession in an ironic light in the last two strophes by casting doubt on the stability of his own desire for this particular girl. He claims that Lalage is more loved not only than Pholoe and Chloris (who are mentioned together, presumably as acquaintances of the poet-speaker, at 3.15.7–8) but also than Gyges. The poet in fact devotes the last strophe to this youth, whose looks are so delicate that if he were placed in a crowd of girls, a spectator would be unable to determine his sex (21–24). Horace ends his ode by focusing on Gyges's flowing hair and sexually ambivalent looks ("solutis / crinibus ambiguoque vultu" [23–24]), leaving the impression that he has transferred his fixation from Lalage to the good-looking boy.

Here, as elsewhere in the *Odes*, the lyric poet differs sharply from the elegist by implying a self-awareness of the irony of his situation as lover.[68] Horace's Gyges, like Narcissus, is a particularly beautiful, youthful male. But, in *Odes* 2.5, it is a middle-aged lover who focuses on this object of desire, almost as an afterthought, as he seems to extricate himself from his passion for a too youthful female by recalling other desirable young women and finally this young male. The girl will seek a husband, and the boy similarly will move beyond his liminal state and become a lover, a pursuer in his own right. The implication is that the poet will then move on to some other amorous object. Horace thus reveals his detachment from any fixed erotic obsession in the very process of elaborating on an apparently intense desire. Ovid's echo of this passage encodes Horace's realization that the beloved is so desirable in part because she is unattainable and that fixation on the beautiful image of desire (male or female) is inherently temporary.

A second set of double similes that immediately follows the analogy of apples and grapes illustrates the evanescence of images in their physical state. Moving quickly from Narcissus's self-infliction of wounds to his general physical deterioration, Ovid thus describes the process of the youth's disintegration:

. . . sed, ut intabescere flavae
igne levi cerae matutinaeque pruinae
sole tepente solent, sic attenuatus amore
liquitur et tecto paulatim carpitur igni. (487–90)

[But just as tawny waxes are accustomed to melt by a thin flame or morning frosts by the warming sun, so he, attenuated by love, dissolves and is gradually worn away by a hidden fire.]

Wax and frost are appropriate analogues for Narcissus's deterioration, the first representing a change of state and the second a virtual disappearance. The latter recalls *Idyll* 7 of Theocritus, where the shepherd-singer refers to Daphnis "wasting like snow" (76). Self-absorbed and resisting love, both characters are ultimately reduced to a state of liquefaction and are absorbed into the waters that provided the backdrop for their laments.[69]

In narrating Narcissus's fate after death, Ovid continues to associate the youth with a fixation on the image. Even as a spirit of the dead, Narcissus is intent on his own reflection in the waters of the Styx (504–5): although only an *imago* now himself, he still seeks his own *imago*.[70] Ovid then shifts his attention to the issue of Narcissus's earthly remains. Here, he describes what happens after the nymphs prepare a bier for the dead youth:

nusquam corpus erat, croceum pro corpore florem
inveniunt foliis medium cingentibus albis. (509–10)

[Nowhere was there a body; they find a reddish-yellow flower, with white petals surrounding the center.]

In this passage, the poet has created a visual image of the flower by clever verbal framing. The adjective and noun for the white petals, along with the participle modifying them, surround the word for the center: the flower thereby takes shape in the verse itself. Significantly, Ovid does not linger over this poetic pictorial image: there is no elaboration, no expansion. The flower image disappears at the end of this tantalizing, but very brief, description. Furthermore, the phrase "pro corpore" implies that the flower is a replacement, a *substitution* for Narcissus rather than a metamorphosis of him.[71] The flower itself is thus only an image of Narcissus, a fragile, transitory object of the natural world ironically memorializing the youth's fixation on his static reflection.[72]

As this chapter has shown, Ovid exploits the underlying paradoxes of elegy so as to reveal that Narcissus embodies the "narcissistic" nature of that genre. On the one hand, the poet constructs Narcissus as the consummate image of beauty through the specific language and tropes by which elegy envisions the mistress, in particular Corinna in the *Amores*. On the other hand, the youth himself enacts the problem of an impossible love by showing a mastery of the conventions of the genre in his lament. The elegiac variations on the theme of separation from the beloved, replete with paradoxes, such as simultaneously inciting and suffering the flames of passion (464), capture the paradox of Narcissus's dilemma. Elegy's discourse of desire, furthermore, is closely bound up with a narcissistic conception of love for the mistress who is the product of the poet-lover's own imagination. As he continues in his lament to gaze in awe on his own reflection in the water, Narcissus absurdly literalizes an unstated paradox of that genre.

Later in the *Metamorphoses*, the poet evokes the Narcissus episode by an ironic perspective on elegiac conventions. Alison Sharrock has pointed to connections between Narcissus and the Pygmalion episode in book 10.[73] Segal has commented on Ovid's ambivalence toward Pygmalion: although his marvelous ability to provide shape to formless material is admirable, the sculptor acts like a parody of the lover in elegiac poetry by his excessive attentions to the statue which he has created before it is transformed into a woman by the favor of Venus.[74] By having Pygmalion behave like an elegiac lover as he falls in love with his own creation, the poet reveals the sculptor's affinity with Narcissus. Pygmalion's implicit self-love likewise has disastrous consequences, though not immediately but rather down the generational line, when his great-granddaughter falls in love with her father. Cinyras then unwittingly commits incest with Myrrha, and the result is another example of perfect beauty, their offspring Adonis.[75]

The poet looks back to Narcissus through the lens of elegy again in book 13, where he recalls the doctrine of self-knowledge derived from the *Ars*. There, Polyphemus boasts that he knows himself after seeing his reflection in water ("certe ego me novi liquidaeque in imagine vidi / nuper aquae" [840–41]). As with Tiresias's prophecy about Narcissus, Ovid exploits the semantic range of the verb *nosco*, exposing the absurd incongruities of the Cyclops's attempts at seduction through song.[76] The verb form *novi* can mean "I have recognized" as well as "I know": Polyphemus "knows" himself now because he has finally seen his face in some sort of mirror. For the intellectually limited Cyclops, self-knowledge is primarily visual.[77]

In addition, by conjoining a boast of self-knowledge with a description of the lover's best features, Ovid has the grotesque shepherd recall Apollo's instructions on amorous success. The Cyclops proceeds to describe his most attractive features: his great size, by which he surpasses Jupiter; his hair overshadowing his shoulders like a grove; the bristles on his skin; and his singular eye, as large as a shield and comparable to the sun (842–53). As Polyphemus highlights through a pictorial style his abundance of hair and his unique eye, the poet exposes the absurdity of the shepherd's implicit claim to the self-understanding that

Apollo advocates for the successful lover in *Ars* 2. Ovid has thus made a kind of reductio ad absurdum of the elegiac concept of self-knowledge, from Narcissus's admission of his desire for himself to Polyphemus's ignorant boast about his own looks.

By the end of the poem, Ovid leaves elegy behind. His last episode containing major elegiac elements occurs in book 14 in the period of the Alban kings; it serves as a bridge to the historical material concerned with the foundation of Rome. In the story of Pomona and Vertumnus, the god in disguise as an old woman narrates the cautionary tale of Iphis and Anaxarete (698–758) after his appearances in various male forms do not succeed in moving the virgin obsessed with tending her orchards. This inset narrative takes the conventions of elegy to an extreme, for when the hard-hearted Anaxarete is totally unmoved by her suitor's *paraclausithuron*, Iphis finds a resolution to his dilemma in suicide. Although Pomona does finally yield, Vertumnus's tale per se does not produce the desired effect of eliciting her favor.[78] Given the meaning of Vertumnus's name as the "turner," it is fitting that elegy in the *Metamorphoses* disappears at the very moment in which the importance of *change* is in fact accepted.

2

The Metamorphic Medea

In the first half of book 7, Ovid recounts the story of Medea, the paradigm of the dangerous female in Greek myth. The poet could assume the reader's familiarity with the long literary history of this formidable female. Euripides, in particular, explored the intransigent nature of this character in his tragedy detailing Medea's horrifying deeds in Corinth. His Medea threatens the very fabric of civilized life when she kills her own children as well as her rival and the king in order to get revenge on her faithless husband by leaving him with no hope to continue his family line.

The Greek playwright reveals Medea's highly problematic status as Other. She is the foreign wife from far-off Colchis who is now dismissed by Jason for a young Greek bride. Yet she is able to exploit the appearance of total vulnerability so as to set in motion a plot by which she gains mastery over the situation. Although urged by the chorus of Corinthian women to accept what cannot be changed, Medea cunningly manipulates Creon into deferring her exile for one day by playing on his sympathies as a father and, by promising to end his childless state, obtains the guarantee from King Aegeus of Athens that once she has fled Corinth he will grant her refuge.

In her appeal to Aegeus, Euripides reminds his audience of the source of Medea's dark powers through her connection to the chthonic goddess Hecate rather than to the Olympian gods: her expertise with magic and drugs enables her to secure Aegeus's help as well as to bring about the horrifying death of the princess Glauke and her father King Creon through the stratagem of a poisoned garment.[1] Euripides symbolically characterizes his heroine with violent images pertaining to the sea, wild beasts, and inanimate nature, which suggest that she has perversely appropriated a male heroic persona in her struggle with Jason.[2] By the end of the play, Medea has succeeded in rendering Jason utterly helpless but seems detached from the human realm altogether, as she appears on high, ready to flee in her magic chariot, and refuses Jason even the comfort of embracing his dead sons.

This dark figure entered into epic in a less awesome, but nonetheless complex, manifestation. In the *Argonautica*, Apollonius brings out the paradoxical nature of this barbarian princess: on the one hand, infected by Eros, she struggles over the conflict between loyalty to her family and her feelings for the hero, but on the other, once she provides the necessary help for Jason to retrieve the Golden Fleece, she has fully implicated herself in her brother Apsyrtus's murder. The Hellenistic poet, furthermore, makes Medea's connection to the dark powers of magic increasingly sinister from her first appearance in book 3 to her destruction of Talus, the last survivor of the race of bronze and the guardian of Crete, in book 4.[3] Although the epic ends with an apparently bright picture of the victorious Jason returning to Greece with his new bride, the specter of Euripides' terrifying character lurks in the background.

Medea was the exemplar of the dangers of female cunning, especially when spurred by unbridled anger, for the patriarchal society of Rome as well as of Greece. Both Ennius and Accius wrote tragedies on Medea in Latin, and Vergil's Dido bears the stamp of this intractable heroine. Ovid himself was drawn to this powerful character well before the *Metamorphoses*: his *Medea*, which unfortunately did not survive antiquity, recast the events previously dramatized by Euripides in Greek and by Ennius and Accius in Latin.[4] *Heroides* 12 envisions Medea's response to Jason when he has just deserted her for the daughter of King Creon.[5]

The episode in the *Metamorphoses* has a much broader sweep, encompassing the entire course of Medea's career from her infatuation with the handsome leader of the Argonauts and subsequent decision to aid him in his quest for the Golden Fleece to her rejuvenation of Jason's father Aeson and treacherous murder of King Pelias and finally to her failed attempt to poison King Aegeus's son Theseus and subsequent flight from Athens (1–424). In a movement from seemingly innocent to overtly threatening and dangerous, the Medea of book 7 appears to be similar to Apollonius's heroine. But Ovid plays with the reader's expectations about Medea's nature more extensively than his Greek epic predecessor. Ovid's quick shift from the inexperienced young woman struggling with her feelings of love for the handsome stranger to the accomplished witch is somewhat unsettling.[6] Her innocent demeanor in the first part and her sinister behavior in the final sections demand a complex characterization. The poet extends the implications of Medea's aggressiveness and cunning in particular, connecting these qualities to his larger epic project.

Ovid only briefly mentions Medea as the vengeful wife who causes the gruesome death of Jason's new bride and her father and murders her own children to punish her faithless spouse (394–97). Instead, in the first section, he reconceives the episode in Apollonius's *Argonautica* in which Medea agonizes over her love for Jason and then decides to help the hero complete the tasks imposed by Aeetes and seize the Golden Fleece. In the second section, he focuses on Medea's powers of witchcraft, especially by expanding extensively on the technical aspects of her craft and revealing the consequences of her machinations.

My discussion explores paradoxical elements of Ovid's Medea in light of the poet's own rather dissonant relationship to the epic tradition. I first examine Medea's soliloquy for its surprisingly powerful rhetoric. The poet, I believe, implies Medea's affinity with himself through an allusion to Horace that evokes his own high poetic aspirations throughout his story of this mythical heroine in book 7. Although numerous characters in the *Metamorphoses* allude to earlier works of literature in their speeches, Medea is distinctive: the poet endows her with a self-consciousness that suggests the young woman's awareness of her own literary past. Allusions to the abandoned wife of Euripides' *Medea* and *Heroides* 12 and to the young heroine of Apollonius's *Argonautica* imply that Medea only apparently reflects the vulnerability of her Hellenistic epic counterpart and that she anticipates her own future as an aggressive, masculinized character in the Greek tragedy and in Ovid's epistle. In her self-presentation, Medea both exploits previous literary versions of her character and employs considerable rhetorical skills so as to become a controlling force in the narrative. The impact of her rhetoric even extends beyond this episode, for her soliloquy serves as the archetype for the speeches of other misguided heroines later in the poem.[7]

Second, in an analysis of Medea's flight on the dragon chariot from Iolcus, I consider how Ovid extends the implications of Medea's transgressive nature. After tricking the daughters of Pelias into killing their father, Medea takes flight from her crime on a course which the poet elaborates in considerable detail. As Ovid describes this journey, he reveals how her trajectory encompasses earlier myths that are both recherché and morally problematic. This character, moreover, embodies the paradox that Ovid's epic both draws heavily on Hellenistic poetry and at the same time undermines its Callimachean poetics. By adding this account of her flight from Iolcus to the traditional story of Medea's manipulation of her metamorphic skills with Pelias, the poet implies his own ability to transform his inherited material and to create a new kind of epic poem. As he charts Medea's course over the Aegean Sea, Ovid makes her flight an image of the second half of the *Metamorphoses*.

Medea's Love for Jason

The young Colchian princess certainly elicits the sympathy that critics have perceived on account of her struggle over the conflicting forces of love and duty.[8] Medea indeed even draws the reader into her frame of mind through her charming naïveté and expressive powers. She acknowledges that Jason's fate is in the hands of the gods but immediately pleads for his safety: "vivat, an ille / occidat, in dis est; vivat tamen!" ("It is up to the gods whether he lives or dies, but nevertheless, let him live!" [23–24]). Here, she not only conveys emotional tension; she also cleverly employs an anaphora by repeating the subjunctive form *vivat* but changing its grammatical function from an indirect question to a hortatory command. In the context of her soliloquy, Medea's rhetorical skill is rather surprising, since she herself calls attention to the uncivilized nature of her homeland ("barbara tellus" [53]).

Medea's expressions of concern about Jason's response build up to a climax in which marriage becomes the reward for her help. She considers that, after being saved by her ("per me sospes" [40]), Jason will leave in order to become the husband of another ("ut per me sospes / . . . virque sit alterius" [40–41]). Yet, because his noble birth and his appearance (*vultus, gratia formae*) rule out the possibility of ingratitude on his part, she is assured of his good faith (*fidem* [46]), to which she will summon the gods as witnesses. She then reinforces the hero's indebtedness to her through a binding commitment: "tibi se semper debebit Iason, / te face sollemni iunget sibi" ("Jason will always owe himself to you; he will join you to himself with the sacred torch," [48–49]). The very structure of her language lends a concreteness to her expectations. Through the anaphora of the second-person pronoun and the asyndeton running the two clauses together, the heroine rhetorically yokes Jason's obligation to her with its fulfillment in marriage.

Medea's mention of conjugal bliss overtly seems to reinforce the impression of a naïveté, but an allusion to Horace connects her closely to

Ovid as poet. Here, imagining herself with her husband, she conveys
her ecstasy in hyperbolic terms: "quo coniuge felix / et dis cara ferar et
vertice sidera tangam" ("Happy with him as my husband, I will be
called dear to the gods and will touch the stars with my head" [60–61]).
Medea's boast echoes the end of *Odes* 1.1, where Horace claims that if
his patron Maecenas places him in the ranks of the Greek lyric poets, he
will "strike the stars with the top of his head" ("sublimi feriam sidera
vertice" [36]).[9] Medea seems to appropriate this status in the poetic
sphere for herself, especially as she begins to project an increasing
awareness of her literary counterparts in Euripides and Apollonius.
Ovid, to be sure, makes the heroine utter his own desires: he stakes a
claim to greatness not only by this dazzling poetic monologue and by
his more sustained adaptation of the myth of Medea in book 7 but also
by complementing this echo of *Odes* 1.1 with an echo of *Odes* 3.30 in the
epilogue at the end of book 15.

Medea's thoughts of leaving Colchis with Jason as her husband give
rise to heightened poetic powers.[10] As she imagines herself with the
hero on the dangerous sea voyage back to Greece, Medea creates a ro-
mantically enticing picture of herself safe in the arms of her husband:

nempe tenens, quod amo, gremioque in Iasonis haerens
per freta longa ferar: nihil illum amplexa verebor,
aut, siquid metuam, metuam de coniuge solo. (66–68)

[Indeed, holding the one I love, clinging to Jason's chest, I will be borne over the
vast seas: embracing him, I will be afraid of nothing, or if I fear anything, I will
fear for my husband alone.]

Here, three participles denoting strong physical contact (*tenens, haerens,
amplexa*) produce a compelling picture of the young woman in the em-
brace of the hero. Ovid has Medea subtly lure the reader into adopting
her point of view. A male would find it flattering to identify with the
protective hero who holds the young princess in his arms and who is
the object of her adoration, while a female might relate to her intrepid,
yet caring, frame of mind.

By appearing to know her literary past and to articulate her own
future, Medea further embodies poetic powers that align her with Ovid
himself. In a discussion of Medea in both *Heroides* 12 and *Metamorphoses*
7, Stephen Hinds has pointed out the epic character's "correction" of a
geographical error concerning the Symplegades when she recounts her
travels with Jason in the epistolary poem.[11] A similar kind of literary
self-awareness by Ovid's heroine, I believe, pervades her monologue.

However engaging she may be, Medea alludes to elements of her story in the Greek tragic and epic versions that are at odds with the merely naive aspects of her self-presentation.

Scholars have long recognized the debt to Euripides' Medea in the young woman's acknowledgment of the difficulty of ending her passion for the stranger. As she faces her dilemma, she feels pulled in opposite directions: "sed trahit invitam nova vis, aliudque cupido, / mens aliud suadet" ("But a strange force carries me away against my will, and desire urges one thing, reason another" [19-20]). She then sums up her predicament: "video meliora proboque, / deteriora sequor!" ("I see and approve of the better course, but I pursue the worse!" [20-21]). With this moral insight, Medea echoes her Euripidean counterpart, who asserts that although she understands the evil course on which she embarks, her rage is stronger than her reason (1078-79).[12] Carole Newlands observes that in the analogous passage in Euripides' play Medea decides to go through with the murder of her own children; she concludes, however, that the words spoken by Ovid's love-struck young woman have a very different effect from the model in Euripides.[13]

This echo of the vengeful wife, however, is reinforced as Medea continues to evoke Euripides' dark heroine through her language. Medea follows this allusion to the tragic character's determination to proceed on her hideous course with a suggestive collocation of words: "quid in hospite, regia virgo, / ureris?" ("Why will you burn for a stranger, royal maiden?" [21-22]). The juxtaposition of *hospite* ("guest" as well as "stranger") and "regia virgo" suggests the relation of Jason to Glauke, the daughter of King Creon of Corinth, in Euripides' play. The verb *ureris* here, of course, has the figurative meaning of erotic passion. But it also evokes the horrific condition of literal conflagration that the Corinthian princess experiences after putting on the crown and the robe that Medea's children have offered as gifts.[14] Just after the tragic heroine gives voice to her moral dilemma, a messenger from the palace describes in considerable detail the fire shooting from the young woman's head and then engulfing her entire body (1186-1201). Medea's words here ironically prefigure her later act of causing another royal maiden literally to burn over her love for the handsome guest.

In her soliloquy, Medea employs poetic figures that recall her unspeakable act of infanticide as dramatized in Euripides' play. As the Colchian princess ponders what will happen if she does not help Jason, she imagines him combating the fire-breathing bulls, the militant crop of earthborn men, and the deadly serpent guarding the fleece (29-31).

Her reaction is then to castigate herself for cruelty in allowing such a fate: "tum me de tigride natam, / tum ferrum et scopulos gestare in corde fatebor" ("Then I will acknowledge that I was born from a tigress, then that I bear iron and rock in my heart" [32–33]). William Anderson notes that the image of a heart of iron or stone goes as far back as the *Iliad*, where Patroclus reproaches Achilles for refusing to re-enter battle after Machaon is wounded (16.33–34).[15]

The source of the comparison here, however, would seem to be Euripides, who applied it specifically to Medea. The chorus thus addresses the revenge-driven wife:

τάλαιν,' ὡς ἄρ' ἦσθα πέτρος ἢ σίδα-
ρος, ἅτις τέκνων
ὃν ἔτεκες ἄροτον αὐτόχειρι μοίρᾳ κτενεῖς. (1279–81)

[Oh, wretched one, how indeed you were rock or iron, you who will kill the crop of children that you bore with a death inflicted by your own hand.]

The context in the tragedy is especially pointed: the chorus makes the remark as it hears Medea's children scream in pain and ask each other how they can escape their mother's onslaught (1270–74). By alluding to Euripides, Ovid has Medea predict how she will be perceived at a later stage in her career. Moreover, by using the strong verb *fateor* ("to acknowledge") here, Medea makes her statement seem to be almost a retort to Euripides, a rejection of the criticism against her in the tragedy.

Medea's insistence that, if she fails to assist Jason, she was born of a tigress has a complex background vis-à-vis the tragic heroine. Euripides' Medea is castigated as a savage beast for her heartless actions against her children. Jason calls her a lioness with the wild nature of the monster Scylla when he sees her about to escape from Corinth in the chariot of the Sun with the bodies of their slain children (1342–43). In response, Medea with bitter sarcasm encourages the helpless hero to call her a lioness or Scylla, since she has achieved her revenge (1358–60). After she refuses to let him kiss or touch his children's bodies, Jason invokes Zeus to witness his injury from this fierce lioness (1405–11).

As scholars frequently observe, Vergil drew on Euripides' tragedy for his characterization of Dido in *Aeneid* 4.[16] The Augustan poet has the angry Dido employ a comparable image of a wild animal when Aeneas reveals his intention to seek a new kingdom in Italy. Using the image of a tigress rather than a lioness, Vergil has the Carthaginian queen direct the analogy against the hero as she reproaches him for his callousness in abruptly deciding to leave her. Her response is to lash out and deny

Aeneas's divine parentage by claiming that the Caucasus begot him on its rocks and that Hyrcanian tigresses nursed him (365–67). Like the tragic Medea, Dido is enraged that the hero has spurned her love after she saved him and his men from death and provided him a share in her kingdom (373–75). Unable to prevent his departure, Dido similarly wants revenge; she hopes that a painful fate will cause him to lament his cruelty and even predicts that she will continue to torment the hero after her death (382–86). In Medea's soliloquy in the *Metamorphoses*, the tigress analogy, along with the image of rocks, evokes Vergil's dark heroine, an earlier literary descendant of Euripides' Medea. Although Dido uses the tigress image in reference to Aeneas, Medea here appropriates it for herself. By reversing Dido's criticism of Aeneas for his lack of gratitude for her assistance, she affirms the necessity of her aid to Jason.

Medea's ingenuous expectations about her life after accompanying Jason back to Greece with the Golden Fleece are ironic against the background of their source in Euripides' play. As she contemplates the positive results of helping Jason recover the fleece, Medea envisions a *titulus* (56), presumably a public monument engraved with her praises as savior of the Argonauts. Such an emblem of heroic stature would normally be awarded to a male rather than to a female. More realistically, she expresses her expectation that she will benefit from experiencing a superior country and cities with a longstanding tradition of art and culture, whose fame has reached even Colchis (57–58).

Although Medea's enthusiasm here could elicit sympathy for its naïveté, her references to the advantages of Greece recall Jason's reproaches to her in Euripides' tragedy. There, the hero criticizes her for being angry that he has taken a new wife. He emphasizes all the benefits that she has received from her association with him: a home in Greece instead of a barbarian land, the rule of law and justice, and fame among the Greeks for her services (536–41). Here, Medea evokes the bitter clash between the hero and the foreign wife whom he has rejected, in which the tragic heroine responds with total scorn to Jason's enumeration of the benefits of Greek civilization. By pre-empting Jason's chauvinistic attitude toward Greek culture in Euripides' play, Medea implicitly reflects Ovid's tendency to undermine the traditional hero's stance of superiority.

Through allusions to the *Argonautica* in Medea's soliloquy and in her meeting with Jason, Ovid exploits the epic background of this myth so as to reinforce the heroine's transgressive nature. The echoes of Apollonius's story of Medea's love for Jason imply a more aggressive character than the Greek poet's naive heroine, one who is by no means simply manipulated by the hero.[17] Somewhat surprisingly, Medea openly expresses her desire to be celebrated (*celebrabere* [50]) as the savior of the Greek youth, in particular by a crowd of mothers ("matrum turba"). The source for this detail, as Anderson notes, is Jason's speech to Medea in book 3 of the *Argonautica*.[18] In that passage, the hero, sensing the young woman's agitation, reassures her by stating that he and his companions will spread her fame back in Greece and that their wives and mothers will do the same (990–94).

Ovid's reader familiar with Apollonius's epic, however, would perceive the irony of this allusion. There, Jason's persuasion of the gullible Medea includes a somber myth foreshadowing the hero's desertion and the heroine's desire for revenge. For Jason encourages Medea by mentioning the case of Ariadne, who helped Theseus and was later rewarded with the distinction of an honorific constellation in the heavens called Ariadne's Crown (997–1006). But he conceals the fact that the celestial honor was a favor bestowed by Dionysus out of love, not a reward for Ariadne's services to Theseus and the band of Greek heroes on Crete. By the echo of Apollonius here, Medea not only appropriates Jason's words but also points forward to the analogous scene later in book 7, in which Jason does not manipulate Medea but instead does her bidding.

Medea's insistence on receiving an oath before aiding the hero implies that she resists the model of the Colchian princess in the *Argonautica*. In her soliloquy, Medea asserts that Jason will swear an oath to her and that she will compel the gods to be witnesses as a guarantee of his good faith (46–47). In doing so, she recalls the oath that Apollonius's heroine asks of Jason as she takes the drastic step of fleeing from Aeetes' palace before she drugs the serpent guarding the Golden Fleece. There, the frightened young woman reacts to her desperate plight, after she has defied her father by giving Jason the magic potion to conquer the bulls and to encounter the earth-born men. First, Medea pleads with the Argonauts to rescue her: "rusasthe dusammoron" ("Save ill-fated me" [4.83]). Then, she addresses Jason individually and promises to subdue the serpent and obtain the fleece for him. When she asks the hero to honor his promises to her so that she may not become a source of reproach for lack of kin (90–91), Apollonius emphasizes the anguish of the young woman, describing her as "*akêchemenê*" ("grieving" [92]).

Ovid's Medea elicits an oath from Jason much earlier than Apollonius's heroine, before providing any help. In her encounter with Jason in the grove of Hecate, she thus states her demands without diffidence:

quid faciam, video, nec me ignorantia veri
decipiet, sed amor! Servabere munere nostro!
servatus promissa dato! (92–94)

[I see what I am doing, and not ignorance of the truth but love will deceive me! You will be saved by my service; saved, make your vow!]

The poet then indicates that the hero made a pledge to guarantee his success in overcoming the dangers by invoking three deities: Hecate, the indigenous divinity of the grove, and Medea's grandfather Helius (94–97). By stating the hero's oath in indirect discourse, the poet allows Jason no personal voice and reduces the immediacy of his presence. Whereas Jason in the *Argonautica* is in complete control of his initial meeting with Medea and shows his ability to manipulate the Colchian princess through his clever speech, here Medea dominates.

Ovid reinforces the power of his heroine by a subtle use of imagery in this scene. Whereas Apollonius emphasizes the intervention of Eros after Hera and Athena request the aid of Aphrodite on behalf of Jason (3.6–166), Ovid subtly shifts the focus to Medea herself by eliminating divine agency. Through a simile, however, he alludes to Eros's wounding of Medea in the *Argonautica*. Here, he describes the hero's effect on the young woman when she first sees him in the grove of Hecate:

utque solet ventis alimenta adsumere, quaeque
parva sub inducta latuit scintilla favilla,
crescere et in veteres agitata resurgere vires
sic iam lenis amor, iam quem languere putares,
ut vidit iuvenem, specie praesentis inarsit. (79–83)

[And just as a small spark which was hidden in ashes is accustomed to feed on the breezes and to increase and to take on its former strength when fanned, so now as she saw the youth, the mild love, which you would have thought was already flagging, burst into flame at the appearance of the man in person.]

Ovid once again cleverly adapts the traditional image of fire for sexual passion. His simile recalls Apollonius's description of Medea after she first sees Jason.[19] The Greek poet here describes the young woman's emotions:

And as a poor woman whose job is to spin wool piles up twigs around a blazing brand so that she may kindle a fire at night beneath her roof, when she has woken up very early, and the flame greatly increasing from the little log consumes all the twigs together, so in secret baneful Love, coiling around her heart, blazed. (3.291–97)

Like Apollonius, Ovid contrasts the small size of the ember with the powerful flame erupting from it. But he diminishes the pathos of his predecessor's simile by eliminating its backdrop of a laboring woman who must rise at a very early hour and start a fire in order to perform the work by which she ekes out a living. Ovid does not supply a context within his simile but instead focuses entirely on the fire generated. He thus makes his Medea less human and more like a force of nature than her counterpart in the *Argonautica*. Furthermore, "oulos erôs" ("baneful love") can signify either the psychological force or the god Eros, who has just shot Medea with his bow, and this ambiguity adds to the pathos of Medea's plight. But the dynamic of the plot involves divine manipulation: intent on promoting the hero's cause, Hera and Athena prevail upon Aphrodite to make Medea fall in love with Jason. On the narrative level, then, the Colchian princess is the victim of higher powers working to achieve their own interests. In the *Metamorphoses*, struck by the hero's appearance, Medea finds Jason's *face* divine ("nec . . . mortalia ora" [87–88]). By alluding to, but at the same time rejecting, divine causality, Ovid further internalizes Medea's passion and suggests her powers to bring about the desired consequences, however dreadful, on her own terms.[20]

Ovid insinuates a reversal of masculine and feminine roles in Medea's meeting with Jason, in sharp contrast to the analogous scene in the *Argonautica*.[21] Whereas Jason in the Greek epic dominates the meeting and adroitly manipulates Medea in the grove of Hecate, here he is passive. There, he speaks to the heroine at great length, reassuring her of his sincerity and flattering her (3.975–1007); she, on the other hand, is able to respond only with difficulty after a considerable amount of time has passed (1025). Here, Jason utters no direct speech at all.[22] Ovid merely summarizes the hero's request in the briefest terms: "et auxilium submissa voce rogavit / promisitque torum" ("He both asked for help with a hushed voice and promised her marriage" [90–91]). Although grammatically modifying *voce*, the word *submissa* ("hushed," "lowered") adds to the characterization of Jason in Ovid's episode: it reinforces his subordination to Medea and his feminized nature in contrast to a subtly masculinized Medea.

Although Medea in *Metamorphoses* 7 is a late descendant of the heroines of Euripides' *Medea*, Apollonius's *Argonautica*, and even *Heroides* 12, she creates the impression that she is a controlling voice in the manner of the narrator. Medea's echo of *Odes* 1.1, in which Horace expresses a desire for high status in lyric, aligns her with Ovid as poet. Ovid, of course, makes allusions to other literary texts, but Medea's self-assertive manner suggests her own awareness of her background in literary myth. Even as she elicits sympathy for her plight, the heroine evokes critical moments in the tragic and epic versions of her story. Ovid thus enables Medea to appear simultaneously an innocent ingenue and a powerful, dominating woman. He thereby hints at Medea's usurpation of the powers traditionally reserved for the heroic male. The clever Medea figuratively transforms herself more fully as her story unfolds. She thus comes to symbolize the multiple forms by which metamorphosis may be envisioned in Ovid's poem.

The Flight of Medea the Witch

After Medea applies her skill with drugs to restore Aeson to youth, she then engages in a more sinister use of magic by deceiving the daughters of Pelias with her deliberately ineffective concoction and then murdering the king. Ovid prefaces this section of Medea's story by explaining her motivation: "neve doli cessent" ("so that plots may not cease" [297]). Her concern is thus to sustain her need for trickery rather than to further Jason's dynastic ambitions. Ovid would doubtless have perceived Apollonius's gloss on the name of Medea in the phrase "mêdea kourês" ("the plots of the young woman" [3.826]).[23] He thus suggests the very essence of Medea by pointing to this etymology of her name in Greek, for *dolus* ("trickery") is the Latin equivalent of *mêdos* (plural, *mêdea*).

Medea at this point illustrates the meaning of her name implied in Ovid's etymological pun, for she proceeds to deceive the Peliades, convincing them that her witchcraft will rejuvenate their father by draining the blood of an old sheep and transforming it into a lamb. By pretending to use the same effective magic potion and ritual on Pelias, she gets the women to stab the old king. After she herself completes the murder, Medea flies swiftly from the scene by air. The poet asserts that without her magic dragons ("pennatis serpentibus" [350]), Medea would not have escaped punishment for this hideous crime.

Medea's very means of escape endows this morally flawed character with a special status.[24] Aerial flight in the *Metamorphoses*, whether by Phaethon in the chariot of Sol in book 2 or by Daedalus on wings of his own devising in book 8, is a form of liberation from normal human constraints that implies common ground with the creative experience of the poet himself.[25] As we will see in chapter 3, Ovid renders Daedalus's creation of wings highly problematic by connecting his flight in the narrative with the fate of his unfortunate nephew Perdix. Medea's journey from Iolcus to Corinth appears to have had no precedent in prior versions of the myth. The poet's own invention, it is a virtuoso display of geographical and mythical lore that scholars have felt serves little real purpose.[26] A close examination of this passage, however, shows that Ovid connects many of the myths mentioned in Medea's flight to thematic concerns and to the unique nature of his epic, especially as it unfolds in the second half.

First of all, the content of several of the myths in this travelogue concerns the loss of children and the response of a parent or, in one case, a grandparent to that loss. Most of these myths are now obscure, but they seem to have had Hellenistic sources. Antoninus Liberalis attributes to Hyginus Alcidamas's loss of Ctesylla (368–70) and Hyrie's of Cycnus (371–81), and to Boius Eumelus's rash act of killing his son Botres for violating sacrificial procedure that leads to the man's despair (390). The story of the river god Cephisus's lament for his grandson who was transformed into a seal (388–89) is otherwise unattested. In two of these myths, the parent bears either a direct or an indirect responsibility for the death of the child. The reference to Alcidamas merits particular consideration. As Medea passes over Carthaea, Ovid refers to *pater* Alcidamas about to marvel at the metamorphosis of his daughter into a dove (369). According to Antoninus Liberalis 1, an Athenian named Hermochares tricked a certain Ctesylla into reading aloud an inscription on an apple to the effect that she promised to marry him. Although agreeing to give Hermochares his daughter in marriage, Alcidamas violated his oath to the man, who called upon the gods for revenge. As a result, they brought about the young woman's death in childbirth but then transformed her into a dove and called for rites to be instituted in her honor.

The myth of Alcidamas has important thematic links with Medea's own actions in Corinth. With his reference to this story about the loss of a child, Ovid does not inform the reader of Alcidamas's pain or sense of responsibility for his daughter's death. Instead, he refers to the man's astonishment at her metamorphosis ("miraturus erat" [370]). The poet similarly does not mention Medea's feelings about killing her children and reports the deed obliquely: "sanguine natorum perfunditur impius ensis" ("The impious sword was drenched with the blood of her children" [396]). He only tersely conveys his distance from Medea's dreadful act in a brief statement: "ultaque se male mater Iasonis effugit arma"

("The mother, having badly avenged herself, fled the arms of Jason" [397]).[27]

The poet, furthermore, ignores an element in literary versions of the two myths with socio-religious implications. In the myth of Alcidamas, the institution of a ritual to commemorate the unfortunate young woman who paid the price for her father's violation of an oath also suggests the eventual outcome of Medea's crime: at the end of Euripides' tragedy, the heroine herself tells Jason that she will establish annual rites to atone for the blood guilt (1381–83). In his brief reference to this myth, Ovid keeps the human and moral issues under the surface, though his contemporary reader would presumably have been aware of the details in Nicander's account.

The flight narrative hints at the morally problematic nature of Medea's witchcraft. Here, Ovid describes Medea's passage over Rhodes:

Phoebeamque Rhodon et Ialysios Telchinas
quorum oculos ipso vitiantes omnia visu
Iuppiter exosus fraternis subdidit undis. (365–67)

[Rhodes belonging to Phoebus, and the Telchines, dwellers in Ialysus. Hating the eyes of those men who spoiled all things with their very gaze, Jupiter hid them under his brother's waves.]

By the epithet *Phoebeam*, the poet calls attention to the patronage of Rhodes by the sun god Helius. That divinity is the grandfather of Medea, a fact which Apollonius emphasizes when the heroine seeks refuge with her aunt Circe after murdering her brother Apsyrtus, for the sorceress recognizes the young woman by her flashing eyes, a characteristic of the race of Helius (4.725–29). Like the Telchines, Medea is capable of bewitching with her brilliant eyes those whom she loathes.[28]

Ovid's reference to witchcraft connects both the Telchines and Medea to a debate about poetics. In his preface to the *Aetia*, Callimachus singles out the Telchines as his literary enemies, hostile critics who carp at him for not producing long works.[29] Responding with disdain for these opinionated backbiters, the Greek poet defends his relatively short poems by reference to their quality: they are all the "sweeter" for being carefully constructed, in contrast to the unpolished work of continuous narrative espoused by the Telchines (frag. 1.1–20).

The Medea section is by far the longest continuous narrative on a single character in the *Metamorphoses*. Does Ovid paradoxically imply that it threatens to expand into a virtual epic by itself? The narrative recounting Medea's magic with Aeson is unusually lengthy (179–293), filled with details about the setting, Medea's invocation of the gods associated with magic, the arcane herbs sought for the potion, and the procedure of rejuvenation itself. Medea's deception of Pelias's daughters then mirrors the previous narrative in the details of her magic, though in a more abbreviated form (300–356). The poet does not stop Medea's story until the moment that her cunning use of magic *fails*. At that point, he dismisses her with only a single line: "effugit illa necem nebulis per carmina motis" ("She escaped death in a cloud created by her incantation" [424]). Fleeing unceremoniously from Athens into an undefined exile, she disappears from the poem for good. Much like the Telchines in Callimachus's *Aetia,* Medea thus symbolizes a narrative, motivated by an obsession with cunning and the arcane, that threatens to proliferate indefinitely.

Immediately after his reference to the Telchines, however, Ovid suggests his affiliation with Callimachus and Hellenistic poetics in his reference to the next two myths. The story of Alcidamas, recounted by Nicander, incorporates the motif of an apple inscribed with a message binding the reader of it to an amorous relationship with its author. Like Ovid in *Heroides* 20 and 21, Nicander presumably imitated Callimachus's story of Acontius and Cydippe in the *Aetia* involving the motif of a similarly inscribed apple, which causes a young woman unwittingly to commit herself to the author of the words.[30] The poet then mentions the story of Cycnus and Hyrie, a quintessentially Hellenistic tale elaborated in some detail rather than summarized in a very sketchy form.

Ovid's account of the myth of Cycnus and his mother is in fact eleven lines (371–81), more than three times the length of each of the other sixteen myths mentioned in this travelogue. It involves a handsome youth who orders a suitor named Phylius to perform the extraordinarily difficult tasks of subduing wild creatures, such as vultures, a lion, and a bull; when Phylius in disgust at Cycnus's coldness refuses to hand over the bull, the youth jumps off a cliff and, as he falls, is metamorphosed into a swan. His mother Hyrie is so filled with grief that, as she weeps, she dissolves into a lake, which then takes its name from her.

Ovid's version differs from Nicander's as reported by Antoninus Liberalis principally in the name of Cycnus's mother and in her metamorphosis. In Antoninus Liberalis 12, the woman is called Thyrie and is transformed into a bird rather than a lake.[31] Although it is possible that Ovid found his variant on the name in some other source, there is no evidence that he did not make the change himself. The difference in the initial letter ("h" as opposed to "th") correlates with the change in the metamorphosis in Ovid's text.

The poet here seems to suggest a connection between the name Hyrie and water. The Greek verb *oureo*, "to make water," which lacks the initial aspirate, is similar.[32] Another name for this lake in antiquity was Hydra, which is also connected linguistically with water (from *hudor*) and might have provided the poet an incentive for changing Thyrie to Hyrie.[33] Furthermore, the Latin verb *urinor* (or *urino*) may have suggested to Ovid a clever double play: since it means "to plunge into water," a proper name related to this verb would not only conjure up an association with water but would also recall the woman's act of jumping into the lake in Nicander, which then brought about her transformation into a swan. Ovid in a typically Hellenistic manner shows how a minute change in orthography can effect a linguistic metamorphosis that substantively alters the meaning of the text.

Ovid's use of the myth of Cycnus here draws attention to the poetics of the *Metamorphoses*. The youth's metamorphosis into a swan is itself suggestive of Callimachean poetics.[34] This story not only involves the transformation of the youth and his mother, but also suggests the instability of a name itself as the marker of a unique and meaningful identity. As the second of three myths relating the transformation of a Cycnus into a swan, this one combines the predominant elements of the other two: the erotic in Cycnus's relationship with Phaethon (2.364–80) and the heroic in Cycnus's encounter with Achilles (12.73–147). The story of Cycnus and Phylius is an odd integration of the two motifs, serving as a parody in miniature of the theme of heroic labor motivated by love. It foreshadows Ovid's humorous treatment of numerous tales interweaving the heroic and the erotic in the last half of the poem, including the Calydonian hunt that centers on Meleager's passion for Atalanta in book 8 and Achelous's contest with Hercules for Deinaira in book 9, which will be discussed in chapter 3.

Ovid's summary amusingly deflates underlying epic pretensions. The myths of Hercules' labors provide an ironic model, for Cycnus plays the role of Eurystheus vis-à-vis Hercules as he imposes on Phylius the task of bringing back vultures, a lion, and a bull (373–74). In Antoninus Liberalis's summary, Hercules even provides help to Phylius in subduing the bull.[35] But the larger issues of divine hostility and political power inherent in the Hercules myth are lacking in this personal love story. Furthermore, the language of high emotions here evokes humor rather than empathy. Phylius becomes angry (*iratus* [375]), refusing to persist

in his efforts when the return of his love is too meager (*stricto* mean-
ing "pulled in," "tight" [375]); Cycnus, in turn, is outraged (*indignatus*
[377]). The poet reduces the behavior of the arrogant lover to mere pet-
ulance, for Cycnus cries out bluntly, "cupies dare" ("You will wish to
give it" [377]). One might have expected a degree of eloquence in the last
words spoken by the son of Apollo as well as of Hyrie, especially since
this offspring of the god of poetry in his metamorphosed state produced
the soulful swan song. Cycnus's final act seems too abrupt and inade-
quately motivated to elicit pity. With no further verbal response on his
part, this haughty youth simply throws himself off a cliff.

Ovid's summary of the Cycnus myth here is a distillation of his nar-
rative technique in recounting the story of Meleager and Atalanta and
the Calydonian boar hunt in book 8, the myth of Hercules and Ache-
lous in book 9, and the Trojan War in books 12 and 13. Heroic activity in
those narratives is similarly deflated as it is interwoven incongruously
with erotic elements.[36] Parody or caricature is the predominant mode. In
the Calydonian hunt, for instance, Theseus dissuades his companion
Pirithous from attempting to shoot at the boar by using language of
love: "cui 'procul' Aegides 'o me mihi carior' inquit / 'pars animae con-
siste meae!'" ("To him the son of Aegeus said, 'Stand far away, oh dearer
to me than myself, part of my very soul!'" [8.405–6]).[37]

Even without an intrusion of the erotic, heroic endeavor elicits
humor more than awe. Achilles' fight with the warrior Cycnus, a son of
Neptune, is rather an endurance test. With considerable impatience, the
Greek hero is forced to undergo a variety of postures and gyrations be-
fore finding a means of snuffing out his enemy's life.[38] Frustrated that
four spear shots fail to penetrate Cycnus's chest, Achilles jumps from
his chariot and pummels the man's head. Then, after Cycnus trips over
a rock, he swings him around and thrusts him to the ground; with
knees on his chest, he strangles the man with his helmet straps (12.96–
144). The metamorphosis of Cycnus into a swan then serves an unex-
pected purpose. As he is about to strip the dead warrior, Achilles finds
the armor empty (145–47): with no body as a war prize, the great Greek
hero is deprived of concrete proof of his valor and a source of material
gain from any ransom for the body.[39]

Ovid hints at a defining characteristic of his poem, the element of
chance, immediately following the myth of Cycnus and Hyrie. The poet
specifies that the next place Medea passes over is in close proximity to
Lake Hyrie and the valley of Cycnus: "adiacet his Pleuron, in qua trepi-
dantibus alis / Ophias effugit natorum vulnera Combe" ("Near them

lies Pleuron, in which Combe, the daughter of Ophius, escaped wounds from her sons on quivering wings" [382–83]). Since nothing is known of the myth of Combe beyond what Ovid says here, it is difficult to assess its significance in the context.

The site is perhaps mentioned principally because the name itself reinforces the fact of its proximity to Lake Hyrie. The word *pleuron* in Greek in fact means "ribs" or "side." The name, functioning grammatically as the subject, is then explained by its verb *adiacet* ("lies beside"). This place happens to be near a more significant one for the poet. Ovid's play with the meaning of the name here points to the element of chance as a governing principle in this epic. Indeed, many events recounted in the *Metamorphoses*, as the poet observes at various points, occur fortuitously at the same time or in succession.[40] Eschewing any significance of a providential nature in such collocations, Ovid exploits the literary potential of chance occurrences as a means of moving his narrative forward.

Elsewhere in the travelogue of Medea's flight from Iolcus, Ovid alludes specifically to his own narrative of the Trojan War as a subject bereft of heroic meaning. Here, as the witch passes over the Troad, he singles out a grave: "quaque pater Corythi parva tumulatus harena est" ("and where the father of Corythus was buried with a small amount of sand" [361]). As Anderson notes, this line refers to Paris and his degrading burial, totally lacking the magnificence that a hero of royal stock would expect.[41] Ovid in his narrative of the Trojan War in books 12 and 13 dismisses Paris as a warrior but mentions him three times in a cynical manner. At the beginning of book 12, in referring to the honor of a cenotaph for Priam's son Aesacus, he records the absence of Paris, "who afterward brought a long war to his homeland along with the wife he had stolen [*rapta*]" (5). In the contest over the arms of Achilles in book 13, Ulysses also disparages the man when he recalls going to Troy as an ambassador to retrieve Helen: "Paris, his brothers, and his comrades in theft [qui rapuere sub illo] hardly kept their wicked hands away" (202–3). Finally, when Neptune can no longer bear the destruction of Troy and sends Apollo to take on Achilles, the god discovers Paris in the midst of carnage shooting arrows here and there at a few insignificant Greeks ("rara per ignotos spargentem cernit Achivos / tela Parim" [600–601]).[42]

The poet here does not even name Paris but instead refers to him obliquely in a way that draws attention to the Trojan's shame. For this son of Priam was exposed at birth lest he fulfill a dreadful prophecy that he would be a source of destruction to Troy but survived by chance; raised as a shepherd, he later wed the nymph Oenone and had a child by her named Corythus.[43] This Corythus goes unmentioned in the surviving accounts of the Trojan War, though his reputed death at the hands of his own father reinforces the propriety of Ovid's allusion to Paris's unheroic burial here.[44] When he later describes the fate of Achilles' body, Ovid implicitly recalls Paris. The "parva urna" (614) that contains Achilles' ashes is analogous to the "parva harena" covering Paris's remains.

The implied comparison between Paris and Achilles is revealing. The poet pays lip service at least to Achilles' reputation as the greatest of all heroes. He contrasts the disparity between the hero's physical remains and his fame: although his ashes hardly fill a small urn, Achilles survives through his glory, which fills the world (615–17). Yet by immediately asserting that Achilles' very shield served to incite strife (*bella* [621]), Ovid connects that hero inherently to violence. In the contest over his arms, as we will see in detail in chapter 5, Ajax and Ulysses both stake a claim to having had the closer relation to the great hero in their individual efforts to win. Although the true successor to his cousin on the basis of martial skills, Ajax cannot win a war of wits against Ulysses and takes his own life. Even as a ghost, Achilles perpetuates bloodshed by demanding the sacrifice of Polyxena to satisfy his need for honor (13.441–48). If his skepticism about heroism undercuts Achilles' glory, the poet does not deny that hero's power. By contrast, Paris's total lack of merit as a warrior wins him only silence or open disdain in Ovid's text.

Immediately after this reference to Paris, Medea proceeds on her journey in the vicinity (the poet does not name another geographical area but instead refers only obliquely to a metamorphosis). Here, the place itself responded to an animal transformation: "et quos Maera novo latratu terruit agros" ("and the fields which Maera frightened with her strange barking" [362]). Commentators note that this Maera is otherwise unknown but point to an analogue in Ovid's account of Hecuba's metamorphosis into a dog: after the body of her beloved son Polydorus washes up on the shore, Hecuba in her inconsolable grief seeks revenge on the treacherous Thracian king Polymestor by gouging the man's eyes out; when the king's followers try to subdue her, she is transformed into a dog (13.537–78). Rather than just offering a brief parallel to a more elaborate myth, the reference to Maera specifically makes an allusion to Hecuba's metamorphosis, by which Ovid continues to anticipate obliquely his Trojan War narrative.

The key, I believe, lies in an etymological play on the name Maera. The only other mythological character known as Maera is the dog that revealed to Erigone the location of the corpse of her father Icarius, murdered by drunken shepherds to whom he had given the gift of wine. After the young woman commits suicide by hanging herself from a tree over her father's body, the protagonists in the myth are honored by being metamorphosed into stars, with Maera becoming Sirius.[45] Appropriate to its association with the Dog Star, the name Maera (or Maira) is related to the Greek verb *marmairô*, "to sparkle."[46] In the *Metamorphoses*, Ovid creates his own etymology for Hecuba after she is transformed into a dog. Here, he recounts the fate of Hecuba in her new form: "veterumque diu memor illa malorum / tum quoque Sithonios ululavit maesta per agros" ("And then, too, for a long time, mindful of her old evils, she howled sadly over the Sithonian fields" [13.570–71]).[47] Hecuba is the Maera who evokes terror in those who hear her strange barking, for her sorrow drives her to howl through the landscape. She has become in essence *maesta:* the adjective, related to the verb *maereo*, "to grieve," explains the name Maera, suggesting the overwhelming grief that she expresses in her new physical form through howling (*ululavit*).

In addition to supplying his version of the Trojan War, Ovid in Hellenistic fashion also alludes to another major section of the second half of the *Metamorphoses*, the narrative of Orpheus in book 10. The poet in fact recalls the death of his great singer near the very beginning of this passage when he mentions Medea's flight over the Aegean along the coast of Asia Minor. After stating that the heroine passed over Pitane, he refers more allusively to the next site: "factaque de saxo longi simulacra draconis" ("and the image of the long serpent made from rock" [358]). As Anderson notes, Ovid here refers to the island of Lesbos, which is situated opposite Pitane and was the scene of the petrification later described in book 11.[48]

This transformation involves the great bard Orpheus. After the Thracian women have mutilated the body of the singer whom they despised for scorning them, Orpheus's severed head, still retaining the power of song, washes up on the shore of Lesbos; it would then have been the prey of a snake if Apollo had not turned the creature to stone (50–60). There, Ovid suggests the frightening aspect of this hideous creature even when rendered harmless, for the snake became stone just as it was preparing to devour Orpheus's head: "in lapidem rictus serpentis apertos / congelat et patulos, ut erant, induration hiatus" ("And he froze the serpent's open mouth into stone and hardened the gaping jaws just as they were" [59–60]). Here, the description of the snake is more abbreviated. But the poet creates a coiling effect in his description of the calcified snake by structuring the verse with a synchesis, in which the two sets of adjectives and nouns are in interlocking order.

The immediate context provides no indication of the poet's reason for alluding to Orpheus's fate. The travelogue, however, contains at least one myth that points to the content of the narrative devoted to Orpheus's songs in book 10. The poet thus refers to Medea's passage over Cyllene: "in qua cum matre Menephron / concubiturus erat saevarum more ferarum" ("on which Menephron was about to lie with his mother in the manner of savage beasts" [386–87]). The theme of incest in fact looms large in Orpheus's songs: the tale of Myrrha's love for her father Cinyras (300–502) is by far the longest in that sequence.[49]

Because of the scandalous nature of the subject matter, Orpheus prefaces his account with an apologetic address to his audience: he urges fathers and daughters to stay away or to disbelieve or to be assured that the crime was punished (300–303). Orpheus thus appears to justify this story through the moral tone of his narration, by focusing on the young woman and underplaying the self-interest of the father.[50] Myrrha pays the penalty by suffering banishment and then metamorphosis just as she is in labor with her child. Cinyras plays the role of a morally outraged victim as he draws his sword and drives his daughter out of the kingdom. But this character is problematic, if not technically culpable: while his wife participates in a fertility ritual to Ceres in which she is prohibited from sexual activity, he seeks sexual pleasure with a young girl who, he is told, is the same age as his own daughter (431–41). Ovid's reference here to Menephron's incestuous relations as *saevarum more ferarum* would seem to point to Myrrha, who in Orpheus's narrative tries to justify her desire for her father by analogy with the sexual habits of cows, horses, goats, and birds (324–29).[51] The speciousness of her argument, however, does not register with the crazed mind that Orpheus depicts, and Myrrha proceeds on her perverted course.

The narrative of Medea's flight from Iolcus contains much material that is difficult to assess, both because of Ovid's compression of these myths and because of the lack of external support for several of them. But it is clear that the poet suggests a complex vision through his evocation of the themes of loss and suffering. He alludes, for instance, to varied levels of responsibility for the death of a child and reactions to that loss by a parent. As I mentioned, Alcidamas is indirectly the cause of Ctesylla's death. Eumelus himself, however, kills Botres in anger over the boy's inappropriate consumption of a sacrificial animal, and his remorse is implied in the word *lugentis* (390). If the former myth hints at the callousness of Medea in Ovid's narrative, the latter has a parallel in the rash decision of Althaea in book 8 to end Meleager's life. There, she is enraged that her two brothers have been killed in an argument with the hero over giving the spoils of the Calydonian boar hunt to Atalanta. Although wavering over the conflicting obligations of piety, Althaea in the end chooses to privilege her brothers over her son. But, in despair, she commits suicide by the sword (531–32).

Preceding a major infusion of material derived from the heroic tradition, the imaginative travelogue that Ovid creates here through his surrogate's flight is a microcosm of his revisionist approach to epic. Ovid avoids the fate of becoming a version of the Telchines, who not only exploit magic for negative purposes but also symbolize a preference for long-winded narrative on a heroic subject. By contrast, the allusions to Hellenistic poetics in this section convey Ovid's light, witty approach to his mythical material.

Medea's flight encapsulates the poet's rejection of traditional heroism and his embrace of more unconventional themes for his own epic. Ovid thus implies the emptiness of the heroic ethic by alluding to the myths of Paris and Hecuba, which reflect problematically on the significance of burial and on the effect of war on the defeated. The narrative of books 12 and 13 develops this skeptical approach to the war and its aftermath from a variety of perspectives, through parody of traditional heroic exploits and repeated illustrations of the mechanical brutality of war.[52]

Ovid hints at the major theme of incest through the myth of Menephron. He develops this subject in the second half of the poem not only through Orpheus's story of Myrrha's incestuous love for her father but also through his extended tale of Byblis's passion for her brother Caunus, whom she tried to seduce by resorting to the elegiac strategy of a love letter (9.450–665). Ovid also incorporates a more prominent role for the artist, whose failures he explores as fully as his talents. His allusion to Orpheus here points forward to his complex portrayal of the archetypal poet in books 10 and 11. There, Ovid fully reveals the paradox of the bard's existence: on the one hand, his sublime powers keep his audience spellbound but, on the other, the antagonism that he arouses highlights his precarious position in the world outside the narrow confines of art. As we will see in chapter 4, Orpheus's narratives reflect an insidious form of self-absorption.

Medea's flight on the magical chariot, recounted in a clever variation on the geographical excursus, thus serves as a dynamic image of the poet's own narrative in the second half of the poem. At the beginning of book 7 she seems to take control and metamorphose the earlier versions of her monumental mythical character, but in her flight from crime she further reflects the etymology of her name with its connection to cunning. The problematic heroine symbolizes Ovid's own production of clever plots that subvert traditional mores and undermine conventional notions of order on all levels.

3

Daedalus and the Labyrinth of the *Metamorphoses*

As the center of the *Metamorphoses*, book 8 assumes a Janus-like position, pointing both backward and forward in a complex narrative movement. First, the theme of a young woman's disastrous passion, which we explored in chapter 2 with the myth of Medea, is revisited in Scylla's betrayal of her father because of her infatuation with Minos (1–151). An extended section on Minos's return to Crete follows, focusing on the myths of Daedalus (152–262). The narrative then turns to Greek heroes, who loom large through book 13: the myth of Meleager occupying a long central section (273–546) is followed by the reception of Theseus and his companions by the river god Achelous (547–884).

Ovid includes an account of Daedalus at work on the Cretan labyrinth, the tortuous paths of which are so confusing that even the architect himself almost fails to find his way out (158–68). The poet's attention to the labyrinth at this point in the poem recalls Daedalus's signal feat in the ekphrasis of the temple doors of Apollo in *Aeneid* 6 (24–30). Vergil similarly incorporates the myth of Daedalus in the pivotal middle book of his poem, mediating between the Trojan past and the Roman future, at the point when Aeneas arrives in Italy, consults the priestess of Apollo, and descends into the underworld for emotional support and guidance from his father in his quest for a new kingdom.[1]

The inevitability of suffering and the value of heroic labor underlie Vergil's conception of the labyrinth in its context in *Aeneid* 6. The poet associates the labyrinth with both the genius and the personal tragedy of the archetypal architect, who sculpts the maze on the temple doors yet cannot bring himself to depict the flight from Crete that cost his young son his life. Vergil also connects the labyrinth with the struggles of the hero who, after viewing the designs on the temple doors, winds his way through the twisted paths of the underworld as one of many labors in his effort to resettle the Trojan exiles.

These fundamental epic concerns emerge as well in *Metamorphoses* 8. Ovid explores the architect's personal loss by narrating the story of Daedalus's flight and his son's disastrous fall. The poet also incorporates a diverse array of heroes engaged in a variety of endeavors; he focuses in particular on Theseus, who successfully emerges from the labyrinth and is later entertained by the river god Achelous, and Meleager, who leads the effort to rid Calydon of the ravaging boar. As we will see, however, Ovid differs markedly from Vergil on these epic issues.

This chapter explores the significance of the labyrinth as the central image of the *Metamorphoses*. My view is that Ovid conceives the labyrinth as a metaphor for the design of book 8 and, by extension, of the *Metamorphoses* as a whole, specifically in contrast to the *Aeneid*. As typical, Ovid is expansive where Vergil is concise: he adds a simile comparing the winding structure to the river Maeander, which has no counterpart in the ekphrasis in the *Aeneid*. In the process, the poet alludes to his predecessor's etymology for the labyrinth yet simultaneously employs the circuitous river as a symbol of the inherently devious nature of the *Metamorphoses*.

In this first section, I discuss Daedalus as a major figure of the poet, not only as architect of the Cretan labyrinth with its twisting paths and but also as inventor of wings for human flight. Ovid reflects on the complex nature of the archetypal artisan through the troubling ways by which he enacts repetition in the sphere of father-son relations as well as in his architectural masterwork. The poet adds to the labyrinthine nature of his narrative here by following the story of Icarus's disastrous flight with an account of Daedalus's nephew Perdix, in which he implies disturbing parallels to the fate of the artisan's son.

I examine how repetition, a seminal element of Ovid's poetics, assumes a special significance throughout book 8.[2] My discussion focuses in particular on the narrative of Theseus's escape from the labyrinth; Meleager and the assemblage of heroes in the Calydonian boar hunt; Althaea's inner turmoil over her conflicting loyalty to her son and her brothers; and the hospitality of Achelous. Theseus, significantly, is present through much of book 8, most prominently at the conquest of the Minotaur on Crete and at the river god's reception of the hero. As we will see, in Achelous's cavern he figuratively reenacts his struggles in the labyrinth.

The final section consists of an extended account of Achelous in his role not only as host but also as storyteller. Although espousing the social value of hospitality intrinsic to epic, the river god perverts his function as host, literally and symbolically denying his guests sustenance. Countering a tale of piety related by the old hero Lelex, Achelous elaborates on the myth of Erysichthon, popularized by Callimachus, but eschews the lightly ironic wit of the Hellenistic poet for an exaggerated rhetoric with a superficially moral basis, grossly misapplying echoes of Vergil. He continues his rhetorical excesses in the account of his own contest with Hercules at the beginning of book 9. Ovid, I believe, creates a potential self-image, a parodic version of the poet, through the river god's extreme failure as narrator to respect limits poetically, not least by his rhetorical excesses in the sphere of the marvelous.

Daedalus and the Labyrinth

Ovid wittily describes the twists and turns of the labyrinth (158–68). In particular, the phrase "variarum ambage viarum" ("by the winding of its various paths" [161]) epitomizes the poet's ability to exploit the mimetic power of language: the punning genitives enclosing the word for "winding" create the impression of confusing repetition. The poet illustrates the devious design of the labyrinth most elaborately by comparing it to the Maeander:

non secus ac liquidis Phrygius Maeandrus in undis
ludit et ambiguo lapsu refluitque fluitque
occurrensque sibi venturas adspicit undas
et nunc ad fontes, nunc ad mare versus apertum
incertas exercet aquas, ita Daedalus inplet
innumeras errore vias vixque ipse reverti
ad limen potuit: tanta est fallacia tecti. (162–68)

[Just as the Phrygian Maeander sports in his clear waters and flows back and forth in an ambivalent course and, rushing on, sees the waves coming at him and directs his uncertain waters now to the source, now to the open sea, so Daedalus fills the countless paths with windings and could himself barely return to the threshold: so great is the deceptiveness of the structure.]

The use of an extended simile making the Maeander an analogue for the labyrinth may be original with Ovid, but a virtuoso poetic description of that river seems to have had a programmatic significance by the Augustan period. As A. S. Hollis notes, Seneca the Younger refers to the Maeander as the "poetarum omnium exercitatio et ludus" (*Epistulae* 104.15).[3] This form of "practice" and "play" seems to have involved literary competition, if one can judge by Seneca's own version, which imitates the *Metamorphoses* passage.[4] Ovid's Augustan predecessor Propertius also showed his skill at poetic play with the Maeander: "atque etiam ut Phrygio fallax Maeandria campo / errat et ipsa suas decipit unda vias" ("and even how the deceptive river Maeander wanders over the Phrygian plain and its very waters confound its course" [2.34.35–36]).

This image of the Maeander symbolizes expansive forms of literature, especially epic, the high genre that the elegist dismisses along with tragedy in favor of elegy.[5] In place of the buskin of Aeschylus, Propertius urges his addressee Lynceus to relax his limbs for soft dances: "ad molles choros" (42). The reference to *mollis* privileges the lower style of elegy over the grander—and, by implication, more pompous—mode of tragedy.[6] Through his description of the Maeander, Propertius cleverly illustrates his own Callimachean principles: the chiastic word order of "Phrygio fallax Maeandria campo," followed by another interlocking pattern with "ipsa suas decipit unda vias," neatly conveys the sense of a winding course, and the personification of the *unda* confounding (*decipit*) the river's course playfully conveys a sense of nature's power.

In the Maeander simile here in the *Metamorphoses*, Ovid shows that epic can accommodate the light, witty aesthetic espoused by the elegist. His description collapses the distinction between river and river god: Maeander not only plays in the waves ("liquidis . . . in undis ludit") but also flows back and forth ("refluitque fluitque") and, even while rushing on (*occurrens*), watches (*adspicit*) the waves coming at him. The poet conveys an impression of the Maeander's errant course by employing the compound verb *refluo* and its root form joined with a double connective -*que*, which mimics the sense of a back and forth flowing movement. Ovid in his epic, then, surpasses the elegist through his mimetic devices and a more expanded personification of this natural force.

Ovid, furthermore, differentiates himself from Vergil in this simile by using the phrase "ambiguo lapsu" to describe circuitous flow of the river. He thus associates the winding structure of the labyrinth closely with the verb *labor*, "to glide" or "to flow." Ovid shows that he was aware of the wordplay in the following passage in *Aeneid* 6, in which Vergil periphrastically describes the labyrinth sculpted by Daedalus on the doors of Apollo's temple: "hic labor ille domus et inextricabilis error" (27).[7]

It is well known that Vergil makes a striking etymological play by deriving the word "labyrinth" from the noun *labor*, thus associating the structure with toil and struggle, concepts closely linked with his hero and the ultimate foundation of Rome.[8] The poet's etymology for Daedalus's architectural achievement is especially appropriate here in book 6. Illuminating Vergil's extensive wordplay in the ekphrasis, Frederick Ahl has commented on his punning with the word *pater*, which reinforces the thematic significance of paternity in this section of the *Aeneid*.[9] At this point, Aeneas himself views the representation of the labyrinth while on his way to consult the Sibyl in order to reunite with his father, who then shows the hero a vision of the ultimate fruits of his labors: the founding of Rome and its culmination in the rule of Augustus (789–886).[10]

The *Aeneid* in its entirety has strong structural and motival links to the labyrinth.[11] As Penelope Doob has cogently shown, the mazelike design of Vergil's epic is achieved through the pronounced *labores* and *errores* in the first half of the poem and through individual episodes with intri-cate patterning.[12] Even the quintessentially labyrinthine book 3, with its highly circuitous plot, focuses on the hero's effort to fulfill divine prophecy by searching for a new homeland for the survivors of Troy.

Ovid dissociates his labyrinth from the grueling labors of the Vergilian hero. The phrase "ambiguo lapsu," with its etymological play connecting the verb *labor* with the labyrinth, characterizes the form of the *Metamorphoses*, its sinuous movement from tale to tale with clever, if tenuous, transitions between individual episodes and books. The adjective *ambiguus* frequently refers to the transformations experienced by his characters, the shape changing of gods, and the metamorphoses suffered by humans in the poem.[13] Like the Maeander, Ovid's poem shifts in direction yet is always looking back.[14] Particular features contributing to its labyrinthine nature include the interlacement created by the interruption of a tale with an inset story; the recollection of an earlier tale through similarities of plot line; the juxtaposition of stories with contrasting or interrelated themes; and the frequent generic shifts, incorporating the elegiac, the tragic, and the pastoral, from one episode to another and even within individual tales. Ovid's specific recall of his own earlier poems, as we will see in his allusions to the flight of

Daedalus and Icarus in the *Ars amatoria,* adds to the sense of retreading the same paths. Whereas the intricate structure of the *Aeneid* mirrors the hero's search for order, the *Metamorphoses* is labyrinthine in its emphasis on a process undermining the very possibility of stability.

Ovid further defines his poetics by contrast to Vergil in his description of the playfulness of the Maeander ("liquidis . . . in undis / ludit"). As we saw in chapter 1, *lusus* is an important Augustan literary concept that characterizes Ovid's elegiac poetry.[15] Ovid extends this poetic "play" to epic, as he incorporates light subjects not normally included in traditional epic and often parodies more serious subject matter.[16] The adjective *liquidus* describing the waves of the Maeander further connects the simile to poetics, for the word occurs among Roman writers to characterize a fluid, smooth style.[17] Here, *liquidus* may be a Latin equivalent of the Greek *katharos,* used by Callimachus at the end of the *Hymn to Apollo* (2.111) to oppose the clear stream flowing from a sacred fountain to the garbage-laden Euphrates, a symbol of the antithesis between the elegance of his own small-scale poems and the lack of polish of the more traditional longer works preferred by his detractors.[18]

In contrast to Callimachus's pure spring but much like the Euphrates, the river Achelous appears here as both a swollen stream and a divinity who boasts of sweeping away trees and boulders, riverside stables with their flocks, cattle and horses, and even strong men in his torrent (552–57). As the narrator of the tale of Erysichthon and in book 9 of his own contest with Hercules, Achelous is a long-winded, overly dramatic speaker whose tumid style matches his swollen flood ("imbre tumens" [250]). The allusions to the *Aeneid* in both stories suggest the speaker's preference for Vergilian high style.[19] The poet's incorporation of such an inflated style is an amusing, if surprising, shift away from his *liquidus lusus,* characterized by an easy flow and light wit.

The Flight of Daedalus and Icarus

The center of the Daedalus episode, the inventor's flight from Crete with his son Icarus (183–235), illuminates the difference between Ovid's and Vergil's imaginative use of the labyrinth. Although literary accounts of Daedalus prior to the Augustan age, including tragedies by Sophocles and Euripides, have not survived, contemporary Roman poets offered complex, sometimes negative, perspectives on Daedalus's creativity.[20] Horace in the *Odes* uses the flight of Daedalus and Icarus as an image of artistic hubris, in particular a misplaced aspiration to the high genre of epic (1.3) or an inappropriate extension beyond the proper bounds of lyric (2.20 and 4.2).[21] Ovid boldly picks up where Vergil left off with only a poignant comment about what was absent from Daedalus's sculptures: "tu quoque magnam / partem opere in tanto, sineret dolor, Icare, haberes" ("You, too, would have a large part in such a great work, Icarus, if grief allowed it" [30–31]).[22] Whereas Vergil abruptly ended his ekphrasis with that empathetic gesture, Ovid fully elaborates on Daedalus's flight with Icarus.

Ovid begins by paying considerable attention to the young boy in this episode. As Daedalus concentrates on constructing the wings, Icarus plays with the materials. The poet offers a highly visual description of the boy's amusement:

... puer Icarus una
stabat et, ignarus sua se tractare pericla,
ore renidenti modo quas vaga moverat aura
captabat plumas, flavam modo pollice ceram
mollibat, lusuque suo mirabile patris
impediebat opus. (195–200)

[The boy Icarus stood around, and unaware that he was handling a source of danger to himself, now snatched at the feathers which the wandering breeze had wafted, with his face beaming, now softened the yellow wax with his thumb, and hindered his father's marvelous work with his play.]

This passage is to some extent a quotidian vignette in a typically Alexandrian manner juxtaposing the *lusus* of Icarus with the *labor* of Daedalus. The narrator, however, foreshadows the boy's death by commenting on his ignorance of the danger inherent in his playthings. As the controlling poet, Ovid adds to the labyrinthine nature of this section, for the image of Icarus softening the wax is later recalled when the wax on the wings softens naturally by proximity to the sun (225–27), catapulting the young boy to his death.

Ovid self-reflexively turns to his own earlier version of the flight in the *Ars amatoria* (2.22–98). His use of this earlier version adds to the complex twists of his literary labyrinth.[23] Ovid incorporates, for instance, the concept of the "middle way" from the didactic poem but makes it more complex here. Daedalus's lecture to Icarus on flying a middle course repeats the artisan's general strictures about the dangers of flying too low or too high in the *Ars*. In both versions, Daedalus explains that the wings will be damaged by the sun's heat if Icarus flies too high or by dampness from the sea if he flies too low (203–205; *Ars* 2.59–62). Ovid even repeats verbatim the essential injunction ("inter utrumque vola" [206; *Ars* 2.63]), along with the emphasis on Daedalus's own leadership ("me duce" [208; *Ars* 2.58]).

Although he shows that, after putting the wings on, Daedalus is anxious for his son and his hands trembled—"et patriae tremuere manus" (211)—Ovid in this section nevertheless reinforces Daedalus's lack of a deep concern for his son.[24] He puts Daedalus's emphasis on the "middle way" in a negative light by looking back to the flight myth of Phaethon in *Metamorphoses* 2. There, the god Phoebus is unable to persuade the youth to reconsider his request to drive the chariot of the Sun.[25] To make the best of a bad situation, Phoebus warns his son that flying too high will burn the heavenly abodes and too low, the earth; a middle path is therefore the safest: "medio tutissimus ibis" (2.137). Daedalus similarly admonishes his own son: "medioque ut limite curras" (203).

If Ovid makes Daedalus a kind of Phoebus figure, he shows the artisan falling short of his divine counterpart. Although lacking forethought over the potential consequences of offering an open-ended promise, the Sun god initially tries to discourage Phaethon's foolhardy desire, emphasizing that the awesome appearance of the heavenly bodies may cause him to lose control of the chariot. But after failing to dissuade his son, the god advises him to stay between the twisting Serpent on the right and the oppressive Altars on the left (138–40). By contrast, Daedalus assumes that Icarus should pay no attention whatsoever to the constellations: "nec te spectare Booten / aut Helicen iubeo strictumque Orionis ensem" (206–7). Instead, he instructs the boy to proceed simply by following him ("me duce carpe viam" [208]). Phoebus's point that Phaethon seeks what even the other gods cannot perform (60–61) is lost on his eager son. Daedalus, however, does not even contemplate such limitations on mortals. His self-absorption distances him further from the pathos of Vergil's artist and father.

Daedalus and Perdix

In the narrative following the death of Icarus, Ovid exposes another form of repetition with Daedalus's behavior in the familial sphere. The poet increases the labyrinthine effect of the narrative by relating the story of Perdix, which is not found in the other extant literary accounts of Daedalus, out of chronological sequence. Seeing Daedalus place his son's body in a tomb, a partridge (*perdix*) applauds vigorously with its wings and sings joyfully (236–38). The poet then provides the reason for Daedalus's *longum exilium* (183–84): the artisan pushed his nephew off the Acropolis but then lied about the boy's fall ("lapsum mentitus" [251]).[26]

In the Perdix story, Ovid emphasizes that the artisan repeats himself with destructive results. The poet makes the relationship between Daedalus and Perdix virtually that of father and son, since the artisan's sister had handed her child over to her brother as his ward and apprentice. Daedalus's envy of (*invidit* [250]) the boy is connected to his egoism as supreme artisan, for by his invention of the saw and the draftsman's compass, essential tools for the work of architects and artisans, Perdix in effect reversed the relation of master and pupil. Recalling his earlier description of Daedalus in the phrase "naturamque novat" (189), Ovid suggests that Perdix is the one who truly transformed nature. The young boy saw patterns from which he created something entirely new: he thus made the first saw by using the backbone of a fish as a model.

Ovid reveals the negative nature of Daedalus's labyrinthine repetitions more fully as the story of Perdix unfolds, for his actions with his nephew have disturbing parallels with the flight from Crete, so disastrous for Icarus.[27] Ovid specifies that Perdix was twelve years old when sent to live with Daedalus (242–43), which appears to be about the age of Icarus at the time of the flight.

Although Daedalus intended to murder his nephew by thrusting him off the Acropolis, Pallas, the protector of inventive genius, metamorphosed him into a partridge while he was still in the air (252–53).[28] Indirectly responsible for his nephew's transformation to a bird, Daedalus is, of course, directly responsible for his own son's attempt to fly, which Ovid describes in a simile comparing the two to real birds as they begin their flight: "velut ales, ab alto / quae teneram prolem produxit in aera nido" ("just as a bird that has guided its tender offspring into the air from a high nest" [213–14]). Ovid implies that Daedalus and Icarus took off by leaping from a cliff.[29] Here, he calls attention to the special nature of the cliff from which Daedalus cast Perdix, "sacraque ex arce Minervae" (250). The artisan thus violated the sacred precinct of the very goddess to whom he owed the utmost piety.

By associating Perdix with Icarus through the concept of the "middle way," Ovid sustains a negative view of Daedalus. When he hurls his nephew off the Acropolis, Daedalus causes the boy in his metamorphosed state forever to be afraid of high places. Ovid elaborates on the partridge's fear of heights as he concludes the story of Daedalus and Perdix:

non tamen haec alte volucris sua corpora tollit
nec facit in ramis altoque cacumine nidos;
propter humum volitat ponitque in saepibus ova
antiquique memor metuit sublimia casus. (256–59)

[Nevertheless, this bird does not raise its body on high, nor does it make its nests on the branches of the very top. It flits near the ground and places its eggs in hedges, and mindful of its prior fall, it fears the heights.]

The hendiadys of the phrase "in ramis altoque cacumine," which makes the words "alto cacumine" grammatically equivalent to *ramis* instead of subordinate to it, calls attention to the problem of height. By his murderous act, Daedalus keeps his nephew from ever flying too high ("non tamen haec alte volucris sua corpora tollit" [256]). The *perdix* does not remain too close to the ground, either, for at the beginning of this story, the poet locates the bird on an ilex tree: "Hunc miseri tumulo ponentem corpora nati / garrula ramosa prospexit ab ilice perdix" ("A chattering partridge from a spreading ilex tree saw him placing the body of his unfortunate son in a tomb" [236–37]).[30] Thus, the *perdix* perches on the branches of trees, though not on the highest ones. While flitting above the ground ("propter humum volitat"), it builds its nests in hedges to protect its young ("ponitque in saepibus ova" [258]). The *perdix* would therefore seem instinctively to represent the principle of *mediocritas*.

Daedalus tried unsuccessfully to persuade Icarus to take a middle path so as to avoid dampening the wings in the sea or melting the wax by proximity to the sun. Ironically, Perdix is now compelled to follow Daedalus's prescriptive "middle way" in a manner that emphasizes the discrepancy between his present limitations as a bird and his earlier brilliance as a youth. This perversion of the middle way after the unfortunate Perdix is metamorphosed underscores Daedalus's failure as both father and mentor.

By making repetition negative in the case of Daedalus, Ovid implies that it is potentially problematic for himself as poet. But, as we will see, his literary labyrinth with its varied forms of repetition incorporates a wide range of content and perspectives: at the end of book 8 Ovid casts a glance at himself with an amused detachment that contrasts with the obsessive self-absorption of his archetypal architect.

Theseus and the Labyrinth

Sustained allusions to Theseus's journey through the maze add to the impression that book 8 is overall the most labyrinthine section of the *Metamorphoses*.[31] After the architect undergoes his convoluted journey, the narrative takes numerous unexpected twists and turns, which frequently include the very hero who conquered the Minotaur. Earlier in book 8, Ovid summarizes what happened after Daedalus built the labyrinth:

Quo postquam geminam tauri iuvenisque figuram
clausit et Actaeo bis pastum sanguine monstrum
tertia sors annis domuit repetita novenis,
utque ope virginea nullis iterata priorum
ianua difficilis filo est inventa relecto. . . . (169–73)

[After he enclosed the double figure of a bull and a youth and the lot, repeated every nine years, on the third time subdued the monster fed twice on Actaean blood, and when the difficult door entered again by none of the previous ones was found by rewinding the thread. . . .]

The poet here uses periphrastic language in intricate clauses condensing the story of the Cretan king's concealment of the Minotaur and punishment of the Athenians, which ended when Theseus slew the monster and returned safely out of the labyrinth. He de-emphasizes the hero by not mentioning Theseus's name and referring to his actions only obliquely through passive verb forms ("the door *entered* again . . . *was found*") in this contorted passage.

Ovid then names the hero specifically in the course of summarizing his involvement with Ariadne:

protinus Aegides rapta Minoide Diam
vela dedit, comitemque suam crudelis in illo
litore destituit. (174–76)

[Straightway, after seizing the daughter of Minos, the son of Aegeus set sail to Dia and cruelly deserted his companion on that shore.]

Although called by the lofty patronymic *Aegides,* Theseus is associated only with the inglorious acts of theft and desertion. By contrast, in summarizing Theseus's successful exit from the labyrinth, the poet emphasizes that the hero owed this feat to the young woman ("ope virginea" [172]).

As we will see, Theseus figuratively reenacts his journey through the labyrinth in the unfolding of the second half of book 8. But, with his valor further reduced, he is caught in the toils of the narrative, first as a participant in the humorously involved account of the Calydonian boar hunt and then as a guest in the confines of the river god Achelous. Theseus indeed finds himself in a *second* labyrinth while in the cave of Achelous (horned, like the Minotaur). The hero does not make his escape until book 9, when he by chance finds an opportune moment to flee.

The Meleager Episode

In the section revolving around Meleager, Ovid provides an extensive account of the hunt and of the hero's demise that is intricately labyrinthine. The Calydonian boar hunt recasts an archetypal Greek myth of heroic valor, the importance of which is attested by its exemplary status in book 9 of Homer's *Iliad* and in Bacchylides' *Olympian* 5, a victory ode for Hieron, and by Sophocles' and Euripides' tragedies on the subject.[32] Prior to the Augustan period in Roman literature, Accius produced a version of Meleager's story apparently influenced by Euripides, who made the hero's love for Atalanta a central feature of the plot.[33] Although the tragedies are no longer extant except in fragments, the popularity of Accius's play in the second century B.C. indicates the compelling nature of this myth. For it embodies a powerful tension between heroic prowess and human passions: the hero responds bravely and effectively to the divine vengeance brought on by his father, yet by failing to control his anger, he himself provokes the intrafamilial strife that ultimately results in his own death at the hands of his mother. Ovid puts his own stamp on this complex myth, first by offering a largely comic rendition of the traditional heroic material of the boar hunt and then by emphasizing the internal struggle of the hero's mother as the familial drama unfolds. Both episodes involve conspicuous forms of repetition, prompted by the manifestation of a type of *monstrum*, which contribute to the effect of a narrative labyrinth.

Ovid retains the traditional motivation and participants but draws special attention to the boar itself and to the landscape of the hunt. As in earlier accounts, after King Oeneus neglects Diana in honoring the gods with the first fruits of the harvest, the goddess sends a boar to ravage the fields around Calydon. Meleager then leads an elite band of heroes in pursuit of the beast (270–97). The boar here is a monstrous hybrid, breathing fire like the mythical Chimaera, yet it rises to almost heroic status through its sheer strength. Extended similes usually reserved for the epic hero are here applied to the beast, though not to the human protagonists who pursue it. As if to underline the boar's superiority to the warriors on the hunt, Ovid compares the animal to an example of Roman war technology: in its rapid assault, it is like a missile propelled from a catapult ("moles adducto concita nervo") at defensive walls and towers crowded with troops (357–58).[34]

The hunt for the boar takes place in the mazelike setting of a forest: "silva frequens trabibus, quam nulla ceciderat aetas" ("a woodland thick with trees, which no age had cut down" [329]).[35] As the heroes engage in myriad attempts to spear the boar, the narrative points to the intrinsic meaning of the labyrinth as confusion, which Ovid aptly rendered earlier by the punning phrase "variarum ambage viarum" ("by the winding of its varying paths" [161]). These surprisingly inept warriors enact intricate, circuitous movements as they rush about in pursuit of, and at times in flight from, the boar. They frequently retreat in unheroic fashion when their spear casts have missed the mark. The narrator wryly observes, for instance, that Nestor might have perished before the Trojan War (365–66) if not for his skill at pole-vaulting. That hero uses his spear to leap up (*insiluit*) onto the branches of a tree from which he can safely look down (*despexit*) at the "enemy" (*hostem*) (365–68). A seemingly endless repetition of spear casts produces the same result: the boar is unfazed, though grazed under the ear by Atalanta (380–83).

The slayer of the Minotaur himself fares no better than any other participant. After the boar has gored Ancaeus, Theseus offers a rationale for cowardice, incongruous with the heroic ethic, so as to keep his dear friend Pirithous out of harm's way: "licet eminus esse / fortibus: Ancaeo nocuit temeraria virtus" ("It is permissible for brave men to stay back; a rash courage harmed Ancaeus" [406–7]). The hero then makes his own attempt with the spear. Well balanced ("quo bene librato" [409]), though apparently less well aimed, Theseus's shot is deflected by the branches of an oak tree. This futile repetitiveness ends only when Meleager hits the boar firmly in the back with a fatal shot on his second try (414–19).

When Meleager's success leads to friction within the group, there is an abrupt shift in tone from the burlesque to the intensely dramatic. When the hero awards the spoils to Atalanta, a beautiful Arcadian huntress, his two uncles seize the booty and are fatally stabbed by Meleager (437–44). The narrative then takes on a tragic cast as Althaea, learning that her son has killed her two brothers, is torn over her conflicting loyalties. Accosted by the Fates at Meleager's birth, she has kept a brand hidden in a secret recess within the intricate confines of the palace (451–58). Althaea now makes the momentous decision to retrieve the *fatale lignum* (479).

Ovid employs repetition to represent the distraught woman's chaotic state, both physically and mentally. In a long soliloquy, Althaea expresses her emotional conflict in her erratic shifts from one stance to another: she first offers her brothers the "evil pledge" of her womb, but as her hands fail, she asks their forgiveness; then thinking of her son living and ruling while her siblings lie dead, she wants the same fate for him; she immediately remembers the pains of childbirth but then exclaims her wish that Meleager had died in the flames at birth; finally, she affirms the power of the image of her dead brothers and proclaims their victory (489–508).

The tormented woman, furthermore, conveys her inner conflict through a rhetoric replete with paradoxes and double entendres. When asserting at the beginning of her speech, for instance, that she will kill Meleager, she refers to her son by metonymy as her own womb: "rogus iste cremet mea viscera!" ("That pyre will burn my womb!" [478]). Since the word *viscera* also refers more generally to the vital organs, she thus implies that in killing her son, she will symbolically kill herself.[36] In his account of her act of suicide later, Ovid repeats Althaea's own language by noting that she thrust a sword *per viscera* (532).

After Althaea's suicide, the Meleager narrative makes a final shift in tone, from the tragic to the bathetic. The focus now moves to Meleager's sisters, who effusively lament their brother's death. Here, the poet interrupts the flow of the narrative by intruding his own persona as he protests his lack of power to do justice to the girls' laments:

non mihi si centum deus ora sonantia linguis
ingeniumque capax totumque Helicona dedisset,
tristia persequerer miserarum dicta sororum. (533–35)

[Not even if a god had given me a hundred mouths with tongues and a huge talent and all of Helicon could I represent the plaintive words of the wretched sisters.]

Exaggerated in itself, the poet's disclaimer seems even more disproportionate to the situation when viewed against its literary background in epic.[37]

The archetype in *Iliad* 2 (488–90) introduces the catalogue of ships, listing the major heroes with troops drawn from all of Greece to help retrieve Helen, including those who were no longer present in the tenth year of the war (494–760). Although Homer alludes to the awesome task of memory for an oral poet, he is considerably more restrained in his rhetoric than Ovid: he refers to the possession of ten tongues and ten mouths rather than a hundred. In his own adaptation of Homer's passage in *Aeneid* 6, Vergil puts the sentiment into the mouth of the priestess of Apollo as she concludes her exposition of the sinners in Tartarus to Aeneas. Since that realm houses the wicked from every age, the Sibyl's insistence that she could not discourse on all forms of crime or their punishments even if she had "a hundred tongues, a hundred mouths, and a voice of iron" ("non, mihi si linguae centum sint oraque centum, / ferrea vox" [625–26]) aptly suggests the scope of human depravity.

By recalling his two models in *Metamorphoses* 8, Ovid draws attention to the absurdity of his own protestation, for the sisters of Meleager cannot compare in number to the troops assembled for the Trojan War or to the sinners housed in Tartarus. Furthermore, the poet may slyly be using his hyperbole to comment not on the pathos but rather on the *volume* of the sisters' laments, so loud and shrill that no poetic language could represent it. Immediately after, making no further references to their words ("tristia . . . dicta" [535]), he moves on to detail their movements: beating their chests black and blue, fondling and kissing the corpse, holding the funerary urn to their chests, lying on the tomb, and finally embracing the name engraved on the stone, made wet by their tears (536–41). His account of their acts here conveys bathos more than pathos.

Ovid then describes in some detail the avian metamorphosis experienced by all of the sisters except Gorge and Deianira (542–56). But by failing to mention any name for these new birds, he hints at his source Nicander, who mentioned the fact that the Meleagrides preserved their brother's name after being transformed into guinea fowl.[38] These raucous-sounding creatures, which according to Varro were called *gallinae Africanae* in Latin (*De re rustica* 3.9.18), were thought to fight around the tomb of Meleager.[39]

Apparently sustaining a high epic tone through his allusion to his two great predecessors, Ovid has in fact significantly lowered the register of the narrative after the dark tragedy of Althaea. From the parody of the expedition against the Calydonian boar to the tragic drama of the hero's mother to this final twist to the myth of Meleager, the poet has led the reader through surprising variations on an archetypal heroic myth. Denied a version all of a piece, consistent with traditional epic, the reader experiences a labyrinthine movement through the narrative as he encounters bewildering shifts on stylistic and generic levels and, in addition, must untangle intertextual allusions that resist the significance of their models in Homer and Vergil.

Achelous in Flood

In his dual status as a torrent and a river god, Achelous recalls the simile describing Daedalus's labyrinth as simultaneously a river in course and a divinity amazed at the water's movements in opposite directions. At this point in the narrative, Achelous as a river in flood takes on a primary function of the labyrinth: its natural grotto becomes a confining space that at least temporarily keeps Theseus and his companions from their journey back home. As the narrator of the most extended tale in book 8, the divinity in his anthropomorphic form produces a bizarre, labyrinthine narrative on the crime and horrific fate of the impious Erysichthon that incorporates a lengthy digression on the personified Fames at its center. Furthermore, by alluding to Vergil in Achelous's narrative of Erysichthon and of his own fight with Hercules over Deianira, Ovid recalls the arduous labors memorialized in the *Aeneid* but displaces them into an overwrought tale of impiety and punishment and a comically hyper-epic contest.

The poet characterizes the river god as a socially conscious, yet at the same time overbearing, host. He observes that Achelous received Theseus, Pirithous, Lelex, and others whom he "had deemed worthy of an equal honor" ("parili fuerat dignatus honore" [569]) and that he was "most delighted with such a great guest" as Theseus ("laetissimus hospite tanto" [570]). The river god has the trappings of a sophisticated host of a Greek symposium, as he reclines propped on his cushion ("innixus cubito" [727]) and entertains with elegant dinnerware, cups bedecked with jewels ("in gemma posuere merum" [573]) with which nymphs serve wine to the guests after the main course.[40] But Ovid suggests that Achelous is guilty of a breach in symposiastic etiquette, for contrary to both Greek and Roman custom, he offers the wine neat (*merum*) rather than diluted with water.

Although ostensibly overjoyed to receive Theseus in his home, Achelous dominates as much over the hero as over his other guests. The god in fact focuses his attention overtly on Theseus alone, the only guest present whom he addresses. Yet, ironically, the hero is virtually silent throughout. He speaks only three times: he barely frames a question about the landscape (574–76), expresses his approval of Lelex's story of the pious Baucis and Philemon and his desire to hear more about divine powers of transformation (726–27), and at the beginning of book 9 inquires about the cause of the god's groans and his maimed forehead.

At each comment by Theseus, the river god responds in considerable detail. First, after the hero asks about the islands in the distance, he explains how the Echinades came into being. Later, he offers the extended tale about the metamorphic powers of Mestra and the impiety of her father Erysichthon. Finally, as he refers to the sensitive subject of his single horn,. his groans end book 8 ("gemitus sunt verba secuti" [884]), but the god immediately proceeds to answer Theseus's question about the cause of his loss at the start of book 9 (1–2) with an account of his contest with Hercules (9.4–88). Betty Rose Nagle points out that Ovid reverses the traditional epic roles by having the hero listen as the host tells stories and notes that the grandiose phrase "Troezenius heros" (567) describes not Theseus himself but rather his comrade Lelex.[41] Only this older, minor hero is able to assert himself at any length through his story of the miraculous transformation of the pious old couple who received Jupiter and Mercury in their humble abode (624–710).

The extended story of a reception of gods in human disguise recalls an important Hellenistic literary version of hospitality to a hero. It is well known that Lelex's tale of the pious Baucis and Philemon, who receive Jupiter and Mercury as guests in their humble abode, evokes the principal episode of Callimachus's *Hecale*, which focused on the old woman's reception of Theseus on his way to conquer the Marathonian bull.[42] As Callimachus appears to have done, Lelex provides minutiae of the meal which the old couple served to their divine guests: in the first course, olives, preserved plums, endive, radishes, cheese, and eggs and in the second, nuts, figs, dates, grapes, and a honeycomb (664–77).[43] The simple abundance satisfies the two gods, who cause the wine bowl to replenish itself (679–80) and refuse to allow the couple to slaughter their only goose (684–88). Here in book 8, then, Theseus listens to a tale that mirrors a major literary work in which he himself was the guest, having sought refuge in the cottage of the old woman to escape from a storm.[44] Apparently pleased to hear this reminder of his own adventure, Theseus asks for more tales about such marvelous power of the gods (726–27).

Achelous's Tale of Erysichthon

Responding to the hero's request, Achelous recounts the bizarre tale of Erysichthon, whose extreme impiety contrasts with the devotion of Baucis and Philemon. Although this story has a model in Callimachus's *Hymn to Demeter,* the protagonist here is unremittingly wicked rather than merely foolish.[45] Whereas the Hellenistic model is narrated in a light vein with comic overtones, Achelous tells his tale in a hyper-epic style frequently echoing Vergil.[46]

My discussion focuses on Achelous's depiction of Erysichthon's hubris through epic marvels, which have close analogues in the *Aeneid.* Unlike Callimachus, who explains that the young man intended to build a dining hall with the lumber from the huge tree, Achelous leaves Erysichthon's hubristic desire unmotivated. Insistent on possessing the largest tree in Ceres' grove, the man adamantly refuses to yield, even though the venerable oak was adorned with offerings of garlands and votive tablets. When his servants hesitate to carry out his orders, he himself seizes and wields the ax (743–57). Achelous then describes the tree's humanlike response to the imminent attack:

contremuit gemitumque dedit Deoia quercus,
et pariter frondes, pariter pallescere glandes
coepere ac longi pallorem ducere rami. (758–60)

[The oak of Deo trembled and made a groan, and the leaves and acorns equally began to grow pale and the long branches began to take on a pallor.]

Finally, when he makes a gash in the tree, blood pours out from the bark ("fluxit discusso cortice sanguis" [762]).

As Otis points out, this passage alludes to the hero's account of discovering the dead Polydorus in *Aeneid* 3, primarily through the motif of the blood flowing from the tree.[47] When Aeneas breaks off branches of cornel and myrtle to adorn an altar, blood trickles from the shafts: "huic atro liquuntur sanguine guttae / et terram tabo maculant" ("Drops of dark blood flow from it and stain the earth with gore" [28–29]). In contrast to Erysichthon, Vergil's hero is performing an act of piety, unaware that Polydorus was treacherously murdered.

Achelous's personification of the tree incongruously incorporates details from both Vergil and Callimachus. The oak's trembling has an analogue in the Polydorus episode, where the hero himself shudders at the sight of the blood dripping from the tree ("mihi frigidus horror / membra quatit" [29–30]). Vergil also mentions a groan that comes from the mound when Aeneas continues to pluck the shafts (39–40), but it is the voice of Polydorus's spirit rather than the myrtle branches. In Callimachus's story of Erysichthon, the Hellenistic poet comments that, when struck, the poplar "calls out an ill-boding melody to the others" ("kakon melos iachen allais" [39]).

For the pallor of the tree, Ovid may have found a source in Callimachus's *Hymn to Delos*, where the ash nymph Melia stops dancing and her cheeks grow pale ("hupochloon esche pareiên" [80]) as she grieves for the tree whose life span coincided with her own. Logically extraneous to his narrative, the personification of the tree through details from Callimachus as well as Vergil suggests that Achelous has inflated the marvelous largely for its own sake rather than for a serious moral point.

Whereas Callimachus in the *Hymn to Demeter* mentions only the tree's ill-boding sound when it is cut, Achelous expands on the response of the dryad coexistent with the oak. Here, the nymph herself cries out for vengeance:

nympha sub hoc ego sum Cereri gratissima ligno,
quae tibi factorum poenas instare tuorum
vaticinor moriens, nostri solacia leti. (771–73)

[I, most pleasing to Ceres, am the nymph within this wood, who as I die predict that punishment for your deeds is close at hand for you, a consolation for my death.]

The nymph's call for revenge evokes another model, the impious father of Paraebius in book 2 of the *Argonautica*.[48] The prophet Phineus explains to Jason and his comrades that when the man impetuously cut an oak, the hamadryad inhabiting it responded with a cry for revenge against not just him but his innocent son as well (476–83). Apollonius's passage presumably influenced the Polydorus episode, but Vergil makes his scene more vivid by quoting rather than paraphrasing the voice emanating from vegetative life. By making a more overt allusion to Apollonius, Ovid cleverly draws attention to a literary model that Vergil himself manipulated for his own baroque effect. But, by having Achelous incorporate marvels from these diverse sources in an incongruous manner, he also exposes the rhetorical excesses of his overly dramatic narrator.

Erysichthon's act of cutting down the oak is, as Anderson notes, a kind of figurative anti-sacrifice.[49] Achelous embellishes the marvel of the blood gushing from the tree with an epic simile drawn from the sphere of religious observance:

haud aliter fluxit discusso cortice sanguis,
quam solet, ante aras ingens ubi victima taurus
concidit, abrupta cruor e cervice profundi. (762-64)

[Blood flowed from the ruptured bark just as bloody gore is accustomed to
pour forth from the severed neck when a huge bull falls as a victim before the
altar.]

The simile, furthermore, alludes to another context of the marvelous in
the *Aeneid,* adding to the overdone quality of the scene in book 8. Here,
Vergil describes the death throes of the priest Laocoön:

clamores simul horrendos ad sidera tollit:
qualis mugitus, fugit cum saucius aram
taurus et incertam excussit cervice securim. (2.222-24)

[He sends terrible screams to the heavens, just like the bellowing when a
wounded bull has fled from the altar and has thrust off the unsteady ax from its
neck.]

This simile culminates one of the most dramatic episodes in the
Aeneid: Laocoön and his two young sons are attacked by a pair of ter-
rifying snakes with huge red crests and burning eyes filled with blood
after the priest urged the Trojans not to receive the Wooden Horse within
their walls and attempted to pierce this icon of Greek cunning with his
spear (40-56, 201-27). The victim in both similes is a bull at the altar,
though Vergil emphasizes the pain and desperate flight of the victim
rather than the blood gushing from the wound of the fallen animal.

The immediate context of Vergil's simile reinforces the inappropri-
ateness of Achelous's echo. Laocoön is actually in the process of sacri-
ficing a bull when the snakes appear (201-2): the simile comparing the
man himself to the very beast which he was offering to the gods renders
his fate all the more horrifying.[50] It exposes his nature as a real victim,
one who helps to ensure the fall of Troy as the precondition for the foun-
dation of Rome. Erysichthon in the *Metamorphoses* simile, by contrast, is
the agent of destruction, and his "victim" is a tree, though it is the larg-
est in Ceres' sacred grove and its resident nymph cries out for revenge.
In Vergil's passage, the fear of the bystanders has far-reaching historical
consequences: the terror that grips the entire assembly ("novus per pec-
tora cunctis / insinuat pavor" [228-29]) precipitates the fall of Troy. It
yields to the mistaken belief that Laocoön was killed for impiety and
to preparations for welcoming the Wooden Horse into the city. Here,
Achelous similarly emphasizes the horror of those around ("obstipuere

omnes" [765]) but simply has one anonymous individual try to prevent Erysichthon from striking the tree a second time. The result is merely grotesque, as the man is quickly decapitated by the villain (765–69).

Vergil's own internal narrator Aeneas, furthermore, recounts the horrifying death of Laocoön as well as his discovery of Polydorus when Dido, entertaining the shipwrecked hero in her palace, asks him to tell about the capture of Troy and his wanderings in the years following (753–56). Aeneas's powerful rhetoric in bringing to life the drama of the Greek attack on Troy and its personal consequences for himself arouses compassion in his host, though ultimately with tragic consequences. Ovid's internal narrator has all the drama but none of the depth of Vergil's hero, who is motivated by a selfless desire to persist in his divinely ordained mission. In spite of the river god's inflation of the episode, Erysichthon is just one bizarre individual, unrelated to larger historical events. By contrast to Aeneas, Achelous has no obvious personal motivation for his story but rather just seems to be carried away by his own narrative.

The main section of Achelous's tale, the strange allegory of Fames and its effect on Erysichthon, also alludes to Vergil's use of the marvelous. Brooks Otis suggests that Fames is "certainly more than reminiscent of Fama and Allecto."[51] Garth Tissol notes that, like Allecto in *Aeneid 7*, Fames here is a strong emotion conceived as an infection.[52] The prominent metaphor of fire, furthermore, echoes Vergil's description of Allecto's effect on Amata. The extended passage in the *Aeneid* (323–571) enacts Juno's anger at the Trojans' attempt to settle in Latium, as she summons the Fury from the underworld to infect with her poison the queen Amata, the hero Turnus, and even the hounds on the hunt with Ascanius so that the Trojan prince will kill a pet stag and thereby incite the Latins to battle. As the Fury envelops Amata's bones with fire ("ossibus implicat ignem" [355]), so the flame increases unabated in Erysichthon's throat ("implacataeque vigebat / flamma gulae" [845–46]).

When Allecto moves on to infect Turnus, Vergil uses an extended simile of a large cauldron of water boiling over after logs are heaped on the fire (462–66) to convey the Rutulian hero's lust for battle. Achelous employs a similar comparison of a fire never refusing sustenance but demanding more as the supply of fuel increases (837–39). Whereas Vergil integrates the metaphor to foreground the passions motivating the resistance to Aeneas and the Trojans at the onset of the war in Latium, here its use is startling. The fire metaphor would more readily suit a context of thirst, which is naturally associated with heat, rather than hunger.

The river god elaborates in detail on the vast scope of Erysichthon's hunger (830–42). The most telling rhetorical feature of this passage is paradox, which virtually takes over the narrative at the end of this section:[53]

> . . . quo copia maior
> est data, plura petit turbaque voracior ipsa est,
> sic epulas omnes Erysichthonis ora profani
> accipiunt poscuntque simul: cibus omnis in illo
> causa cibi est semperque locus fit inanis edendo. (838–42)

[The greater the amount he was given, the more he seeks, and he is more voracious because of the very abundance; thus, the mouth of the wicked Erysichthon receives and at the same time demands all banquets. All food is the cause of food for him, and the place always becomes empty by eating.]

Both form and content in this section threaten the very essence of Ovid's poem. As Leonard Barkan observes, the description of Erysichthon's ceaseless consumption, including a simile of the sea absorbing the earth's rivers (835–36), ultimately functions as a "gruesome parody of the metamorphic links within the universe."[54]

Given the extremes to which Achelous goes to convey Erysichthon's hunger, it is odd that he does not mention any specific food at all until the very end of the story. The river god explains that after depleting his patrimony, Erysichthon sells his own daughter to purchase more food. But when she prays for help to Neptune, who took her virginity, she finds herself transformed into a fisherman and delights in her ability to deceive the master who searches the shore for her. Erysichthon then repeatedly sells the girl to new masters (848–74). After Mestra's clever efforts fail to satisfy her father's unabated appetite, Achelous describes how the man's hunger finally ceased.

His conclusion to Erysichthon's story differs drastically from the version in Callimachus's *Hymn*. There, when he has depleted the resources of the royal house, consuming mules, cattle, horses, and even a cat, the son of the king sits at the crossroads begging for food (107–15). But, in accord with the rest of his narrative, the river god here ends with a hideous extreme and one final paradox:

> ipse suos artus lacero divellere morsu
> coepit et infelix minuendo corpus alebat. (877–78)

[He himself began to tear away his own limbs with lacerating bites, and the wretch nourished his body by diminishing it.]

Achelous has lost sight of both the deeper theme of impiety underlying his story and the obligations of *hospitium* owed to his guests. It may be poetic justice that the man who turned his flesh and blood into chattel should literally eat his own flesh. But the river god seems oblivious to the situation of his own audience. Theseus makes no comment on this story, nor does the poet refer to the reaction of the guests, as he did at the conclusion of Lelex's tale. Their response may simply be revulsion, for the heroes in fact have not finished dinner but are awaiting the second course.

Achelous's Contest with Hercules

Achelous immediately turns to a new subject by raising the issue of his own metamorphic powers:

Quid moror externis? etiam mihi saepe novandi est
corporis, o iuvenis, numero finita potestas. (879–80)

[Why should I linger over others? I, young man, also have the power—though limited in number—of often transforming my body.]

He then mentions his bull form by referring specifically to horns: "armenti modo dux vires in cornua sumo" ("Now, as the leader of the herd, I acquire strength in my horns" [882]). But, in a revealing ellipsis, he exclaims: "cornua, dum potui" ("horns, while I could!" [883]). As Achelous points to the missing horn and groans (883–84), Theseus asks about the loss (9.1–2).[55]

Ostensibly, the river god is loath to tell the story of his mutilation: "Triste petis munus. quis enim sua proelia victus / commemorare velit?" ("You request a sad service. For who, when defeated, would want to recount his battle?" [4–5]). But his reluctance to oblige the hero is underscored with irony. Commentators have noted that this passage echoes Aeneas's words to Dido when she asks to hear the story of the fall of Troy and his wanderings (2.2–8). There is, furthermore, an allusion to Sophocles. In the prologue of the *Trachiniae*, Deianira explains to her nurse that she feared marriage when the dreadful river god presented himself as a suitor but was relieved when Heracles came forward and won the contest with Achelous (4–21). Claiming that she herself

cannot tell the details of the struggle, Deianira asserts that only some-
one who watched without fear (*atarbês* [23]) could do so. Ovid's reader
might well be amused to recall Deianira's speech: as the river god's ac-
count of the contest unfolds, one can only infer that Achelous is not
suited to be the narrator of the story.

As Achelous proceeds, a disjunction between the content and the in-
flated style is reinforced by misplaced allusions to Vergil. First of all, the
river god perceives himself as the native hero resisting the intrusion of
the outsider in his struggle with Hercules: "nec gener externis hospes
tibi missus ab oris" ("nor am I a son-in-law sent to you as a stranger
from foreign shores" [19]). So, too, Turnus views Aeneas as an inter-
loper, in spite of an oracle from Faunus informing Latinus that a son-in-
law will come from foreign shores ("externi venient generi" [7.98]). Al-
though unheroically relying on metamorphosis to elude his opponent,
the river god bolsters his image as an epic hero through similes that
echo the *Aeneid*. When describing his resistance to Hercules' repeated
thrusts, Achelous compares himself to a rock beaten by the sea:

haud secus ac moles, quam magno murmure fluctus
oppugnant: manet illa suoque est pondere tuta. (40–41)

[Not other than a massive rock that waves assault with a resounding crash; it
remains firm through its weighty mass.]

Anderson notes that the god's use of the simile of a rock battered by
mighty waves to describe his resistance to his opponent is rather ill con-
ceived since he himself is a river.[56] The analogy seems all the more ab-
surd in light of Achelous's emphasis on the power of his waters in flood
at the beginning of the episode.

The analogy further undercuts Achelous's heroic self-image by re-
calling a simile in *Aeneid* 10. Vergil thus describes Mezentius standing
firm against the onslaught of Tyrrhenian troops:

Ille (velut rupes vastum quae prodit in aequor,
obvia ventorum furiis expostaque ponto,
vim cunctam atque minas perfert caelique marisque,
ipsa immota manens) . . . (693–96)

[He, just as a cliff, which extends into the vast sea, subject to the fury of the
winds and exposed to the deep, endures all the force and threats of both sky
and sea, itself remaining unmoved . . .]

Although the Tyrrhenian troops respond en masse because of their ha-
tred of the cruel tyrant, Mezentius successfully counters with repeated

spear casts against his foes, who do not dare to face him in hand-to-hand combat with the sword (715). The impious Mezentius is in fact a ferocious warrior. Achelous, by contrast, proves himself to be a coward. In addition, the allusion to Mezentius as a storm-beaten cliff adds another level of irony, since Vergil's exemplar of the *contemptor deum* underlies Achelous's characterization of the impious Erysichthon.

A final echo of the *Aeneid* encapsulates the ludicrously exaggerated nature of Achelous's rhetoric. The river god thus describes his determination not to give way to his rival:

non aliter vidi fortes concurrere tauros,
cum pretium pugnae toto nitidissima saltu
expetitur coniunx: spectant armenta paventque
nescia, quem maneat tanti victoria regni. (46–49)

[Not otherwise have I seen brave bulls charge, when the sleekest wife from the whole glade is sought as the prize of battle; the herds look on and tremble, not knowing to which the victory of such a great kingdom awaits.]

As is well known, Ovid alludes to a simile in *Aeneid* 12 comparing Aeneas and Turnus to bulls.[57] Here are the first five lines of Vergil's passage:

ac velut ingenti Sila summove Taburno
cum duo conversis inimica in proelia tauri
frontibus incurrunt, pavidi cessere magistri,
stat pecus omne metu mutum, mussantque iuvencae
quis nemori imperitet, quem tota armenta sequantur . . . (715–19)

[And just as in huge Sila or on the highest point of Taburnus, when two bulls charge, with brows turned for deadly battle, the cowherds retreat in fear, the whole herd stands silent with fear, and the heifers wonder which will rule the glade, which all the herds will follow . . .]

Like Vergil, Achelous points to the significance of the contest by emphasizing that an audience watches in suspense, waiting to find out which one will dominate. Whereas the river god boasts in his simile that a kingdom (*regni*) is at stake, the Augustan poet, maintaining a focus on the rustic image, refers to a glade (*nemori*). In the *Aeneid*, a kingdom is in fact at issue in the contest between Aeneas and Turnus, and all the Trojan and Italian troops, even King Latinus himself, turn their eyes to the two rivals who are the referent of Vergil's simile (704–9).

The heroic self-image which Achelous projects through the bull simile reflects a kind of victory on the level of rhetoric rather than deed.

Even more than Turnus with Aeneas, Achelous is no match for Hercules. Yet the river god creates the impression of equal skill: "ter sine profectu voluit nitentia contra / reicere Alcides a se mea pectora" ("Thrice without success the son of Alceus wished to throw my chest back from himself" [50-51]). He employs a heightened rhetoric by appealing to the epic device of a "threefold" attempt and by naming his opponent through the lofty patronymic form Alcides (even though he earlier challenged Hercules' paternity [23-26]).[58] The river god then turns a simile into a metamorphosis when he undergoes a third and final transformation into a bull. In fact, his manifestation in bull form results not only in defeat but in humiliating mutilation, as Hercules grasps one of the horns and breaks it off: "rigidum fera dextera cornu / dum tenet, infregit truncaque a fronte revellit" ("While he held the hard horn with his fierce right hand, he broke it and wrenched it from my forehead, left maimed" [85-86]).

Achelous says nothing more about the contest over Deianira. Having achieved a success only rhetorically, Achelous quickly offers an aetiology of the *cornu copiae:* "naides hoc pomis et odoro flore repletum / sacrarunt, divesque meo Bona Copia cornu est" ("Naiads filled it with fruits and fragrant flowers and made it sacred, and Kindly Abundance is prolific through my horn" [87-88]). Signaling that the river god has nothing further to say (*dixerat;* "he had spoken" [89]), Ovid immediately resumes the role of narrator.

Ovid concludes Achelous's reception of Theseus by cleverly evoking the issue of the river god's failure of hospitality. The poet makes pointed references to the god's broken horn. First, he mentions that an attendant nymph, dressed in the manner of Diana, brings out the second course in the horn. Although the cornucopia is teeming with fruits ("praedivite cornu" [91]), it is unclear if the heroes partake of its bounty. As soon as he mentions the ripe fruits of autumn constituting the second course ("autumnum et mensas, felicia poma, secundas" [92]), the poet notes that dawn arrived ("lux subit" [93]). Not even waiting for the flood waters to subside, the heroes abruptly take their leave: "et primo feriente cacumina sole / discedunt iuvenes" ("And as the sun first struck the rooftops, the heroes departed" [93-94]).

Since a considerable amount of time has elapsed from the end of the first course, when it was light enough for Theseus to notice the Echinades in the distance, the guests would presumably be rather hungry. Ovid suggestively leaves open the heroes' response to the grotesque details of Achelous's narrative: the blood flowing from the oak tree and gushing from the sacrificial victim in his bull simile as indicators of Erysichthon's impiety; the long description of Fames with her "place for a stomach" (799–808) prefacing the sinner's punishment by unmitigated hunger; and finally his self-cannibalization. It may well be that Achelous's tale has left his guests with no appetite.

At the very end of this story, Ovid refers to the horn as he mentions the river god's descent into his waters: "vultus Achelous agrestes / et lacerum cornu mediis caput abdidit undis" ("Achelous hid his rustic face and his head bereft of its horn in the midst of the waves" [96–97]). Referring again to the horn periphrastically as "an adornment that had been taken away" ("ablati . . . decoris" [98]), he leaves the river god "concealing the loss" ("celatur . . . damnum" [100]) with willow and rush. By calling attention to the horn so strongly at the end, the poet encourages the reader to reconsider Achelous's own earlier allusions to this anatomical feature. In the contest with Hercules, Achelous alludes to the potency of his horns: "vires in cornua sumo" ("I take up strength in my horns" [9.82]). The river god's insistent reference to bulls in his narration is not fortuitous: it evokes his anxiety over the loss of the symbol of his virility and suggests his need to compensate by extremes in the realms of reception and rhetoric.

Ovid cleverly interweaves the motifs of narration and guest-host relations. As an analogue to Achelous's storytelling, he subtly hints at the excesses of the god's dinner in his references to the wine served neat and the appearance of the serving nymph dressed as Diana. The poet, moreover, attributes a symbolic significance to dining in Lelex's story that can be interpreted as an implicit criticism of Achelous: the genuine fulfillment provided by the simple meal of Baucis and Philemon has a counterpart in the pleasure that the guests take in the tale, narrated with a light humor about the incongruities of the rustics' humble entertainment. Lelex himself explains that the old couple's cheerful attitude compensated for any deficiency in the elegance of the food: "nec iners pauperque voluntas" ("Their goodwill was neither sluggish nor impoverished" [678]). At the end of that tale, Ovid affirms that "both the story and the narrator had moved everyone" ("cunctosque et res et moverat auctor" [725]).

Contrasting the skepticism of Pirithous and the belief of Lelex, Denis Feeney observes that both must serve as models for the reader of the *Metamorphoses*.[59] Adapting Feeney's insight on the importance of reading underlying this section of the poem, I suggest that Ovid also reflects on this issue through a clever characterization of Achelous. The river god's anxiety about the loss of his horn provides an explanation for his extremes as a narrator, especially his lack of control in overemphasizing the marvelous through echoes of Vergil, Callimachus, and Apollonius in the tale of Erysichthon and in inappropriately applying heroic similes from the *Aeneid* in the account of his contest with Hercules. In these extended narratives, Achelous fails as a storyteller in part because Ovid shows him to be a poor "reader" of the *Aeneid*, interpreting the text egoistically and being absorbed in its dazzling effects. He, furthermore, ignores the impropriety of his rhetorical excesses for the guests who listen to his stories. Achelous both misses the point of his "sources" and pays inadequate attention to his audience. In his capacity as both host and narrator, the river god has ensured that the heroes led by Theseus will escape from their confinement in his "labyrinth."

Ovid in *Metamorphoses* 8 ultimately draws the reader fully into the narrative labyrinth. Throughout the book, of course, the poet's "ideal" reader is engaged in recognizing the forms of repetition at work: Ovid's replay of his earlier version of the flight of Daedalus and Icarus in *Ars* 2; the involved narrative of the Calydonian boar hunt with the vainly repeated attempts of the heroes to spear the beast; the psychologically motivated indecision of Althaea impelling her to shift back and forth in her quandary over piety to her brothers or to her son; the juxtaposed tales of Baucis and Philemon and of Erysichthon, based on two myths recounted by Callimachus but here narrated in antithetical styles; and the numerous allusions to Vergil woven into the tale of Erysichthon.

In the Achelous episode, Ovid more specifically relates repetition to the problem of reading as Theseus listens to Lelex's tale of Baucis and Philemon, which replays his own visit with the kindly old Hecale recounted in Callimachus's epyllion. From "reader" who approves this variation on a Callimachean subject, Theseus becomes a model for the reader of another kind of narrative altogether. Consumption of food provides a symbolic link between the two, revealing which is the superior tale. As the controlling poet who alludes to the *Aeneid* throughout the *Metamorphoses*, Ovid of course "reads" Vergil in far more diverse, complex ways than this surrogate narrator. In his behavior as host and storyteller with Theseus and his companions, Achelous humorously serves as a negative model for the poet's own relationship to his reader. The poet, however, has situated the river god's storytelling in a context from which the reader, unlike the hero Theseus, can take his clues and thus find in the pompous river god's narratives a source of entertainment and enlightenment.

4

Orpheus and
the Internal Narrator

O rpheus dominates book 10, first in Ovid's story of the death of
his wife on their wedding day and his journey to Hades to
retrieve her (1–147) and then as the narrator of an extended
series of erotic tales (148–739). The bard in the *Metamorphoses*, however,
seems far from the tragic figure in Vergil's *Georgics*.[1] Ovid represents
the bard appealing to Pluto and Proserpina in the underworld with a
long and oddly unimpassioned speech.[2] His Orpheus, furthermore, ap-
pears more immature than tragic in failing to heed the restrictions im-
posed on him as he exits the underworld with Eurydice.[3]

When he sings his song to his audience of beasts and trees, however,
Orpheus reveals his powers as a storyteller in an Ovidian vein. The
very trees that provide the setting and are moved by his singing (86–
105) reflect a connection to the refined poetry espoused by Ovid.[4] His
tales are the typically Hellenistic kind of narrative favored by Ovid,
emphasizing erotic themes and destabilizing traditional heroic values
(148–739).[5] Much like Ovid's throughout the *Metamorphoses*, these sto-
ries exhibit a generic range, incorporating elements of tragedy as well
as of erotic elegy.[6] In both form and content, Orpheus's song stands out
as a *mise en abyme* of the *Metamorphoses*.[7]

The heart of Orpheus's song is a series of interrelated tales that be-
gins with Pygmalion's love for his own creation, a beautiful statue which
is transformed into a woman through the agency of Venus and becomes
the mother of a daughter named Paphos (220–97). His most extended
tale in this section shares the incest theme that Ovid elaborated in the
story of Byblis in book 9:[8] Paphos's granddaughter Myrrha, whose

passion for her father Cinyras is brought to fruition with the help of her nurse, is driven away and ultimately metamorphosed into a tree, which gives birth to a beautiful boy (298–518). Orpheus concludes his song with the tale of Venus's affair with Adonis, the offspring of the incestuous union of Myrrha and Cinyras, who is gored to death by a boar and then metamorphosed into a flower (519–739).

Although the bard never refers to the events of his own life in his song, scholars have recognized that Orpheus's loss of Eurydice and his adoption of a new sexual orientation significantly affect his tales. Some view his effort in positive terms, emphasizing his idealistic perspective on the power of art and his concern not only with his own lost love but also with the nature of love per se.[9] But others have raised the question of the bard's biases and failures of perception, pointing to the narcissism of his view of the artist and an underlying misogyny in his song.[10]

This chapter focuses on Orpheus's final tale, the love affair of Venus and Adonis, which provides an aetiology for the ritual known as the Adonia. Orpheus yields a major portion of the tale to the goddess herself, who relates the story of Hippomenes and Atalanta to her beloved (560–704). Surprisingly, critics have failed to consider why the bard allots so much of this section of his song to Venus's story of Hippomenes and Atalanta. It is, in fact, almost twice as long as his own narrative of the goddess and her young lover. This doubling of embedded narrators complicates the concerns and desires reflected in the story.

As we will see, Venus's narrative is inherently narcissistic, driven by issues of desire and power and ultimately having an unintended effect on her audience that results in tragedy. First, I discuss the importance of valor in Venus's tale of Hippomenes and Atalanta as it applies to the hero and affects the goddess's lover. Then, I consider complex forms of role changing and substitution involving the goddess, her young lover, and the characters of the inset tale. Ovid's allusions to the mythical model of incestuous passion in Phaedra's love for her stepson Hippolytus add another level of complexity to Venus's relations with Adonis. I consider how the goddess's promise that Adonis's existence will be renewed through metamorphosis and that he will be commemorated in an annual ritual are paradoxically destabilized by the bard's narrative. The chapter then moves on to show ways by which Orpheus himself is significantly implicated in the story of Venus and Adonis, revealing the bard's own self-absorption and his failure to heed his larger audience. Finally, I suggest that the poet of the *Metamorphoses* resembles his surrogate in his own self-involvement and in his obliviousness to the effect of his work on his most powerful "reader."

Venus's Admonition to Adonis

Venus has a twofold purpose in telling Adonis the story of Hippomenes and Atalanta: to explain her hatred of lions and to warn her young lover about the danger of such beasts to hunters (542–52). The goddess states that, after she enabled Hippomenes to win his race with Atalanta by means of three golden apples, he failed to show her gratitude; she therefore caused the couple to have sex in the temple precinct of Cybele, who then transformed them into lions (686–704). Venus indicates the danger of these wild animals for Adonis by detailing their metamorphosis from human to beast, with their fingers becoming claws, long tails lashing the sands, and fierce growls replacing speech (698–702). She then draws attention to their ferocious teeth, tamed by the bit for Cybele's chariot ("dente premunt domito Cybeleia frena leones" [704]).

Venus directly admonishes Adonis about the dangers of such wild animals. Here, she addresses him in the language of paradox: "in audaces non est audacia tuta" ("Boldness against the bold is not safe" [544]).[11] She reinforces her appeal by hinting at the consequences for herself: "parce meo, iuvenis, temerarius esse periclo" ("Refrain, young man, from being rash to my detriment" [545]).[12] At the end of her tale, the goddess again warns Adonis to avoid such wild creatures: "genus omne ferarum, / quod non terga fugae, sed pugnae pectora praebet, / effuge" ("Flee every kind of wild animal that does not furnish its back to flight but its chest to battle" [705–7]).

Given her explicit warnings, it is odd that the majority of Venus's narrative appears to bear little relation to her purpose of explaining her enmity toward lions and their danger for Adonis. The goddess first recounts the failed attempts of the various suitors to defeat Atalanta from the perspective of Hippomenes, who happened to be a spectator; she then describes in detail the latter's own decision to compete with Atalanta, the young woman's unexpected attraction to the intrepid challenger, and the race itself. Only the last 19 of the 145 lines of Venus's story deal with the punishment of the pair by metamorphosis into lions. To a large extent, Venus's narrative is about *desire*, in which the goddess herself, not just Hippomenes and Atalanta, is implicated.

Desire in Venus's Story of Hippomenes

The focus of Venus's narrative is Hippomenes' passion for Atalanta. The goddess builds up to the hero's decision to compete for the swift maiden by presenting Hippomenes' own reaction to the race in which so many young men struggled, only to forfeit their lives with their defeat. At first, Hippomenes is skeptical of such a perilous venture. But at the sight of Atalanta's face and her unclothed body ("ut faciem et posito corpus velamine vidit" [578]), he changes his mind, admitting to the suitors the value of the prize they were seeking (580–82).

Here, unlike other extant versions of this myth, Venus makes Atalanta struggle with her incipient passion but quickly succumb to her passion.[13] Reluctant to compete with Hippomenes, the maiden first acknowledges his handsome appearance: "'quis deus hunc formosis' inquit 'iniquus / perdere vult?'" ("'What god unjust to the good-looking,' she says, 'wishes to destroy him?'" [611–12]). She then denies her attraction but immediately qualifies her statement: "nec forma tangor (poteram tamen hac quoque tangi)" ("Nor am I touched by his beauty [I would nevertheless have been able to be touched by it, too]" [614]). Using the rhetoric of elegy, Atalanta singles out the feminine quality of his face: "at quam virgineus puerili vultus in ore est!" (631).[14] Although attributing her feelings of concern for him to his youth and courage (615–16), she repeatedly refers to Hippomenes' love for her. She even admits that he has moved her to thoughts of marriage: "unus eras, cum quo sociare cubilia vellem" ("You were the only one with whom I would have been willing to share a marriage bed" [635]).

This mutual desire motivated by beauty, suggesting that Hippomenes and Atalanta are to some extent interchangeable, has a corollary in the story of Venus and Adonis. The goddess interrupts her narrative with a comment to Adonis about the good looks that Hippomenes instantly found so desirable. After singling out Atalanta's face (*faciem* [578]), she observes that the maiden's body was in fact much like her own or his, if he should become a woman: "quale meum, vel quale tuum, si femina fias" (579). Commenting on this odd remark, Betty Rose Nagle emphasizes the connection between love and the loss of individual identity in this story, a problem that relates to Hippomenes and Atalanta in the embedded narrative as well as to Venus and Adonis.[15] Micaela Janan, furthermore, suggests that the goddess is interested in Adonis as a reflection of herself and creates a doppelgänger heroine in Atalanta, who desires Hippomenes because he has a similarly feminine beauty.[16] Yet the goddess also creates a double for herself in Hippomenes, whose passion for Atalanta corresponds to Venus's for Adonis. The two objects of desire, moreover, share a connection in their association with forests and hunting.[17] When Orpheus later resumes the narrative in his own voice, substitution takes on added significance.[18]

Venus's story of Hippomenes and Atalanta, furthermore, is infused with another form of desire: the urge to win the race and take the prize. To explore the implications of that drive, I consider why the goddess devotes so much of her narrative to the race itself, especially to the part that precedes Hippomenes' request for aid and his deployment of the golden apples. Venus subtly idealizes the masculine value of *virtus* by making Hippomenes the more central character in the embedded tale and thereby creates a powerful rhetoric privileging boldness. Paradoxically, she narrates the story of Hippomenes' race through language and tropes that conflict with her purpose of discouraging Adonis from an audacious pursuit of wild animals.

In order to attain his object of desire, Hippomenes must, of course, enter the race against Atalanta. But, more specifically, his desire for Atalanta is closely bound up with a need to prove himself as a hero. As he wonders why he should leave the fortune of that contest untried, he employs a pithy aphorism: "audentes deus ipse iuvat" ("Divinity itself aids those who dare" [586]). In addition to divine sanction, the syntax here also reinforces the value of boldness: the direct object *audentes,* the present participle form emphasizing action, occupies the emphatic position of the first word. A simile immediately following compares the swift young woman to a speeding projectile: "quae quamquam Scythia non setius ire sagitta / Aonio visa est iuveni" ("although she seemed to the Aonian youth to go not unlike a Scythian arrow" [588–89]). Famed for their skill as archers, the Scythians in Latin literature are frequently held up as exemplars of military valor, enhanced by their hardy existence as nomads of the northern regions of the Black Sea.[19] By referring to the "Scythian" nature of Atalanta from the perspective of the civilized "Aonian" Hippomenes, Venus makes the young woman's elemental, unspoiled vigor an idealized example of *virtus.*

The language of Hippomenes' challenge further contributes to the rhetoric encouraging aggressiveness. As a suitor, the hero presumably would not need to do more than simply state his intention of winning Atalanta in marriage by competing with her in the race. But he goes much further, first by asking why she seeks an easily won distinction ("facilem titulum") through defeat of sluggish (*inertes* [602]) competitors and by offering himself as a real challenger: "mecum confer" ("compete with me" [603]). He then refers to the fame that she will receive if fortune does not favor him:

nec virtus citra genus est; seu vincar, habebis
Hippomene victo magnum et memorabile nomen. (607–8)

[Nor is my valor unequal to my pedigree; or if I am defeated, you will have a
great and noteworthy reputation by defeating Hippomenes.]

Here, the last words of Hippomenes' speech urging Atalanta to com-
pete with him place the focus on the glory to be won from *virtus:* his
defeat would serve to magnify her reputation to heroic proportions
("magnum et memorabile nomen").

When Atalanta in her soliloquy articulates her reluctance to compete
with Hippomenes, she too places the youth's bravery in a positive light.
Here, she begins a tricolon consisting of questions by which she at-
tempts to deny simply a physical attraction to the handsome Hippo-
menes: "quid, quod inest virtus et mens interrita leti?" ("What about
the fact that courage and a mind undaunted by death are present in
him?" [616]). The speech emphasizes courage through its primacy in
Atalanta's list, picking up the concluding point of Hippomenes' speech.
In addition, Atalanta praises the youth's bravery here specifically by
stressing that he does not fear death, much as Hippomenes himself ex-
cused the suitors for putting their own lives at risk once he perceived
the value of the prize for which they were competing (580–82).

Modulations of style also enhance the appeal of *virtus.* Venus raises
the narrative to a higher level by including analogies equivalent to sim-
iles in epic poetry. She thus pictures Atalanta and Hippomenes flying
down the racetrack:

posse putes illos sicco freta radere passu
et segetis canae stantes percurrere aristas. (654–55)

[You would think that they could graze the surface of the sea with dry feet and
rush over standing stalks of white grain.]

Here again Venus turns to Adonis and addresses him personally,
drawing him into the scene.[20] The goddess creates the two images of
suprahuman speed over the natural and the cultivated landscape. She
makes them forceful by restricting each to a single hexameter, by using
some poetic diction (*radere* instead of *tangere,* and *canae* instead of
albae), and by employing the metonymy of "pace" for "feet" (*passu* for
pedibus).

Right after this simile, a powerfully rhetorical passage draws atten-
tion to the importance of *virtus.* Here, Venus vividly brings to life the
audience responding to Hippomenes' efforts and urging the youth on:

adiciunt animos iuveni clamorque favorque
verbaque dicentum "nunc, nunc incumbere tempus,
Hippomene, propera! nunc viribus utere totis!
pelle moram! vinces." (656-59)

[The shouts and goodwill increase the youth's high spirits, along with the words of the people saying, "Now, now is the time to press on; hasten, Hippomenes! Now use all your might! Cast off delay, you will conquer."]

The clipped, excited speech of the crowd itself creates an impression of immediacy and urgency. The repetition of *nunc*, first in an anadiplosis and then in an anaphora, reinforces the call for valor. The three consecutive imperatives (*propera, utere, pelle*) heighten the tension in this dramatic display of popular sentiment encouraging the youth's daring.

Venus's narrative creates an effective suspense leading up to the reward for Hippomenes' valor. In her description of Atalanta pausing to pick up one of the golden apples, the goddess initially suggests that Hippomenes will have little trouble winning the race and Atalanta as his bride: "obstipuit virgo nitidique cupidine pomi / declinat cursus" ("The maiden was dumbstruck and swerved from the course out of desire for the resplendent apple" [666–67]). Yet, after the first two apples are thrown, Atalanta reenters the race and succeeds in surpassing Hippomenes. With the third apple, however, Venus says that the young woman seemed to hesitate (676). The goddess herself then forced her to pick it up and, making the apple heavier, slowed the maiden down by the weight of the burden and the additional delay (676–78). Venus thus sums up the results of the race: "duxit sua praemia victor" ("The victor led off his prize" [680]). Valor, then, is shown to reap an appropriate reward.

The undercurrent of an incitement to *virtus* in Venus's depiction of Hippomenes, I believe, has the effect of inducing Adonis to display his own prowess. Indicating that the youth immediately goes off to hunt, Orpheus laconically states: "sed stat monitis contraria virtus" ("But valor is opposed to warnings" [709]).[21] Although the bard's comment may seem reasonable, it is very generalized and, furthermore, follows the puzzling statement that after warning Adonis, Venus left in her chariot: "iunctisque per aera cygnis / carpit iter" ("And, with her swans yoked together, she took off on a journey through the air" [708–9]).

Since the goddess has so forcefully expressed fears for her young lover's safety, it is surprising that the bard leaves her abrupt departure here unexplained. Accepting the youth's action as inevitable, Orpheus does not take an overtly critical perspective on the goddess's speech or behavior. The reader is left to wonder why Venus implicitly encourages Adonis to go off hunting boldly and why she leaves the scene. We now consider possible motivations for Venus's behavior.

Role Changing in Venus's Relations with Adonis

A striking physical change in Venus herself has a significant bearing on her relations with Adonis. The goddess has completely abandoned her usual haunts and radically altered her mode of life to be with the beautiful youth. Having adopted the garb and pursuits of Diana, Venus may seem quaint as she takes up hunting in order to devote herself to Adonis, whom she prefers to heaven itself ("caelo praefertur Adonis" [532]). There is certainly a lightly humorous tone to Orpheus's description of the abandonment of normal haunts and activities by the goddess accustomed to lounge in the shade and to enhance her beauty by adornment ("adsuetaque semper in umbra / indulgere sibi formamque augere colendo" [533-34]).

From one perspective, this alteration may be a typically clever Ovidian mechanism for reducing the stature of an Olympian goddess.[22] But Venus's metamorphosis, albeit temporary, is highly problematic since she assimilates herself to the very goddess who is Venus's antithesis through her hostility to sexuality. Although her role in the story of Adonis is not directly mentioned here, Diana is a divinity whose destructive power lies just under the surface of this episode. For, according to the prophecy made by Artemis at the end of Euripides' *Hippolytus*, she will get revenge for the death of her innocent devotee, the victim of Phaedra's lust, by destroying Aphrodite's own favorite (1416-22).[23] To what extent, then, is Adonis here a victim?

Recent scholarship on this section of the *Metamorphoses* has suggested a link between Artemis in Euripides' play and Venus as a Diana figure here. Exploring Ovid's use of the *Hippolytus* in the Myrrha episode and its aftermath, M. D. Thomas observes that the poet alludes to Artemis's revenge through Venus's assimilation to Diana and that Adonis avenges his mother Myrrha's passion by figuratively serving as a substitute for Cupid.[24] Hardie notes the subtle connection between the goddess's young lover and her son: after comparing Adonis to painted versions of naked Cupids ("qualia namque / corpora nudorum tabula pinguntur Amorum" [515-16]), the bard represents Venus wounded by Cupid's arrow as she kisses her son.[25] Orpheus here relates the incident:

namque pharetratus dum dat puer oscula matri,
inscius exstanti destrinxit harundine pectus. (525–26)

[For while the boy wearing his quiver was giving kisses to his mother, he unknowingly grazed her breast with a shaft that protruded.]

As Hardie concludes, the implication of this passage may be that Cupid inadvertently caused Venus to fall in love with him.[26] Clever verbal patterning here may also suggest something more than a casual accident.[27] The bard's narrative would seem to hint at a complex nexus of potentially literal as well as figurative incestuous desires on Venus's part.

Adonis's function as a surrogate for Cupid is complicated by Venus's relations with her son in the poem. At the beginning of the episode, Orpheus indicates Venus's angry reaction when Cupid grazes her: "laesa manu natum dea reppulit" ("Wounded, the goddess pushed her son away" [527]). In book 5, Calliope in her story of Ceres and Proserpina depicts Venus complaining vehemently about her own lack of power among the gods and urging Cupid to wound Pluto with his arrow (365–68).[28] As Venus expresses her fears to Cupid that Ceres' daughter will remain a virgin (376–77), she promotes an intrafamilial union on the divine level.[29] Although referring to her shared rule with her son (371–72), Venus expects Cupid to follow her orders. Earlier in book 10, the bard mentioned Cupid's denial that he had caused Myrrha to fall in love with Cinyras and blamed one of the Furies instead (311–14).[30] Venus may now have good reason to distrust her son's protestations of innocence. Since she herself is his victim, it is all too clear that Cupid is not under her dominion. If Adonis symbolizes Venus's sexual attraction to her son, he also reflects her need to obliterate those very feelings and to restore her own sense of power.

The incest theme implied in Venus's guise as Diana is, I believe, reinforced by an additional allusion to Euripides. Venus as a huntress recalls not only Artemis, who boasts that she will avenge Hippolytus's death, but also the heroine Phaedra, lovesick for her stepson, in the same play. Here, Orpheus refers to Venus urging on the hunting dogs ("hortaturque canes" [537]) and seeking prey such as stags ("celsum in cornua cervum" [538]). In the *Hippolytus*, Phaedra in a delirium from her illness similarly raves about going to the mountains to hunt for stags, calling to the hounds, and holding a spear poised for the kill (215–21).

Ovid earlier imitated this passage of Euripides' tragedy in *Heroides* 4: Phaedra, acknowledging her desires to her stepson, recounts her fantasies of driving deer into the nets, urging on the hunting dogs, and casting the spear (41–43). Furthermore, she attempts to persuade Hippolytus to take a break from hunting by citing the example of Venus and Adonis:

Saepe sub ilicibus Venerem Cinyraque creatum
  Sustinuit positos quaelibet herba duos. (97–98)

[Often some grassy plot held Venus and the son of Cinyras lying under ilex trees.]

In his elegiac poem, Ovid thus overtly associates the queen who articulates her incestuous desires with the goddess of love, prefiguring the association of Phaedra with Venus in her story in *Metamorphoses* 10.

The analogue with Phaedra, resonating with the illicit passion dramatized in the Euripidean model, is reinforced here by an intratextual allusion, linking the story of Venus's love for Adonis with Myrrha's for Cinyras. In the latter tale, there are clear echoes of the impassioned Phaedra in the young princess's agony over her feelings for her father and in her interaction with her nurse.[31] An association of Myrrha and Venus through the heroine Phaedra is particularly appropriate, for the goddess sanctioned the figurative incest of Pygmalion for his ivory maiden by bringing the statue to life and by presiding over the marriage that resulted in the birth of Paphos, the mother of Cinyras (270–97).

Indirectly responsible for Myrrha's incestuous passion for her father, Venus now experiences such feelings for her own son, transferred to his surrogate. But the model of Phaedra has radically different results for the young woman and the goddess. Myrrha's futile struggle over her passion for her father and the nurse's ill-thought interference end in disaster for the young woman: she flees, with the outraged Cinyras in pursuit, and in her grief is ultimately metamorphosed from human to vegetative form. Venus's "metamorphosis" into Diana, by contrast, is temporary: when Adonis meets with disaster, the goddess is restored to her Olympian splendor.

Adonis's fate is similar to that of his counterpart in the Greek tragedy. Phaedra deliberately brings about her stepson's death because he vehemently reviles her for her incestuous passion, which was communicated through her nurse, and she fears the damage to her good name if he exposes her intentions.[32] After reading the letter with Phaedra's false accusations, Theseus invokes a curse on his son as the cause of the queen's dishonor and suicide, and the innocent Hippolytus is trampled to death by his own horses. Here, in the epic, Venus abandons Adonis to his own inclinations, which prove to be fatal. Unequal to the task of confronting the boar, Adonis only grazes the fierce beast with a weak blow ("obliquo . . . ictu" [712]). When the boar easily dislodges the shaft, the youth desperately seeks some means of escape ("trepidumque et tuta petentem" [714]) but is gored and left bleeding to death on the sand.

Venus's absence at this point may seem fortuitous, but her destination is significant. Cyprus is the very land in which, according to Orpheus, she lost interest because of her passion for Adonis (529–31).[33] Earlier, in her narrative of Hippomenes' race, Venus elaborated on the source of the golden apples in a vivid ekphrastic passage on the sanctuary and the tree with its precious fruit. Recalling the ancient tributes bestowed on her, she describes a sacred precinct called Tamasenum, the best section ("optima pars" [645]) of Cyprus, which early settlers dedicated to her and added as a "dowry" (*dotem* [646]). Her use of the term *dos*, most often applied to the wealth that a bride brought with her into a marriage, suggests the considerable material value of the property. Venus's description of the tree itself draws attention to its unique nature: "medio nitet arbor in arvo, / fulva coma, fulvo ramis crepitantibus auro" ("In the middle of the field a tree with tawny foliage glistens, its golden branches rustling with tawny gold" [648]). The repetition of the adjective *fulvus* emphasizes the precious material of the tree and its fruit; the phrase "fulvo . . . auro" framing the word for branches (*ramis*) further adds to the visual effect. In her departure for Cyprus, Venus may be motivated by her own rhetoric. After warning Adonis with her ambivalent narrative, Venus sets out for the land that symbolizes her concern for power and privilege.

The Transformation of Adonis

The narrative of Adonis's fate after death reveals more about the desires of Venus and, as we will see, implicates Orpheus himself. Although Adonis perishes from the wound inflicted by the boar, Venus decides to preserve her young lover in some fashion. But the goddess couches her promise of survival in a manner that deflects from Adonis himself. On proclaiming that she will create a flower from Adonis's blood, Venus proceeds to apostrophize Proserpina with an invidious reference to the latter's metamorphic powers:

... an tibi quondam
femineos artus in olentes vertere mentas,
Persephone, licuit, nobis Cinyreius heros
invidiae mutatus erit? (728-31)

[Were you, Persephone, once permitted to change a woman's limbs to fragrant
mint, but a transformation of the hero born of Cinyras will be begrudged to
me?]

Venus's words here reveal her obsession with power. She cannot tol-
erate a rival possessing a privilege denied to her.[34] Since in book 5 it was
Venus herself who caused Pluto to be filled with passion for Proserpina
through her agent Cupid, the goddess's complaint may be motivated in
part by a recollection of the power that she wielded. Although obscure,
the myth referred to in this passage involves the resentment of Pluto's
mistress Menta (or Mintha) when Persephone arrived as his wife.[35] It is
not possible to know if Ovid followed a version of the myth different
from our extant sources or if he varied the story himself.[36] But Venus's
allusion to Menta recalls that the goddess of the underworld wished to
eliminate the threat to her own position posed by her avowed rival. The
analogue with Persephone thus further hints at Venus's self-interest in
her transformation of Adonis.

Ironically, Adonis seems to disappear in the very process of Ve-
nus's claim to preserve him. The goddess primarily exhibits self-concern
when she discovers the youth's body lying on the blood-soaked ground.
Her first words are far from an expression of horror or grief for Adonis;
instead they reflect her opposition to the power of the Fates: "at non
tamen omnia vestri / iuris erunt" ("But nevertheless all things will not
be under your sway" [724-25]). Even as she turns to the dead youth, the
goddess still focuses on herself:

... luctus monimenta manebunt
semper, Adoni, mei, repetitaque mortis imago
annua plangoris peraget simulamina nostri. (725-27)

[Memorials of my grief will always remain, Adonis, and a reenactment of your
death repeated annually will represent my lament.]

The only possessive adjectives here refer to Venus's grief, not to
Adonis's death; there is no *tuae* expressed to balance *mei* and *nostri*,
which receive emphasis as the last words in their respective clauses.
Language of illusion, moreover, lends a sense of unreality to the *moni-
menta* that the goddess promises: *imago* implies something "shadowy,"

and the neologism *simulamen*, occurring only here in Ovid, denotes a "copy" or "imitation." Adonis receives no solid monument to mark his remains, even though the language here may recall the concrete powers of art.[37] The ritual that Venus promises will be celebrated largely by courtesans in the Greek and Roman world, commemorating *her* grief and evoking Adonis in a context of riotous drinking, dancing, and sexual license.[38] Ovid elsewhere refers flippantly to the cult of Adonis in his contemporary Rome: the *praeceptor* of the *Ars* singles out celebrations of the Adonia as appropriate hunting ground for erotic conquests (1.75) and encourages female profligacy by asserting that Venus did not allow her grief for Adonis to keep her from giving birth to Aeneas and Harmonia (3.85–86).

In the brief conclusion to the story of Venus and Adonis, Orpheus's comments on the goddess's commemoration of her young lover reinforce its problematic nature. After Venus sprinkles Adonis's blood with nectar, the bard describes the mixture swelling up "ut fulvo perlucida caelo / surgere bulla solet" ("just as a very bright bubble is accustomed to arise in the yellow sky" [733–34]). Although some scholars find a textual problem here in part because of the description of the sky as "tawny" (*fulvo*), details of this simile are suggestive.[39] With the flower in progress likened to a simple bubble floating upward on a hot day, the simile is in a lower poetic register than one would expect after Venus's dramatic proclamation of compensation for Adonis's death, but it appropriately implies that the flower is the essence of fragility. The word *bulla*, furthermore, has a secondary meaning in the sphere of art. An ornament worn around the neck by Roman boys, generally composed of gold for the upper classes, the *bulla* was set aside at the point of manhood.[40] Ironically for Adonis, himself at the threshold of manhood, the *perlucida bulla* is a symbol of his removal from human existence altogether.

Orpheus elaborates suggestively on two features of this new flower. First of all, he compares its blood-like color to the red of the pomegranate: "qualem, quae lento celant sub cortice granum, / punica ferre solent" ("such as pomegranates are accustomed to bear, which conceal their seeds under their pliant rind" [736–37]). The analogy serves as a reminder of the unfortunate consequences of Venus's machinations. For, as Calliope's song in book 5 poignantly reveals, Persephone could not be unconditionally freed from Hades because she had eaten a pomegranate.[41] But the womblike pomegranate with its abundant seeds is a symbol of marriage and fertility as well as of death.[42] The analogue of a pomegranate here, however, has an ironic resonance, for the blood that produces the flower flowed from a wound in the groin ("sub inguine" [715]). As a reminder that Adonis has been unmanned, the pomegranate image thus signifies sterility.

Second, fragility and effacement underlie the bard's account of this flower:

namque male haerentem et nimia levitate caducum
excutiunt idem, qui praestant nomina, venti. (738–39)

[For the winds that furnish its name likewise shake it, barely holding together and perishable because of its excessive lightness.]

Although not mentioning the specific name of the flower, Orpheus alludes to it in his description here. The word *venti* clearly supplies the etymology, for it translates the Greek noun *anemos*, the root of the word "anemone." But, as Janan has pointed out, at the very moment that it signals the name of the flower, the text simultaneously effaces its existence.[43] Adonis, furthermore, does not receive the honor granted by Apollo to Hyacinthus, for the flower does not perpetuate his name. Although Venus has also promised Adonis a lasting ritual, Orpheus in his resumption of the role of narrator expands only on the flower, a sign of absence.

Venus's creation of the anemone and the allusion to the Adonia recall Apollo's response to the loss of Hyacinthus: the god similarly has a flower spring up from the youth's blood, and Orpheus calls attention to the annual ritual celebrated in his honor (209–19).[44] Since the story of Apollo's love for Hyacinthus is Orpheus's first extended narrative, following on the brief account of Jupiter's rape of Ganymede, the bard's song in a sense comes full circle here. But in its emphasis on the notion of absence in the flower commemorating Venus's young lover and of sterility in his cult, the conclusion to Adonis's story differs from that of Hyacinthus. The flower sprung from Hyacinthus's blood is marked with the letters AIAI (215–16), the Greek cry of woe; it thus perpetually unites the lost youth with the god's grief.

Emphasizing the enduring honor of the cult, Orpheus asserts that the Hyacinthia has preserved its traditional form ("celebrandaque more priorum" [218]) with splendid pageantry ("praelata . . . pompa" [219]). As a cult that involved young males and females in elaborate processions, sacrifices to Apollo including slaves as well as citizens, and games attended by the populace, it brought the community together in a movement from grief to celebration.[45] Through the flower inscribed with

Apollo's lament for his young love and the ritual bemoaning his loss, Orpheus appears to validate the god's ability to provide a meaningful commemoration. But his perspective on the goddess's effort to preserve her dead lover is far more dubious.

Orpheus's Role in the Tale of Venus and Adonis

Orpheus's relation to Venus, his internal narrator for so much of the song, is complex. By rejecting women for young boys, the bard has in effect spurned Venus herself.[46] Noting that Hippomenes' fate is much like the bard's, Robert Coleman has suggested that Orpheus derives consolation from the suffering of Venus as compensation for the pain inflicted by the gods on mortals.[47] At the beginning of his story of Venus and Adonis, the bard apostrophizes the youth: "te quoque, ut hos timeas, siquid prodesse monendo / posset, Adoni, monet" ("She warns you, too, Adonis, to fear them, if she were able to help in any way by warning" [542–43]). William Anderson observes that Ovid addresses Adonis "as if he wished us to feel especially close to the boy."[48] I would qualify Anderson's statement, however, by noting that Orpheus rather than Ovid aims for this effect. Furthermore, the imperfect subjunctive verb (*posset*) creates a contrary-to-fact conditional clause, which implies Orpheus's view that Venus could do nothing to deter the youth's natural inclinations. Yet, as I have suggested, the bard's recitation of Venus's tale of Atalanta and Hippomenes reveals a powerful rhetoric: by privileging *virtus*, the goddess produces an impact on Adonis contrary to her expressed intentions for his safety.

If Orpheus is to some extent distanced from the goddess, he also reflects his own preoccupations as he records Venus's story of Hippomenes and Atalanta and recounts the goddess's love and loss. Orpheus merges his voice with Venus's by alluding to his own encounter with the rulers of the underworld. When Venus complains to the Fates that not everything will be under their jurisdiction, the phrase "vestri / iuris erunt" (724–25) echoes Orpheus's own attempt to persuade the infernal gods to defer their claim to his young wife. There, after flattering Pluto and Proserpina about the scope of their powers and kingdom (34–35), he assures them that once Eurydice has reached a full maturity through a reasonable life span (36), she will then belong to them: "iuris erit vestri" (37). Immediately after challenging the Fates, Venus, as we have seen, apostrophizes Persephone in an eristic manner about her metamorphosis of Menta by suggesting that *invidia* may deny her a similar feat (728-31).

Ovid gives priority of place to Persephone both in the bard's approach to the king and queen of the underworld ("Persephonen adiit inamoenaque regna tenentem" [15]) and in their response to his speech ("nec regia coniunx / sustinet oranti nec, qui regit ima, negare" [46-47]). But, after he forfeits the right to regain Eurydice by disobeying the prohibition against looking back at her, the bard places the blame on Proserpina and Pluto rather than on himself as he laments the cruelty of these two gods: "esse deos Erebi crudeles questus" (76). When Orpheus records Venus's angry apostrophe to Persephone, he echoes his own resentment at the queen of the underworld.

In reciting Venus's inset story, moreover, Orpheus reflects his own similarity to Hippomenes. The bard projects a self-image in the idealized portrait of the hero eager to achieve success in the competition with Atalanta. For Hippomenes' entrance in the dangerous race to win the beautiful, as well as fleet-footed, Atalanta has a counterpart in Orpheus's bold descent to the underworld to restore Eurydice to life. But both Hippomenes and Orpheus undermine their heroism by a form of forgetfulness that reflects a failure to respect the gods. The former does not express gratitude to Venus; the latter fails to heed Pluto's stipulation against looking back at Eurydice until they reached the upper world. As Orpheus records Venus's tale, however, disproportionate emphasis is given the heroic side of Hippomenes in comparison to his offense; the youth's positive qualities predominate, validating his heroic stature. Hippomenes' failure to express thanks or offer incense (682-83) is apparently the result of a momentary mental lapse. Wrapped up in his success at winning the girl, the young man is too self-indulgent, not unlike Orpheus in his eagerness on the way out of Hades.

An additional point of contact between the hero and the bard concerns the fate of the beloved. Both unwittingly destroy their innocent objects of desire through an excess of passion.[49] Although Venus says that she caused Hippomenes to engage in sex within Cybele's temple precinct, the hero himself becomes fired with passion when he sees Atalanta running naked and praises her beauty ("laudando concipit ignes" [582]). In his account of Orpheus's journey to the upper world with Eurydice, Ovid is more oblique about the bard's feelings but states that the lover looked back, eager to see ("avidusque videndi / flexit amans oculos" [56-57]).

In fixing his gaze on the object of desire, Orpheus seems to act more like a lover (*amans*) from the elegiac tradition focusing on possessing the beloved than a husband in the process of restoring his young wife to her proper place in the *domus*.[50] The poet's comparison of Orpheus to a man named Olenos emphasizes the overweening self-confidence that is indirectly responsible for the death of a spouse, for Olenos wanted to rescue his wife, who had incurred the anger of a goddess by boasting of her beauty, but instead was turned to stone with her (68–71).[51]

Orpheus concludes his song with a final allusion to his own experience. As he breaks off at the moment that the youth is transformed into an anemone, the bard ends with the word *venti*. To the extent that Orpheus represents himself through Venus, Eurydice corresponds to the unfortunate Adonis. Orpheus's narrative of Adonis's fate implies that the object of desire is irretrievable, that symbolic forms of recovery through metamorphosis and ritual are illusory. The metamorphosis of Adonis into the fragile anemone, whose identity is bound up with the winds that destroy it, recalls the state of Eurydice when Orpheus tried to embrace her after he disobeyed Pluto's injunction. There, Ovid shows that, as a receding shade, or *imago*, she was nothing more than the breeze: "nil nisi cedentes infelix adripit auras" ("The unhappy man grasps at nothing but the moving breezes" [59]).

Orpheus can no longer continue his song at the moment when Adonis's metamorphosis represents his own failure, his second loss of his wife. Never truly commemorated in his song, Eurydice disappears altogether with Adonis. The song thus ends when the tale of Venus and Adonis effaces the bard's efforts at self-validation. Orpheus cannot sustain the fantasy of a creative triumph such as Pygmalion's ivory maiden. Both artist and bard are oblivious to the narcissism underlying that tale.[52]

Like his surrogate narrator Venus, the bard has been inadequately attuned to the audience of his song.[53] In his self-absorption, he sings to the trees and the beasts, who listen to his tales in rapt adoration, and fails to take heed of the presence of the Thracian women, who not only resent Orpheus's change in sexual preference from female to youthful male but also hear the biases expressed through his singing. Their rage against Orpheus has turned them into wild animals (*ferae* [11.37]) who are not susceptible to the enchantment of his music.[54] After tearing apart the beasts of the field, the Thracian women do the same to the bard (37–43).

Although an apparently happy scene, the bard's reunion with his wife in the underworld (11.61–66) suggests his inherent self-concern. Having achieved in death the goal that eluded him in life, Orpheus focuses on his object of desire in the safe haven of the Elysian fields. Playing a game of "follow the leader," the two now exchange roles ("Sometimes he follows as she walks first; sometimes he goes ahead of her" [65]). But much as Narcissus remains fixated on his image in the waters of the Styx (3.503–4), Orpheus looks back at Eurydice: "Euridicenque suam iam tuto respicit Orpheus" ("Orpheus now safely looks back at his Eurydice" [66]). Orpheus's self-involvement is no longer conveyed through the medium of poetry. But, spared any possibility of further separation, the bard perpetually reenacts his original gesture of self-absorption, without the painful consequences.

Orpheus and Ovid

Although Ovid has Orpheus narrate the powerful tale of Myrrha's love for her father, Cinyras, the poet himself is responsible for the underlying dynamic of figurative incest in the bard's song. Orpheus, I believe, is blind to this symbolic level of his tales: because of the self-referential nature of his work, he puts a positive slant on Pygmalion's effort to sculpt the "ideal" female, and the complex layering of incestuous desires in the final tale includes not only Venus's substitution of Adonis for Cupid but also the poet's allusions to Phaedra and Hippolytus in *Heroides* 4. The bard creates a dramatic portrayal of literal incest in which the guilty young woman is driven out of the country by her father and loses her human form.

Ovid's own tale of Byblis, moreover, connects him with Orpheus not only in the incestuous desire of the female but also in a kind of self-absorption by the poet. As noted earlier, the Byblis episode suggests a figurative incest in the poetic sphere as Ovid has the young woman reiterate his elegiac corpus both in her behavior and in her letter to her brother. The poet, furthermore, goes back to his own heroine Medea in book 7 for Byblis's tormented soliloquy. When the young woman, for instance, assures herself that her brother was not born from a tiger and does not have rock or iron in his chest (9.613–14), she repeats the triple analogy by which Medea tries to justify betraying her father in order to help Jason (7.32–33). Ovid's exploration of incest in his own voice thus repeats his literary present as well as past.

As we saw in chapter 1, the poet suggests his fascination with visual images through the character of Narcissus. He has Orpheus indulge in this proclivity, for instance, in the simile connecting Adonis with

Cupid. There, Orpheus describes Myrrha's infant as so beautiful that he resembled the type of naked Cupid one sees in paintings, with or without a light bow (515–18).[55]

We observed that Ovid through the bard even has Venus produce the graphic image of Atalanta and Hippomenes appearing to skim over the surface of the sea or over grainfields as they speed on. This pictorial passage, however, is not original but echoes an image of skimming over grainfields or over the surface of the sea in *Aeneid* 7.[56] Vergil thus describes the warrior Camilla:

> illa vel intactae segetis per summa volaret
> gramina nec teneras cursu laesisset aristas,
> vel mare per medium fluctu suspensa tumenti
> ferret iter celeris nec tingueret aequore plantas. (808–11)

> [She could have flown over the tops of the blades of grain without touching them and would not have damaged the tender ears or could have made her way over the sea, lifted over the swelling waves, and would not have wet her swift feet on the surface.]

This simile describing a powerful exemplar of heroic excellence is part of an extended passage that brings to a close the catalogue of troops assembled to fight against the Trojans.[57] Since the model in Vergil occurs at the end of book 7 in the climax of the catalogue of Latin troops, a reader of the *Aeneid* would likely recall it. Ovid's echo is surprising: to convey Camilla's uniqueness, Vergil appropriately uses highly poetic language and tropes in his double analogy, but Ovid reverses the two components, compresses them, and employs a tighter, less fully poetic style. Yet he places the word *aristas* in the same position as in the *Aeneid* at the end of the hexameter (655; *Aeneid* 7.809), thus leaving a trace of his source.

Immediately afterward, the bard has Venus create the lively scene of spectators encouraging Hippomenes against Atalanta. There, too, the poet echoes a famous scene in the *Aeneid*. In the final stages of the race that begins the funeral games for Anchises in book 5, Vergil shows Mnestheus competing with Sergestus to pass ahead of Gyas and thus to take second place. Here, the captain of the *Pristis* exhorts his men:

> hortatur Mnestheus: "nunc, nunc insurgite remis,
> Hectorei socii, Troiae quos sorte suprema
> deligi comites; nunc illas promite viris,
> nunc animos, quibus in Gaetulis Syrtibus usi
> Ionioque mari Maleaeque sequacibus undis." (189–93)

[Mnestheus urges: "Now, now press upon your oars, comrades of Hector, whom I chose as companions in the final disaster of Troy. Now display that strength, now that courage which you employed in Gaetulian Syrtes and on the Ionian Sea and the turbulent waves of Malea."]

The reduplication of the word *nunc* at the very beginning of Mnestheus's attempt to spur his men on and the anaphora with the same word in the following clause, along with three imperative phrases, produce a powerful rhetorical unit that stands out in the narrative of the boat race. Ovid's echo here is also surprising: the poet duplicates Vergil's unusual double repetition of the adverb *nunc* (through anadiplosis and anaphora) in a triple imperative construction, conveying a collective cry of encouragement, in a context that a reader of the *Aeneid* would easily recognize.

As we saw in chapter 3, Ovid in book 8 significantly engages with his great Augustan predecessor, redefining Vergil's use of the labyrinth as a symbol of his narrative. Yet, at the end of that book, he also makes use of an obsessively Vergilian epic style so as to parody the pomposity of his river god. Ovid, of course, is not an Achelous. But his recollections of the *Aeneid* here seem to be appropriations without engagement, a kind of slippage. The allusions are woven into a context of competition suggesting a more problematic "identification" with Vergil. The poet, in effect, takes on some of the character of his surrogate narrator of book 10, who in his self-absorption conflates his own voice with Venus's in the story of Atalanta and Hippomenes.

Ovid's account of the fate of Orpheus's head looks forward to his own highly personal moment at the very end of the poem. While mentioning that the bard's voice defied death, Ovid emphasizes that Orpheus's tongue continued to sing. But he tells the reader only that the song was "something plaintive": "flebile nescio quid queritur lyra, flebile lingua / murmurat exanimis" ("The lyre laments something plaintive; his lifeless tongue murmurs something plaintive" [11.52]). In projecting his own fate after death in the poem's epilogue, Ovid also refers to the voice and mouth, but with an important difference. He prophesies that he will survive on the lips of men who will continue to read his poem ("ore legar populi") through the ages (15.878–79); he himself will become identifiable with his text. As both the subject and the narrator of a major section of the poem, Orpheus receives a share of the immortality with which Ovid will be endowed through his epic.

The bard, of course, is only one of numerous surrogates for the poet throughout this epic, though perhaps the most compelling storyteller.

Whereas Orpheus perpetually reiterates the self-obsession that defines his voice in Ovid's text, the poet of the *Metamorphoses* lives on in the multiplicity of his tales and their varied perspectives. But Orpheus, for instance, shifts between distance from and identification with Venus both in his recitation of her story and in his own narrative of her affair with Adonis. As those fluctuations suggest, each internal narrator potentially has an ax to grind, and the boundary between narrator and surrogate may be significantly blurred.

5

Ulysses and
the Arms of Achilles

In *Metamorphoses* 13, Ovid continues his account of the Trojan War
from book 12 with the contest of Ajax and Ulysses for the arms of
Achilles, a subject popular not only with epic and tragic poets but
also with professional rhetoricians in antiquity.[1] Devoting nearly half of
the book (1–398) to this contest, the poet sustains the traditional con-
trast between the two heroes: the one is brave but rather taciturn, and
the other is cunning and articulate. But he also provides a surprising
twist: whereas Ulysses reveals the adaptability characteristic of his Ho-
meric counterpart, Ajax here is much different from the grand Sopho-
clean hero whose sublimely intransigent nature drives him to commit
suicide after losing the contest. His metamorphosis into a flower at the
end of the episode reinforces the lack of a lofty, tragic status. As I show,
while devaluing the traditionally noble character of Ajax, Ovid privi-
leges the changeable, though at times ethically questionable, nature of
Ulysses.

Ajax represents the traditional moral as well as social values re-
flected in the *Iliad*. Throughout his speech, he naturally emphasizes his
courage (*virtus*) on the battlefield. But he also reflects the importance of
good faith (*fides*), demonstrated in fair dealing with and loyalty to one's
comrades. In censuring Ulysses for causing Philoctetes to be left on
Lemnos, the hero apostrophizes the abandoned warrior in a gesture of
sympathy as "Poeantia proles" ("offspring of Poeas" [45]) and elab-
orates on the hardships of his life alone on the island (47–54). He also
abhors Ulysses' false charge that Palamedes had betrayed the Greeks

for gold, which cost that hero his life (56-60). Furthermore, critical of his opponent for fleeing the battlefield when Nestor called out for help, Ajax manifests a belief in divine power, affirming that "the gods look on mortal affairs with just eyes" (70). The hero's connection to these traditional values suggests that Ovid's Roman audience would have been predisposed to favor him over his cunning opponent.² By echoing Vergil's description of Ulysses as "hortator scelerum" ("inciter of crimes" [42]), Ajax seems in accord with conservative Roman moralism.³

The centripetal pull of this episode toward the high moral ground reflected by Ajax (and, conversely, against the rather questionable ethics represented by Ulysses) is weakened by an undercurrent of arrogance that Ovid infuses into the hero's speech. The poet suggests his own distance from heroic egoism, a hallmark of the Homeric warrior, through aspects of this hero's rhetoric. Ajax reveals this characteristic in particular by his use of aphoristic *sententiae*. After referring to his resistance to Hector's efforts to burn the ships of the Greeks, he employs this pithy *sententia*: "atque Aiax armis, non Aiaci arma petuntur" ("And Ajax is sought by the arms, the arms are not sought by Ajax" [97]). To be sure, the hero reveals wit by personifying Achilles' arms. But the implicitly egoistic gesture by which Ajax places his own name first in each unit caps an unfortunately crass display of arrogance. For he precedes this *sententia* with a boast by which he in effect places himself above Achilles: "quaeritur istis, / quam mihi, maior honos" ("Greater glory is sought by those arms than by me" [95-96]).

At the end of his speech, the hero utters this challenge testifying to his undaunted courage: "arma viri fortis medios mittantur in hostes: / inde iubete peti" ("Let the arms of the brave hero be sent into the midst of the enemy; then order them to be sought" [121-22]). Ajax here echoes a *sententia* of Porcius Latro, a renowned Augustan *rhetor*.⁴ Ovid's contemporary reader would likely have been familiar with the version of the contest for Achilles' arms by the popular Latro.⁵ Ajax's boastful words, however, lose their force when measured against the vigor of his model.⁶

At the conclusion of this episode, the poet himself employs a pithy *sententia* to undercut Ajax's bravery. He thus summarizes the results of the contest: "fortisque viri tulit arma disertus" ("The fluent man carried off the arms of the brave man" [383]). On the surface, the poet's terse comment might appear to imply sympathy with the loser. But the phrase "fortisque viri tulit arma" is an ironic echo of Ajax's *sententia* at the end of his speech.[7] Ovid's echo serves to highlight the arrogance of Ajax's assumption that he himself will, in fact, be victorious over his opponent.

Ulysses, of course, wins the arms through his ability as an orator. As expected, the clever Greek reveals himself a master in the all-important sphere of *elocutio,* style. On the one hand, Ajax relies heavily on invective, persistently demeaning his opponent. On the other, Ulysses not only responds in kind but also effectively exploits a wide range of tones and emotions.[8] He is, moreover, far superior in the essential area of *inventio,* finding arguments. Whereas Ajax focuses on only one major action on the battlefield, his aborted duel with Hector, Ulysses covers the full range of his martial contests as recounted in the *Iliad* and incorporates numerous examples of his work done in the long intervals between battles. Ulysses also differs markedly from Ajax in *dispositio,* the arrangement of his material, by employing an associative process in which he at several points brings up his own connection to the dead Achilles.[9]

Ovid, however, attributes to the clever Greek more than a facility with the fundamental oratorical skills by which he outclasses his opponent. Ulysses, I believe, in effect blurs the boundaries between rhetoric and poetry, combining the "muscle" of rhetoric with the "brilliance" of poetry.[10] This chapter argues that Ulysses is an imaginative and deconstructive rhetorician analogous to the poet who thoroughly destabilizes the genre of epic in the *Metamorphoses.*[11] The clever Greek reveals impressive metamorphic powers. Through the inventive techniques of his speech, Ulysses shapes an image of himself as a hero, turning weakness into strength, especially by adroitly manipulating the important issues of lineage and valor and even contradicting facts about the Trojan War related in the *Iliad* and the *Odyssey.*

In the sections that follow, I discuss how the clever Greek reflects his transformative powers in his account of the night raid involving the Trojan spy Dolon; his enumeration of his contests on the battlefield; his display of chest wounds as the visible signs of his valor; his discussion of his relationship with Achilles and rescue of his corpse; and his ekphrasis of the great hero's shield. Throughout, he engages in a significant play with language, especially by subtly exploring the semantic range and etymology of words. Ulysses is thereby a surrogate for the poet who so pervasively exploits the malleability of language in the *Metamorphoses* and challenges the authority of "official" epic, Homer as well as Vergil.

Ulysses and Heroic Genealogy: Divine Lineage

Traditional heroic society (and Ovid's own Rome), of course, placed great emphasis on an individual's genealogy. But here Ajax and Ulysses address the issue of lineage in very different ways. Ajax responds in a manner typical of a Homeric hero. Calling attention to his paternity, he identifies himself in high epic style as *Telamone creatus* (22).[12] As one would expect from a Homeric warrior, he emphasizes the heroic deeds of his father, pointing out that Telamon stormed Troy with Hercules and accompanied Jason to Colchis in search of the Golden Fleece.[13] He also asserts that his grandfather Aeacus serves as a judge in the underworld, where Sisyphus pushes his heavy rock (25–26). Formalizing his direct descent from the king of the gods, Ajax boasts that Jupiter acknowledged (*agnoscit* [27]) Aeacus as his son and then refers to himself in the third person as Jupiter's great-grandson: "sic a Iove tertius Aiax" ("Thus, Ajax is the third in line from Jupiter" [28]).

True to his aristocratic nature, Ajax expresses resentment at a perceived blot to his family name in Ulysses' attempt to possess the arms. Although he does refer to Ulysses by the patronymic *Laertiades* ("son of Laertes" [48]), he asserts that his opponent is the offspring of the criminal Sisyphus, eternally punished in the underworld: "sanguine cretus / Sisyphio furtisque et fraude simillimus illi" ("born from the blood of Sisyphus and very similar to him in thefts and trickery" [31–32]).[14] Since he himself shares the line of Aeacus with Achilles, Ajax concludes that Ulysses demeans his noble family by his effort to win the arms: in his view, his opponent attempts to "graft" the name of an unsuitable family onto his own or to "intrude" it ("inserit Aeacidis alienae nomina gentis" [33]).[15]

Ulysses, by contrast, perceives lineage in a more flexible way. First of all, ignoring his rival's scornful reference to his alleged shameful paternity, he focuses on his equality to Ajax in his own descent from Jupiter. He boasts that he is likewise three generations from the king of the gods:

... nostri quoque sanguinis auctor
Iuppiter est, totidemque gradus distamus ab illo.
nam mihi Laertes pater est, Arcesius illi,
Iuppiter huic. (142–45)

[The author of my line too is Jupiter, and I am just as many degrees from him, for my father is Laertes, his was Arcesius, and his was Jupiter.]

Ulysses enhances his claim by his skill with language. As Andreas Michalopoulos observes, the clever Greek reinforces his connection to Jupiter by prominently repeating the god's name at the beginning of two lines and by placing the word *pater* at the caesura of the intervening line, thereby calling attention to a possible etymology of Jupiter's name.[16] In addition, by referring to Jupiter as the *auctor* ("increaser" as well as "originator") of his family line, he implicitly adds to the underpinning of support for the excellence of his lineage in the presumed derivation of Jupiter's name from the verb *iuvo* ("to help"). This play with language, implying a deep understanding of the relation between words and things, is a hallmark of Ulysses' speech. It becomes an important device by which the hero separates himself from his rival and, implicitly, links himself with the poet of the *Metamorphoses*.

Ulysses' Relation to Mercury

Ulysses makes another claim to divine lineage that gives him an edge over Ajax. Here, he asserts his descent from Mercury: "est quoque per matrem Cyllenius addita nobis / altera nobilitas" ("And another source of nobility, the Cyllenian god, has been added to me through my mother" [146–47]). His claim cleverly obscures the fact that it was Anticleia's father Autolycus, the archetypal thief, who was Mercury's son by Chione.[17] But Ovid has already made the reader aware of this biological relationship through the tale of Daedalion in book 11. There, Ceyx tells the story of his brother's grief at the death of his beautiful daughter Chione, with whom Mercury and Apollo had simultaneously fallen in love and whom each had impregnated (293–345). The king of Trachis thus describes Chione's son by Mercury:

alipedis de stirpe dei versuta propago
nascitur Autolycus, furtum ingeniosus ad omne,
candida de nigris et de candentibus atra
qui facere adsuerat, patriae non degener artis. (312–15)

[From the stock of the wing-footed god a versatile offspring was born, Autolycus, talented in all trickery, who was accustomed to make white black and black white, not unworthy of his father's skill.]

This passage not only characterizes Mercury's immediate offspring but also insinuates a connection with a subsequent generation, for the adjective *versutus*, a lengthened form of *versus* ("turned"), is a close

Latin equivalent of the Greek *polutropos*, Homer's signal epithet for Odysseus.[18] The word also serves to connect the cunning hero with the clever messenger god in the *Odyssey*, though Homer does not imply a biological relationship between the two.[19] In Latin, *versutus* is the word used by Livius Andronicus to render *polutropos* in the first line of his translation of the *Odyssey*: "Virum mihi, Camena, insece versutum" ("Tell me, Muse, of the clever man").[20]

Ovid calls attention to this synonym for *callidus* since he uses *versutus* only here in the *Metamorphoses*. As he describes Mercury's cunning offspring, he simultaneously conveys an impression of his metamorphic ability through a clever deployment of rhetoric and grammar: the poet reinforces the unexpected ability of turning white to black and vice versa in the chiastic word order of "candida de nigris et de candentibus atra" and also changes the adjective *candida* to the participial form *candentibus* in the reverse transformation of the second unit.

As his speech progresses, Ulysses increasingly reflects the power of Autolycus and his divine progenitor to make things seem to be what they are not.[21] He thereby reveals an affinity with Ovid, whose close connection to Mercury emerges most clearly in the tale of Pan's pursuit of the nymph Syrinx in book 1. There, the messenger god ironically exploits the power of a love story on his immediate audience, the hundred-eyed monster who guards Io in her transformed state as a cow. Singing his song to the music of the rustic pipes, he cleverly causes his tale to have a stupefying effect, leaving Argus vulnerable to his lethal attack with a sword.[22] By picking up the tale, which Mercury stops when Argus falls asleep, the poet reinforces his close relation to the messenger god.[23] Moreover, as he reaffirms the aetiological nature of this story, motivated by Argus's curiosity about the origin of the unfamiliar pipes, Ovid performs a sly move in the spirit of his divine counterpart by making Pan rather than Mercury the inventor of the instrument known as the *syrinx*.[24] Ovid's propensity to exploit tales ironically for devious purposes has much in common with the verbal cunning of both the messenger god and his Ithacan descendant.

Ulysses and the Night Raid

Ulysses' metamorphic powers can be observed in particular when he makes his case for the arms through material familiar to the reader from Homer. The clever Greek responds at length to his rival's dismissive reference to "Rhesus and the unwarlike Dolon" (98), exemplifying his charge that Ulysses performs feats only at night and with the help of Diomedes (100). Immediately before his account of the night raid with Diomedes, Ulysses summarizes his success at keeping the Greeks from abandoning the war when Agamemnon tested the troops because of a dream sent by Jupiter (216–37), an account that closely corresponds to *Iliad* 2 (1–335). The reader would naturally expect a similar conformity with the Doloneia in *Iliad* 10, especially after Ulysses boasts that Diomedes shares (*communicat*) his deeds with him, approves of him, and relies on him as comrade (239–40). He thus caps this claim of a privileged position: "est aliquid de tot Graiorum milibus unum / a Diomede legi" ("It is something to be the one chosen by Diomedes from so many thousands of Greeks" [241–42]).

It is all the more surprising, then, that Ulysses eliminates Diomedes' role in the night raid altogether. As commentators note, he contradicts Homer's account by claiming that he himself killed not only Dolon (244–45) but also Rhesus and his companions (250). In *Iliad* 10, by contrast, Diomedes does all the killing; Odysseus extracts information from Dolon and drags the bodies of Rhesus and his men out of the way to prevent the Thracian's prized horses from bolting.

In addition to taking credit for his companion's actions in Homer, Ulysses appears to exaggerate his own accomplishment with Dolon by asserting that he learned from the Trojan spy "quid perfidiosa Troia pararet" ("what perfidious Troy was preparing" [246]). That claim in fact reflects the purpose of the mission, as explicitly stated by Nestor in *Iliad* 10 (206–10). But the captured Dolon has nothing to tell the two Greeks about the Trojans' strategic plans; he is able to divulge merely the whereabouts of Hector and his allies. Learning of the newly arrived Rhesus with his wonderful white horses (414–41) from Dolon, they decide to go after the valuable spoils.[25] Although contributing significantly to Greek strategy in the war, Odysseus in the Doloneia succeeds only in eliminating a handful of the enemy and acquiring limited, though valuable, spoils. But, here in the contest, Ulysses may be cleverly playing on the range of meanings of the verb *paro*: his boast can also be interpreted to mean "what perfidious Troy was acquiring," specifically, the fabulous horses of the newcomer Rhesus.

Ulysses shapes his story in particular by embellishing his return to camp in an image of glory. As commentators observe, the Greek makes an anachronistic reference to the Roman custom of a triumph as he thus concludes his summary of the night raid: "atque ita captivo victor votisque potitus / ingredior curru laetos imitante triumphos" ("And so as victor having fulfilled my prayers, I proceeded in the captive chariot resembling a joyful triumph" [251-52]).[26]

Once again, Ulysses deviates significantly from Homer's account. In the *Iliad*, Dolon indeed tells Odysseus that Rhesus's chariot is decked out in gold and silver and that his armor is huge and golden, more fit for gods than for men (438-41). Homer, however, states that Odysseus loosens the horses from the chariot, reins them together, and drives them from the slaughter, lashing them with his bow since he forgot to take the whip from the chariot (498-501). For his part, Diomedes contemplates two options: on the one hand, whether he should seize the chariot with the valuable armor and pull it away with the pole—or perhaps lift it and carry it off—or, on the other hand, whether he should slay more Thracians (503-6). But Athena intervenes, urging him to leave before another god rouses the Trojans (507-11). The two warriors then mount the horses and quickly dash back to the Greek camp (513-14).[27] When Nestor greets them with relief on their arrival, Odysseus responds to the old counselor in a sensible manner: he openly credits Diomedes with killing Rhesus and his men and tempers Nestor's enthusiasm over the horses by asserting that a god could have better horses than these (555-63).

Ovid's Ulysses thus invents the impressive picture of his return in the "captive chariot." Furthermore, he implicitly associates his triumphal procession with the preservation of Achilles' divinely sired horses, which he immediately asserts were the prize demanded by Dolon for undertaking his spying expedition ("cuius equos pretium pro nocte poposcerat hostis" [253]). In *Iliad* 10, however, Odysseus wryly sets Dolon straight about Achilles' horses: the "great gifts" for which he lusted are very difficult for any mortal to control, except the supreme hero born of a goddess (401-4). Homer makes it abundantly clear that Dolon stands no chance of winning those prized horses.

Here, the historical anachronism of the triumph, the glorious celebration of a singular (and single) individual, explains in part why the hero left his comrade out of his account of the night raid. By the image of a triumph, Ulysses begins to re-create himself to some extent as a Roman, seizing opportunities to invent anachronisms that his immediate audience can admire, if not fully comprehend. As he refashions himself by using language and an inventive imagination to transform reality, this hero reveals how much he resembles the poet of the *Metamorphoses*.

Ulysses and Homeric Valor

Ulysses further responds to Ajax's criticism that he operates only at night and always with the aid of Diomedes by elaborating on his feats on the battlefield. Here, Ulysses offers a roster of slain warriors in the manner of the epic poet's narrative of an heroic *aristeia*:

> Quid Lycii referam Sarpedonis agmina ferro
> devastata meo? Cum multo sanguine fudi
> Coeranon Iphitiden et Alastoraque Chromiumque
> Alcandrumque Haliumque Noemonaque Prytanimque
> exitioque dedi cum Chersidamante Thoona
> et Charopem fatisque inmitibus Ennomon actum,
> quique minus celebres nostra sub moenibus urbis
> procubuere manu. (255–62)

[Why should I refer to the troops of Sarpedon devastated by my sword? I routed with much blood Coeranus, the son of Iphitus, and Alastor and Chromius and Alcander and Halius and Noemon and Prytanis, and I sent to death Thoon along with Chersidamas and Charops and Ennomus, driven by a harsh fate, and less famous men who fell by my hand beneath the walls of the city.]

Ulysses' list cleverly renders the impression of a great onslaught of men felled in a display of heroic prowess. As is well known, Ulysses refers to two separate episodes recounted in books 5 and 11 of the *Iliad*. But his compression of Homer's account conceals important facts. Although the first four lines do reflect Odysseus's success in *Iliad* 5, they allude to incidents encompassed within the *aristeia* of Diomedes, the very warrior on whose prowess Ajax claims Ulysses depends. Homer minimizes Odysseus's role in the fighting in book 5 and shows him to be a minor player at this stage of the battle. Although Ulysses boasts of his rout of the Lycian troops, Homer in fact emphasizes Odysseus's failure to engage in combat with the leader of the Lycians. When the poet tersely comments that it was not Odysseus who was fated to kill the illustrious Sarpedon, the son of Zeus (674–75), the reader is left to anticipate Sarpedon's dramatic contest with Patroclus, who enters the battle wearing the armor of Achilles.

The list of men named in the third and fourth lines closely imitates the following passage in *Iliad* 5:

Then he took Koiranos and Alastor and Chromios and Alcandros and Halios and Noemon and Prytanis. (677–78)

Here, Homer refers to the lesser warriors whom Odysseus defeats after deciding not to pursue the wounded Sarpedon.[28] Even more relevant to Ovid's context, although Ulysses reproaches Ajax sarcastically for failing to defeat Hector in hand-to-hand combat (278–79), the echo of *Iliad* 5 refers to the point at which Odysseus himself is stopped by Hector. For immediately after this list of warriors slain by the Greek hero, Homer states that "godlike Odysseus would have killed more of the Lycians if great Hector with the shining helmet had not sharply perceived him" (679–80). Ovid's Ulysses thus cleverly suppresses his own failure while asserting his opponent's deficiency.

In the next two lines, he refers to an incident recounted in *Iliad* 11, in which he kills Chersidamas, Charops, and Ennomus (420–25). Odysseus is then wounded by Charops's brother Socus but succeeds in slaying the man (427–55). Immediately afterward, the Trojans press in, and ironically, Aias has to save Odysseus. It is unclear who the *minus celebres* (261) are, since the Ithacan has no further role on the battlefield in *Iliad* 11.[29] But Ovid may imply that the "less famous men" lack the luster of those named in this passage because Homer did not mention them:[30] heroic glory derives principally from epic poetry.

Ulysses strengthens his case further by employing poetic powers on the level of an epic poet. In the passage at hand, the names of warriors whom Ulysses boasts of slaying agree with the text of the *Iliad*, but the clever Ithacan adds verbal details that make the achievements seem more impressive. He embellishes the names of two warriors, one from the material recounted in *Iliad* 5 and the other in 11. Homer adds no descriptive phrase to the name of the fallen warrior in either case. Whereas Ulysses refers to Coeranus as *Iphitiden*, "son of Iphitus," Homer in the *Iliad* mentions an Iphitus only as the father of Schedius and Epistrophus (2.518) and another as the father of Archeptolemus (8.128). But Ovid has Ulysses play on the name of Coeranus, which is the Latin form of the Greek noun *koiranos*, "ruler" or "master." The patronymic Iphitides would be appropriate, then, since it means "son of the strong man." The word thus serves as a form of etymological gloss that reinforces the purported distinction of the vanquished warrior and adds to the luster of Ulysses' success. Ovid in effect has his orator imitate Homeric practice, since the name Archeptolemus, the son of Iphitus in *Iliad* 8, itself means "leader of the war."

Ulysses similarly expands on Homer's mention of his victim Ennomus by describing him as "fatisque immitibus actum" ("driven by harsh fates"). This descriptive phrase on the inexorable nature of

Ennomus's death in itself is typical of epic style.[31] Furthermore, Ulysses provides an etymological gloss on the man's name by pointing to its origin from the Greek noun *nomos* ("law"). Derived from the verb *nemo* ("to apportion" or "allot"), this word first of all means "anything assigned or apportioned." The hero's linguistic play here heightens the gravity of Ennomus's death as it simultaneously suggests Ulysses' own intelligence.

Unlike Ajax, who mentions no individual contests except for his aborted duel with Hector, Ulysses implies to his discriminating audience that he chooses his opponents well, with an eye to their status and to the potential benefit for the common cause of the Greeks at Troy. By adapting the facts as recorded in the *Iliad* and even outdoing Homer, Ulysses in effect rises to the level of an epic poet.

Ulysses' Chest Wounds

Ulysses reveals his transformative powers further when he responds to Ajax's comments about their respective shields. The clever Greek adds to the image of himself as a Roman and, like his ancestors Autolycus and Mercury, reveals his ability to make things appear and disappear. Ajax contrasts Ulysses' shield with his own, which is so full of spear marks that he actually needs a new one (116–18). Presumably unable to refute his opponent's sarcastic reference to his unblemished (*integer* [118]) shield, Ulysses boasts of the wounds on his body: "sunt et mihi vulnera, cives, / ipso pulchra loco" ("And, citizens, I have wounds, splendid by their very location" [262–63]). Hopkinson notes that by using the word *cives*, the hero in effect lends the impression of being a Roman war veteran.[32] In a gesture mimicking Ajax's directness, Ulysses insists on the superiority of facts to mere words: "nec vanis credite verbis. / aspicite en!" ("Don't trust empty words: just look!" [263–64]).[33] Matthew Leigh has observed that by drawing his garment open and revealing the wounds on his chest, Ulysses employs a strategy not uncommon in the Roman political arena, especially when candidates for public office wished to capitalize on their service to the state in warfare.[34]

Ovid's reader, of course, does not have the opportunity to inspect the hero's chest but must rely on the words by which he communicates to his immediate audience of Greek leaders judging the contest. But by using the imperative *aspicite* in the line quoted above, preceding the word *pectora*, Ulysses points to an assumed etymology for *pectus* connected to vision: his very language seems to offer "proof" of the visibility of his wounds.[35] The poet himself merely comments: "vestemque manu diduxit" ("and he pulled open his garment with his hand" [264]) and then continues to quote Ulysses' words on the subject: "'haec sunt / pectora semper' ait 'vestris exercita rebus'" ("'This chest,' he said, 'has always been engaged for your interests'" [264–65]).

The meaning of this assertion may seem obvious, but the word *pectus* has a wide semantic range. It refers to the chest which Ulysses has exposed to his Greek comrades, but it can also be used in the sense of "mind" or "spirit." Ulysses himself employs the word in the mental sense when he refers to Ajax as "rudis et sine pectore miles" (290). The verb *exerceo*, with its primary meaning "to exercise" or "busy" something, would fit well with *pectora* in a double sense, applying to both mind and body.[36] The inherent nature of the Homeric Odysseus, characterized as *polutropos*, necessitates both physical and mental "turnings" throughout the Greek epic. Here, Ovid reveals the ability of this hero to exploit the multivalence of words so as to conjure up a suitably heroic image of himself.

The verbal ambiguity underlying *pectora exercita* may suggest that Ulysses has no real wounds on his chest to show given that he quickly opens and then, presumably, repositions the upper part of his tunic. Ovid would, of course, expect his reader to recall relevant passages in the *Iliad* and the *Odyssey*. In the single episode in which Odysseus receives a wound in the *Iliad*, a spear shot from Socus hits his shield and penetrates through to the ribs (11.435–38). In the *Odyssey*, moreover, the hero displays his chest in contexts that suggest a lack of extensive scars from wounds.[37] When the naked Odysseus appears before Nausikaa and her companions after being shipwrecked on Scheria, no mention is made of wounds; only the grime from his prolonged exposure to the elements masks the physical appeal that a bath and Athena's attention to his looks soon restore (6.224–37). Similarly, in the games with the Phaeacian youth, Laodamas comments extensively on Odysseus's physique, with a negative reference only to the effects that a long period at sea have presumably had (8.134–39). Later, Odysseus's exposed body elicits no reference to chest wounds in his fight with the beggar Irus. Homer even mentions that after revealing his large thighs, wide shoulders, chest, and thick arms, the hero makes a strong impression on the suitors (18.66–71).

Ovid suggests the fluidity of Ulysses' position about the importance of wounds when he refers to other warriors. Ulysses not only points

with pride to his chest wounds; he also openly disparages Ajax for lack-
ing wounds:

at nil inpendit per tot Telamonius annos
sanguinis in socios et habet sine vulnere corpus. (266–67)

[But the son of Telamon has shed no blood for his comrades through so many
years and has a body without a wound!]

Since a total absence of wounds would be unusual in a ten-year war,
Ovid may wish subtly to remind the reader of the post-Homeric tradi-
tion that made Ajax invulnerable.[38] Yet Ulysses takes a different posi-
tion about Hector when he criticizes Ajax for failing to kill or disable
Hector in their individual contest. After claiming that Ajax received the
privilege of that duel simply by the luck of a lottery system ("praelatus
munere sortis" [277]), Ulysses complains not only that Ajax failed to
win the contest but also that Hector walked off without even being
wounded ("violatus vulnere nullo" [279]). The lack of wounds in that
case clearly makes Hector the superior warrior. In addition to this re-
versal of perspective on the significance of wounds, Ulysses also con-
tradicts the relevant passage of *Iliad* 7 where Aias does in fact wound
Hector in the neck (260–62) during a contest that is then stopped by
heralds at nightfall (279–82).

The inconsistency of Ulysses' positions here is brought into sharp
relief by Odysseus's glorification of the unwounded Neoptolemus in
Odyssey 11. There, Odysseus responds to Achilles' inquiries about his
son Neoptolemus. With considerable detail, he recounts Neoptolemus's
courage in the front lines and his boldness once the Greeks got into
Troy in the wooden horse (513–32). Odysseus concludes his praise of
the young man by emphasizing that after the sack of Troy Neoptole-
mus embarked on his ship completely unscathed: he had never been
wounded by spear shot from a distance or by sword in close combat
(534–38). That passage reflects the ethos of the *Iliad*, which would rate a
warrior highly for avoiding wounds from—and, conversely, for inflict-
ing them on—the enemy.[39] By twisting the significance of wounds
(their presence positive for himself and their absence negative for Ajax,
yet positive for Hector), Ulysses both cleverly uses and inverts the tra-
ditional heroic value system. His cunning deviation thus reflects the
shifting mentality of the son of Mercury, who turns black to white and
vice versa.

Ulysses' chest wounds here, possibly Ovid's own invention, contrast
with Odysseus's famous thigh wound in the *Odyssey*. That single scar,

the mark by which his old nurse Eurykleia recognizes him, symbolizes the Homeric hero's unique nature.⁴⁰ By conceiving of chest wounds for Ulysses, Ovid reinterprets the indelible scar from the boar in Homer. Multiple rather than single, countering the punctured shield of the hero's own rival, ambivalent even in their very existence, the wounds are emblematic of the inherently metamorphic nature of Ovid's Ulysses. Furthermore, as he undermines the exaltation of Achilles' son by his Homeric counterpart in the underworld, Ulysses not only displays his determination to win the contest for the arms but also implies Ovid's own skepticism about the ideals underlying Homer's vision of heroes and warfare.⁴¹

Ulysses and Achilles

Whereas Ajax asserts that he should be awarded the arms because of his extraordinary valor and his kinship with Achilles, Ulysses subtly bolsters his own claims through verbal strategies that suggest a bond between himself and the great warrior. Since Ajax has specifically called for an exchange of Achilles' arms for the Greek ships that he saved from burning by Hector ("date pro tot navibus arma" [94]), Ulysses utters a similar request on the basis of the arms by which he caused Achilles to reveal himself on Scyros, where his mother, Thetis, had hidden him away among the women to keep him out of the expedition to Troy:

illis haec armis, quibus est inventus Achilles,
arma peto: vivo dederam, post fata reposco. (179–80)

[I seek these arms for those arms by which Achilles was discovered: I had given arms to him while alive, I ask for arms back after his death.]

In contrast to his opponent's blunt command, the Ithacan here not only uses verbs of requesting but also employs clever word patterning to suggest the merit of his claim. He encloses the demonstrative adjective *haec*, referring to Achilles' arms, within the phrase composed of the contrasting demonstrative and the word for "arms" (*illis haec armis*); he thus seems already to possess the desired weaponry through language.

Ulysses brings up his discovery of Achilles on Scyros again when he responds directly to Ajax's charge that he had shamefully tried to avoid service in the war by feigning madness ("detractavitque furore / militiam ficto" [36–37]). He answers the criticism by mentioning Achilles' own subterfuge:

Quid, quod me duri fugientem munera belli
arguit incepto serum accessisse labori
nec se magnanimo maledicere sentit Achilli?
si simulasse vocas crimen, simulavimus ambo;
si mora pro culpa est, ego sum maturior illo.
me pia detinuit coniunx, pia mater Achillem. (296–301)

[What about the fact that he claims that I, fleeing service in a harsh war, arrived late at the undertaking that had already begun? Doesn't he realize that he maligns great-spirited Achilles? If you call it a crime to have pretended, we both pretended. If delay is a fault, I was earlier than he. A devoted wife held me back, a devoted mother held him.]

Ulysses here asserts a common bond with Achilles in their mutual attempts to avoid participating in the Trojan War and at the same time manages to reproach Ajax for implicitly disparaging the dead hero. He also subtly reinforces through his language the connection, however demeaning and even dubious, that he shares with Achilles.[42] His repetition of the verb *simulo*, with an effective emphasis on the second form (*simulavimus*), placed immediately after the caesura, implicitly responds to the criticism by Ajax that Ulysses is in fact most similar to the trickster Sisyphus ("furtisque fraude simillimus illi" [32]). Ulysses also links himself with Achilles here by repeating the adjective *pia* in his reference to the concern of both his wife Penelope and Achilles' mother Thetis. He makes the association even more effective in the tightly structured verse through asyndeton and chiasmus (with the reversal of subject and direct object in the corresponding units). He may even suggest a connection between himself and Achilles by word play on *mater:* the adjective *maturior* ("earlier" [300]) is derived from the same root as the word *mater*.[43]

Ulysses' use of the word *munera* here, responding to Ajax's charge that he avoided the war, further strengthens his implied association with Achilles. Shortly after this passage, the Ithacan reaffirms that he shares that fault with Achilles: "crimen / cum tanto commune viro" (303–4). Ulysses would seem to be playing on the etymology of *communis* from *munus* ("service") and to be detracting from Ajax's emphasis on his own family connection to Achilles, for the latter stated that his illustrious lineage would mean nothing to him if he did not have it in common with the great Achilles: "si mihi cum magno non est communis Achille" (30). By exploiting etymological play with *communis* as well as with *simulo*, Ulysses here justifies his own earlier cowardice as he imaginatively connects himself with Achilles.

Ulysses and the Death of Achilles

Ulysses responds to Ajax's sarcastic claim that he could not lift the shield with his timid left hand (111) if he were to win the arms by asserting that he carried off Achilles' arms from the battlefield: "et simul arma tuli; quae nunc quoque ferre laboro" ("And at the same time I bore his arms, which now also I strive to bear away" [285]). As Charles Simmons notes, Ulysses plays on two levels of meaning of the verb *fero:* "Ulysses 'carried' the arms which he now desires to 'carry off.'"[44]

Ulysses, moreover, claims that he carried Achilles' *body* back from the battlefield: "his umeris, his inquam, umeris ego corpus Achillis . . . tuli" ("On these shoulders, I say, on these shoulders, I carried the body of Achilles" [284–85]). By this boast, he again veers from the Homeric tradition. Homer's hero certainly makes no such reference directly to Achilles himself when he meets him in the underworld in *Odyssey* 11, even though it would have been the proper moment to reveal such a feat. Among writers of the epic cycle, Arctinus in the *Aethiopis* recounted that Ajax, not Ulysses, had in fact carried Achilles' body off the field.[45]

The only extant source for Ulysses' claim that he carried off the hero's corpse and his armor from the battlefield occurs in Sophocles' *Philoctetes*. There, the son of Achilles is sent by Odysseus to retrieve Philoctetes because the Greeks are aware of a prophecy stating that they cannot take Troy without this hero, who at Odysseus's instigation was abandoned on Lemnos with a rank, festering wound from a snakebite. Neoptolemus must then explain to Philoctetes the reasons for his supposed alienation from the Greek leaders. He claims that after Odysseus and Phoenix had come for him upon Achilles' death, the Greeks would not allow him to take his father's arms, now in the possession of Odysseus (343–67). The youth then proceeds to recount his angry reaction and Odysseus's response: the Ithacan asserted his right to them because he had carried both the arms and their owner off the battlefield (368–74). Explaining his refusal to remain and help the Greeks in the war, Neoptolemus emphasizes his outrage over Odysseus's insistence on keeping the arms that the dead hero's son would expect to inherit.

Although Sophocles' passage may be indebted to a tradition diverging from the epic cycle, Ovid as a close reader of Greek tragedy would have grasped the ironic implications of Neoptolemus's account of events to Philoctetes. For the youth, who initially has no idea how to persuade the inheritor of Heracles' bow and arrows, is explicitly instructed by Odysseus to make up any convincing lie against him.

Odysseus provides Neoptolemus only a sketchy outline on which to base his fabrication: he is leaving the Greeks because they swore that they could not take Troy without his help but then refused his legitimate request for his father's arms in deference to Odysseus (55-66). When Neoptolemus reports Odysseus's claim that he carried both Achilles and his arms off the battlefield, he would thus be weaving his own fiction, the embellishment of a lie spurred by the cunning Ithacan.

It might seem that this falsehood would be easily detected by the hero's immediate audience and weigh against him. But Ulysses perhaps takes advantage of the chaos of the time when Achilles was killed. The Greeks in general, then, may not be fully aware that Ajax actually carried the hero off the battlefield while Ulysses kept the Trojans at bay. Furthermore, they would not learn the truth at this point since Ajax is not given an opportunity for rebuttal.

Ulysses, moreover, is continuing the strategy that he implemented early in his speech when he claimed credit for everything accomplished by Achilles since he had discovered the great hero on Scyros and persuaded him to join the war: "ergo opera illius mea sunt" ("Therefore his deeds are mine" [171]). Later, when elaborating on his considerable efforts to keep the Greeks from leaving Troy, he extends his claim to Ajax himself. Here, Ulysses asserts that his opponent had ignominiously fled: "quid, quod et ipse fugit? vidi, puduitque videre, / cum tu terga dares inhonestaque vela parares" ("What about the fact that he himself also fled? I saw, and it was shameful to see when you took to flight and prepared to set sail" [223-24]). As with Achilles, he then declares that credit for Ajax's subsequent deeds belongs to him: "tempore ab hoc quodcumque potest fecisse videri / fortiter iste, meum est, qui dantem terga retraxi" ("From this time, whatever that man can seem to have done belongs to me, who dragged him back as he fled" [236-37]).

The clever Greek has thus implemented an imaginative strategy that his alert audience (and the reader) can grasp: his claim of carrying Achilles' body out of the battle is a *fictional device* rather than hard fact. Although he did not specifically name Diomedes as one of those who fled and who thus owe their deeds to him, in retrospect one may assume that Ulysses applied the same rationale with his claim to have killed Dolon and Rhesus. As we observed, however, the hero accords Diomedes an important gesture of respect by acknowledging what a great privilege it is that his comrade shares (*communicat*) his deeds with him (239-42).

Ulysses' Ekphrasis of Achilles' Shield

Whereas Ajax briefly mentions Achilles' arms with a sarcastic reference to its unsuitability for his opponent, Ulysses responds in a manner reflecting the powers of an epic poet. After insisting that Ulysses could not bear the weight of Achilles' helmet nor remain safe in his nightly sorties because of its gleaming gold (107–9), Ajax asserts that the Ithacan could not wield the heavily embossed shield:

nec clipeus vasti caelatus imagine mundi
conveniet timidae nataeque ad furta sinistrae. (110–11)

[Nor will the shield, engraved with a picture of the vast universe, suit his timid left hand, meant for thievery.]

In response to this insult, Ulysses provides a much fuller description of the shield illustrating his point that his adversary is too dim witted to comprehend the significance of the shield's designs:[46]

scilicet idcirco pro gnato caerula mater
ambitiosa suo fuit, ut caelestia dona,
artis opus tantae, rudis et sine pectore miles
indueret? neque enim clipei caelamina novit
Oceanum et terras cumque alto sidera caelo
Pleiadasque Hyadasque inmunemque aequoris Arcton
diversosque orbes nitidumque Orionis ensem.
postulat, ut capiat, quae non intellegit, arma. (288–95)

[Was the sea-blue mother therefore surely concerned for her son so that a rough and stupid soldier would take up the divine gift, a work of such great artistry? For he does not comprehend the engravings of the shield, the river Ocean and the lands and the constellations in the high heavens, both the Pleiades and the Hyades and the Bear, kept out of the sea, and the divergent poles and the shining sword of Orion. He seeks to take arms that he does not understand.]

Whereas Ajax makes a brief, general reference to the shield, in this passage Ulysses offers his audience a kind of poetic mini-ekphrasis in the manner of Homer or Vergil. He implies the encompassing nature of his intellect by presenting a scientific view of the shield, first by indicating the tripartite division of the universe and then by concentrating on its depiction of the heavens. Ovid even appears to associate Ulysses with himself by casting an eye back to his cosmogony at the very beginning of the poem, where he also refers to the nexus of land, sea, and sky filled with stars (1.21–23 and 69–75).

Ulysses' description here is a clever retort to Ajax, not only because it expands on the latter's spare reference to the shield but also because it picks up on his opponent's mention of its engravings. There, Ajax himself may supply an etymological gloss in his claim that "the shield engraved with the image of the vast universe" ("clipeus vasti caelatus imagine mundi" [110]) is unsuited to Ulysses' cowardly hand. As Michalopoulos notes, the participle *caelatus* in that context recalls the views of ancient grammarians that the word *clipeus* was derived from the Greek verb *gluphein* ("to engrave").[47] But Ulysses does Ajax one better here by his emphatic juxtaposition in the phrase *clipei caelamina*, making the relationship of the two words more apparent.[48]

The hero, moreover, extends his etymological play involving the word *caelamen* in this passage. Philip Hardie observes that Ulysses with the word *caelamina* here alludes to Ajax's description of the shield as *caelatus* (110) and shows an awareness of the etymology of *caelum* ("sky") from the verb *caelare* ("to engrave"), according to Roman linguistic theory of the late republic as summarized by M. Terentius Varro (*De lingua Latina* 5.18).[49] In the same passage, however, Varro indicates that he approves of the derivation of *caelo* from *caelum*, given that the verb refers to raising something above the surface.[50]

Ulysses implies his own position in this etymological debate by highlighting words related to *caelum* and thus privileging it in the passage. He not only includes the word *caelum* in the ekphrasis with the phrase "cumque alto . . . caelo" (290) but also refers to the shield as "caelestia dona" (289), thus drawing attention to the word for heaven itself as well as to the creation of the artifact by the god Vulcan. Furthermore, in an epic-style periphrasis, Ulysses describes Thetis as "caerula mater" ("sea-blue mother"). As he appropriately applies the epithet to the domain of a Nereid, Ulysses incorporates another word in the cluster related to *caelum*. The adjective *caerulus*, a poetic variant of *caeruleus*, is subordinated to *caelum* linguistically: in its origin through dissimilation and rhotacism of *caelulum*, the word itself suggests that the sea takes its bluish color from the sky. The clever Greek thus purposefully exploits the etymological resonance of this passage: by making the heavenly bodies his focus in the ekphrasis of the shield, he exposes the possibility of a proper linguistic relationship between *caelum* and *caelare*.[51]

Ulysses' emphasis on *caelum* draws attention to *diversos orbes*, representing the two opposite poles, which appear to substitute for the two opposing cities in Homer's ekphrasis.[52] By including this element, Ulysses further reveals his intellectual acumen in contrast to Ajax's dullness. In this case, Ovid would expect his reader to realize that the discovery of the two poles was an important scientific advance, which was in fact made in Hellenistic times.[53] In the *Fasti*, for instance, the poet refers thus to the ignorance of men in the early Roman period of the kingship: "quis tunc aut Hyadas aut Pleiadas Atlanteas / senserat, aut geminos esse sub axe polos?" ("Who then had perceived either the Hyades or the Pleiades, daughters of Atlas, or that there are two poles under the firmament?" [3.105–6]).

Among several possible meanings derived from its fundamental sense of "circle," *orbis* can be taken as a poetic synonym for *polus*, as appropriate to the epic context. Here, Ovid may have Ulysses imply to the judges, consisting of aristocratic Greek leaders, that his knowledge is extensive and on the cutting edge of thinking from the linguistic to the scientific sphere.[54] At the beginning of the *Metamorphoses*, the poet implements his own interest in cosmological theories as a manifestation of the creative mind.[55] Like Ovid, Ulysses reflects an informed, but not pedantic, penchant for scientific poetry.

The centrifugal pull favoring Ulysses in this episode may be unsettling to some readers since the clever hero appears manipulative and unethical in his effort to win the arms. His claim to feats that he in fact did not accomplish is on the surface of things problematic. Although his immediate audience would take his usurpation of Achilles' deeds in the war with a grain of salt, his boast of retrieving Achilles' corpse and killing Dolon and Rhesus denies Ajax and Diomedes their proper glory. However, Ulysses' rhetorical flourishes claiming his "ownership" of Achilles' and Ajax's *opera* establish the imaginative level on which the specific claims operate. In that sphere, in which the fictionality tempers the underlying ethical problem, Ulysses reveals powers of dramatic narrative akin to epic.

Ulysses is a significant surrogate for Ovid. His connection to the poet revolves around a vision of constant change, on which the *Metamorphoses* is predicated. In the fluid use of wounds, the Greek hero renders this intrinsic element of the martial world relative rather than stable, no longer endowed with a dependable social significance. Even on the

level of language, Ulysses shows his awareness of instability and rela-
tivity.[56] Attuned to the multivalence of words, Ulysses creates the illu-
sion of reality and increases the magnitude of his actions, as when he
exploits the potential meanings of the verb *paro* and the noun *pectus*. By
his clever play with the etymology of *caelum*, he points to conflicting
theories about the origins of words and suggests his own view of the
significance of *caelum* in that debate. In this respect, he takes up one of
Ovid's own poetic trademarks, which the poet inherited from Hellenis-
tic authors such as Callimachus and Apollonius.

Like the poet, Ulysses grasps the importance of symbolic, figurative
levels of meaning. Unlike Ajax, who stresses the importance of his blood
tie to Achilles through their common descent from Aeacus and Jupiter,
Ulysses imaginatively constructs a relationship, even an identity, with
the dead hero through their similarity in trying to avoid the war. Fur-
thermore, by culminating his account of the night raid with a picture of
himself as in a triumph, the Greek casts himself in a particularly im-
pressive light to his immediate audience. As the controlling poet, Ovid
endows Ulysses with the ability to make himself appear to be a general
celebrating the ultimate military honor for a Roman.

By referring to material in the *Iliad* and the *Odyssey*, Ulysses implic-
itly interprets Homer, challenges the Greek poet's authority, and makes
himself his equal. In his own description of Achilles' shield, he distills
the cosmic essence of Homer's great ekphrasis, adding an awareness
of the two poles that was a scientific discovery only in the Hellenistic
period. Although he does not radically alter the account of his fighting
in *Iliad* 5 and 11, he adapts the Greek poet's narrative by suppressing the
fact that he failed to encounter Sarpedon himself, that he was frightened
off by Hector, and that he was rescued by Ajax, and he embellishes his
minor successes with descriptive phrases derived from Homer himself.
Ulysses' account of the Trojan War is in effect a microcosm of Ovid's own
Trojan narrative: much as the clever Greek diminishes Ajax and even
Achilles for his own purposes, so the poet frequently undermines he-
roic grandeur as he diverges from Homer.[57]

Ovid's representation of Ulysses calls to mind the characterization of
Odysseus by Alcinous in *Odyssey* 11. There, the Phaeacian king offers
an ambivalent compliment to the hero for the absorbing account of his
adventures after the Trojan War by claiming that Odysseus seems not to
make up lying tales like a roguish wayfarer but rather shows a graceful
intelligence (363–69). In the *Metamorphoses*, Ovid's hero blurs the dis-
tinction of Alcinous's antithesis and, in doing so, reflects the revisionist

image of the poet himself. But in the process of undermining received tradition, Ovid does much more than pull the wool over his reader's eyes through a witty and pleasurable narrative. He simultaneously encourages the reader to probe the instability of the values that he as poet so frequently challenges.

Conclusion

After the contest for the arms, Ulysses' direct role in the poem ends, as the poet succinctly says that the victor set sail for Lemnos to retrieve the arrows of Hercules (499–501) and then, after tersely narrating the fall of Troy, mentions that the Greek dragged Hecuba away from her children's tombs and took her captive (424–26). Ovid's other surrogates disappear from the poem altogether, but references to Ulysses occur through much of the next book. As we saw, both Narcissus and Orpheus end up in the underworld, obsessed with their own objects of desire. Medea loses even the security of her haven in Athens after Aegeus foils her attempt to poison Theseus (7.406–24). Daedalus fails to make his way back to Athens in his disastrous flight with Icarus and ends up at the court of King Cocalus in Sicily, with Minos in pursuit (8.260–62). Allusions to Ulysses after the Trojan War narrative suggest that for Ovid this most versatile hero is the strongest surrogate of the poet.

Ulysses remains an oblique presence in book 14, mainly but not exclusively in numerous references to his wanderings after the Trojan War. First, as a prelude to the humorous account of Polyphemus's buffoonish serenade of the nymph Galatea, the seer Telemus delivers a prophecy to the Cyclops that he will lose his single eye to Ulysses (13.771–73). Then, Ulysses becomes the subject of recollections about their postwar adventures by Achaemenides and Macareus when the two Greeks happen to meet again at the place soon to be named Caieta in honor of Aeneas's nurse. The former elaborates on the episode in the cave of the Cyclops, emphasizing his terror at being left behind by Ulysses and his men and his ultimate rescue by his former enemy Aeneas (14.167–222). The latter tells of his adventures with Ulysses involving the wind god Aeolus, the cannibalistic Laestrygonians, and the witch Circe.

After keeping Ulysses in the background of book 14 by adapting and fragmenting his story, Ovid casts a final glance at this hero's reunion with his wife Penelope. In his speech to Pomona, Vertumnus claims that, if she chose, the nymph could have more suitors than "the wife of bold Ulysses" ("coniunx . . . audacis Ulixei" [671]). Ironically, as we noted in chapter 1, the god in disguise as an old woman does not succeed in his attempts at persuasion. But his reference to Penelope by periphrasis here calls attention to her success at keeping the suitors at bay and helping to enable the hero to succeed after his return to Ithaca. Ulysses' "boldness" is an allusion to his clever, but risky, strategy for reclaiming his wife and household after his twenty-year absence. Ovid thus, albeit very allusively, takes this particular surrogate to the successful conclusion of his personal journey.

All of Ovid's surrogates whom we have examined are problematic in significant ways. But Ulysses remains in the poet's consciousness, ultimately ending his displacement, whereas the others disappear. What distinguishes this particular figure is, in large measure, his self-awareness. At the end of the contest for the arms, Ovid reveals Ajax's clear lack of that virtue. The defeated hero thus conceives of his imminent suicide as a validation of his superior prowess: "ne quisquam Aiacem possit superare nisi Aiax" ("so that no one can overcome Ajax except Ajax" [390]). The poet, however, puts the great warrior's act in a different light, drawing attention to its irrational basis: "invictum virum vicit dolor" ("Distress conquered the unconquered hero" [386]). By revealing the failure of self-awareness in so many of his characters throughout the poem, Ovid encourages his attentive reader to comprehend its value.

Among the characters discussed here, Narcissus perhaps most strongly contrasts with Ulysses. Although the youth achieves a moment of self-awareness, his recognition of the lack of distinction between lover and beloved is quickly dispelled as he retreats back to his fascination with his image. Even in the underworld, he cannot tear himself away from his reflection in the Styx. In metapoetic terms, the self-involved youth remains an elegiac poet-lover and does not attain epic status.

Even in her manifestation as an inexperienced young princess, Medea reveals powerful rhetorical skills, but in her monologue she becomes the victim of self-deception about her feelings for Jason and the merits of acting on his behalf. This awesome mythical figure displays impressive cunning in devising strategies to rid herself (and Jason) of obstacles, thus symbolizing Ovid's own interest in creating intricate plots revolving around intrafamilial strife and in reducing the status of the traditional hero. But Medea in the *Metamorphoses* is intrinsically defined by scheming and plotting. Ovid's fascination with Medea drives the narrative into an un-Callimachean expansiveness. The poet, however, ultimately puts the brakes on and dismisses this character: when her ruse to murder Theseus is defeated by the vigilance of Aegeus, she instantly exits from the poem.

Unlike his counterpart in Vergil, Daedalus is almost entirely absorbed in his efforts to create complex designs defying normal human boundaries. His desire for supremacy in that sphere ultimately diminishes his humanity. The poet defuses the pathos of Daedalus's grief over Icarus's death by juxtaposing his callous destruction of Perdix over jealousy of his young nephew's talent. Ovid, to be sure, reflects his own aesthetic preference for intricacy and his competitiveness with his immediate predecessor in epic in his account of the archetypal artisan. But Daedalus ultimately fails as a true surrogate poet because he takes such qualities to an extreme.

As the archetypal bard, Orpheus sings of the loves of gods for young boys and of the perverted passions of females. However, he not only narcissistically intrudes his self-interests into his narrative but is also blind to the figurative incest implied in the story of Pygmalion and, as we observed in detail, to the self-absorption underlying Venus's relations with Adonis. Although in his persona as narrator Ovid often adopts a neutral or even positive stance toward such characters, as controlling poet he reveals his own distance from such failures of understanding.

The encounter of Ulysses' two former companions, which Ovid apparently invented, strengthens the poet's connection to the Greek hero, in part through his challenge to the authority of Homer and Vergil. Achaemenides' story to Macareus reflects a markedly different perspective from Homer's account of Polyphemus, because this internal narrator is concerned with his own state of mind after he was left behind on the island of the Cyclopes rather than with the hero's cleverness at getting out of the cave. When he asserts that Ulysses' shouts on escaping from the Cyclops nearly caused Macareus's ship to be sunk (180–81), he alludes to the specific cause of the hero's sufferings at sea as recorded in *Odyssey* 9: the boast that it was Odysseus, son of Laertes, who had blinded him (502–5). Yet in quoting Polyphemus's curse on the Greeks, Achaemenides recalls something different from the Homeric account, a threat to consume even more Greeks (192–97) that encapsulates the source of his own terror.

For his part, in recounting the hero's adventures known to the reader from book 10 of the *Odyssey*, Macareus keeps closer to Homer's tales. He emphasizes, for instance, that Ulysses cried as they all embraced ("flentem flentes amplectitur illis" [305]) after Circe transformed Macareus and his comrades from pigs back to men. Homer similarly has Odysseus acknowledge that he and his men lamented profusely as they reunited (397–99). This emphasis on the Greek hero's very human feelings contrasts strongly with Vergil's persistent condemnation of Ulysses from the Trojan perspective: as we observed in chapter 5, Ajax himself in his speech echoes Deiphobus's criticism of Ulysses as the hardened inciter of criminal behavior ("hortator scelerum" [*Aeneid* 6.529]). Unlike Vergil, Ovid shows Ulysses' multifaceted nature, providing a glimpse of his humanity through the perspective of another character.

When he has Macareus tell Achaemenides that Mercury gave Ulysses the gift of *môlu*, enabling him to encounter Circe without danger (291–94), Ovid deviates from Homer's account. For the Greek remembers how Ulysses employed his protective amulet in a way that differs from the passage in *Odyssey* 10: he states that Circe first attempted to fondle the hero before he threatened her with violence, whereas Homer has him follow Hermes' instructions to present her with force before she makes any attempt to use her female wiles (292–301). In evoking Mercury, moreover, the poet recalls that god's special relation to himself as well as to the Greek hero. His use of the epithet *pacifer* (291, noted by Simmons), in particular, points to Mercury's association with the persuasive powers of language.

Ovid refers to Ulysses again in his story of Cybele's transformation of Aeneas's ships to nymphs after Turnus attempts to destroy them by fire (530–65). He changes Vergil's account in *Aeneid* 9 (69–122) considerably, not least by having Turnus succeed in scorching the ships and at the end by having the nymphs preserve a hatred for the former enemies of their beloved Trojans. The poet says that the nymphs rejoice in seeing Ulysses' ship destroyed and Alcinous's turned to stone by Neptune (563–65). These responses recall two significant events in *Odyssey* 12 and 13, which together reinforce the power of Ulysses' endurance and his ability to transcend misfortune.

The first evokes Ulysses' self-restraint in contrast to his men's inability to withstand the pangs of hunger, for it refers to the death of all of

Odysseus's companions at sea after they ate the cattle of the Sun and the hero's own rough ten days floating with the wreckage (12.403–50). The second alludes to the punishment inflicted on the Phaeacian king for providing the hero transport back to Ithaca (13.125–64). Ovid thereby evokes Ulysses' persuasive powers as a storyteller, for which the hero in the *Odyssey* was rewarded by Alcinous and Arete with valuable gifts as well as conveyance home.

The poet here also recalls this hero as the victim of divine hostility, prevented from returning home and suffering difficult years at sea. Again, Ovid sharply differentiates his Ulysses from the Greek hero in Vergil's antagonistic portrayal as the embodiment of a strictly negative cunning. The poet's allusion here foreshadows the final reference to the Greek in the voice of Vertumnus, who refers to the fact that, in spite of a god's anger, Ulysses himself eventually prevails. Ovid shows that this hero is the fully *versutus* ("much-turned") grandson of Autolycus, not only in his mental agility and his wanderings at sea but also in the varied ways by which his story is embedded in this poem. The labyrinthine narrative in this case has a constructive purpose: by "retracing" Ulysses' wanderings, the poet brings the laboring hero back to his wife and home.

Notes

Introduction

1. Segal 1998, 9–41, examines in particular metamorphoses as manifestations of psychological drives and as illustrations of widely held views about gender in antiquity in which the female body is perceived as an object and the recipient of male aggression and the male body is associated with invulnerability.

2. Ovid asks the gods to "lead down" ("deducite" [4]) the poem, employing a metaphor derived from spinning; *deductus,* the participle form of the verb *deduco,* was used to describe a refined Hellenistic aesthetic in the Augustan period. Wheeler 1999, 8–30, discusses these opening lines of Ovid's poem at length and specifically addresses the metaphor of spinning for refined poetry in the manner of Callimachus.

3. Tissol 1997, esp. 13–15 and 52–61, observes that paradox is especially prevalent in the *Metamorphoses* with respect to characters who are, for various reasons, unable to act. See also Kenney 2002, 76–77, on Ovid's facility with paradox, implemented especially in forms of double theme and variation.

4. Ranging through Ovid's elegiac works as well as his epic, Hardie 2002, 143–72 and 272–92, provides nuanced discussions of this theme in the episodes of Narcissus and Ceyx-Alcyone, respectively.

5. See Wheeler 1999, in particular, on the relevance of book divisions to the distinction between the narrator as oral poet and the implied poet as writer of a text and on the narrator's use of addresses to an unspecific second person, the first-person plural, apostrophes, and rhetorical questions in constructing the fiction that he is performing orally to his "narratorial audience" (Wheeler's term). Throughout his study, however, he tends to focus more on the audience side of the equation.

6. My use of the terms "centripetal" and "centrifugal" derives from the work of Mikhail Bakhtin on the concept of "dialogism" in narrative. Bakhtin 1981, 272–73, associates the "centrifugal" forces with the powerless, the popular, and

the carnivalesque, with types such as the trickster, and with low literary genres. Here, Ovid makes even Arachne's birthplace symbolic of the low as he sets it in contrast with her *nomen memorabile:* "quamvis / orta domo parva parvis ha- bitabat Hypaepis" ("although she was born in a small home and lived in small Hypaepa" [12–13]). The name Hypaepa in Greek itself connotes restriction, as it means "under the lofty": Ovid reinforces its meaning in the verse by using the device of anadiplosis with *parva parvis,* the first adjective modifying *domo* and the second, *Hypaepis.*

7. Rosati 1999, 251, notes that the young woman includes a particularly thoughtless allusion to the violation of Minerva's temple by Neptune's rape of Medusa (119–20).

8. On Arachne's limitations as evidenced by her arrogance toward Minerva, see Barkan 1986, 2, and Harries 1990, 65. Lateiner 1984, 17, stresses Arachne's flaw of failing to admit the "debt of the artist to something greater than him- self"; Barkan 1986, 2, takes a similar position. Leach 1974, 115, suggests that the young woman's desire for widespread fame and her pride in her success are a consequence of her humble background, which leads her to reject a sense of in- debtedness and to insist on her autonomy.

9. Referring to her transformed state, Ovid says that Arachne "works at her webs of old as a spider" ("antiquas exercet aranea telas" [145]). The word *aranea* in Latin, significantly, means both spider and spider's web. The phrase, further- more, points up the aetiological function of the myth by mentioning the Latin word for "spider," which is close to its Greek equivalent, *arachnê* (or *arachnês*).

10. In evoking Envy, the poet may well imply empathy with Arachne. Ovid in the *Amores* brought up the problem of Livor vis-à-vis his own poetry (e.g., 1.15.1 and 39), and in his exile poems he returns to this theme (e.g., *Epistulae ex ponto* 3.1.65, 3.3.104, 3.4.74). The poet here appears to recall Callimachus's com- ments in the *Hymn to Apollo* that Phthonos maligns him because his works do not go on at length. See Hofmann 1986, 233, on the correlation of Livor with Phthonos, a figure who is identified in *Hymn* 2 with traditional epic and who maligns the refined work of poets like Callimachus.

11. See, in particular, Barkan 1986, 4–5, and Harries 1990, 66–67.

12. Hofmann 1986, 223–41.

13. On Ovid's affiliation with Callimachean aesthetics, see esp. Lyne 1984, 9–34; Knox 1986a, esp. ch. 5, "The Roman Callimachus," 65–83; Wills 1989, 143– 56; Keith 1992, 9–20, 43–45; Myers 1994b, 2–5 and ch. 2, "Callimachus' *Aetia* and Framed Aetiological Narratives in the *Metamorphoses,*" 61–94.

14. On this kind of *mise en abyme,* see Dällenbach 1989, esp. 96–106.

15. Cohon 1991, 22–30, proposes this model for the organization of the shield in relation to the shield of Athena Parthenos. See McKay 1998, 199–221, for a structure with three concentric circles: the scene of Octavian's triumphal entry into Rome and his review of the conquered tribes before the Palatine temple of Apollo at the center; scenes from republican history arranged in the middle

circle; and scenes from the kingship in the outermost one. He argues that Vergil represents the events on the shield from the perspective of a triumphal parade, incorporating significant monuments located on the route. Hardie 1985, 121–24, connects the scene of Manlius on the Capitoline with the doors of Augustus's temple of Apollo on the Palatine and, 346–76, discusses the shield as an emblem of moral and theological order.

16. Feeney 1991, 193–94, summarizes the negative aspects of Arachne's weaving as a spider: its vulnerability to destruction, its totally symmetrical designs, and (as asserted by Seneca, *Epistulae* 121.23) its lack of status as art.

17. Harries 1990, 71–72, connects the issue of Arachne's desire to attain an enduring *nomen* for herself with two scenes from Minerva's tapestry: the goddess's contest with Neptune to name the city of Athens and the punishment of Rhodope and Haemus for assuming the names of the gods Jupiter and Juno.

18. The connection between Arachne and Leuconoe's image is noted by Rosati 1999, 250–53, citing classical sources for the spider's delicate thread as a model for the weaver's own.

19. See Myers 1994b, 79–80, on the aetiological nature of the Minyeides' tales and their association with a refined Alexandrian poetic style, suggested by the phrase "levi deducens pollice filum" ("drawing the thread with her light thumb" [4.36]). The unnamed sister thus not only unites weaving with singing but also does her work with a "light" touch.

20. Janan 1994, 433–38, explains the lack of a moral interpretation by proposing that Leuconoe's narrative represents a particularly feminine kind of imagination; her use of the spider web's image on this account reflects a sensually oriented imagination in line with an overall defiance of logic in her description of Vulcan's net.

21. Hardy 1995, 145–46, argues that the narrator progressively shifts the focus in his ekphrasis of both tapestries: he moves from Minerva's emphasis on the gods' power to punish mortals to an empathy with human suffering and from Arachne's focus on the females as victims of rape by the gods to the "generative power" of the divinities. Leach 1974, 117, observes that Minerva certainly *interprets* her opponent's tapestry as representing *caelestia crimina* (which can simultaneously mean "divine crimes" and "reproaches against the gods" [131]). Vincent 1994, 381, however, suggests that Arachne's tapestry is a "scandal" in making divine hypocrisy public; it then induces the goddess to respond as a member of her own class and destroy the woman's weaving.

22. See Nagle 1988a, 101–11, referring to the story as a "miniature *carmen perpetuum*." Hinds 1987a, spurred by the magisterial study of Heinze 1919, is a seminal, extended examination of this episode that compares its use of elegiac elements to Ovid's version of the myth in the *Fasti*.

23. Myers 1994b, 164.

24. Myers 1994b, 159–62; Hardie 1995, 204–14; Hardie 1997, 182–98.

25. Hardie 1997, 187–89. Hardie 2002, 6, also points out that Pythagoras

shares with Ovid a particular kind of visualization, "the ability to see things far removed." Holzberg 2002, 146, observes that Pythagoras's speech, in reflecting structural elements and themes of the *Metamorphoses,* especially through parallels to Ovid's account of the origins of the universe, is a "condensed *carmen perpetuum,*" similar to the Muse's story in book 5 and Orpheus's song in book 10.

26. Segal 1969, 280–84, underscores Ovid's parodic purposes in his use of Pythagoras, noting that metempsychosis was the subject of ridicule by intellectuals of the poet's day and that the emphasis on vegetarianism in the philosopher's speech evokes a host of satirical jibes against that dietary practice in the Greek and Roman literary tradition.

27. See Nicoll 1980, 174–82, on the programmatic significance of Cupid's rebuke to Apollo after defeating the Python in book 1, which recalls his similar criticism of Ovid for attempting epic in *Amores* 1.1. Knox 1986a, ch. 2, "The Transformation of Elegy," 9–26, discusses Apollo as an elegiac poet-lover in the story of Daphne and the characterization of Narcissus through elegiac motifs of madness, pride, spiritual union, and physical deterioration. Hinds 1987a, 99–134, demonstrates that, despite Calliope's concern in book 5 about the elevation of her song, the modulated style of the Muse's story in fact has much in common with the version of this myth in the elegiac *Fasti,* especially in the use of its charming *locus amoenus* (4.417–30). Sharrock 1991, 36–39, views Pygmalion's creation of the ivory statue as an analogue of the lover's construction of the beloved in the discourse of elegy: both sculptor and elegist give life to inert raw material and narcissistically become enamored with the objects of their creativity (or with the creative act itself). Myers 1994a, 225–50, esp. 234–42, discusses the incorporation of numerous elegiac topoi and allusions to Propertius 4.2 in Vertumnus's tale of Anaxarete. Gentilcore 1995, esp. 116–19, shows that Ovid parodies the elegiac convention of *paraclausithuron* in the tale of Anaxarete: the excluded lover's threat of death becomes a reality here when Iphis hangs himself, and the mistress's hardness becomes literal rather than figurative when Anaxarete is metamorphosed into stone. For an overview of Ovid's use of elegy throughout his poetic career, see Harrison 2002, 79–94.

28. See Conte 1986, 31, on Homer's function as the "code model" for epic by incorporating the particular elements and devices of the genre and as the "exemplary model" by providing specific passages for imitation. More recently, Hinds 1998, esp. 20–21, 41–45, 49–50, has debated and refined some of Conte's insights on allusion, especially by considering the role of authorial intention and the adaptability of the code. On Ovid's relation to Vergil, Tarrant 2002, 13–33, considers strategies of emulation, such as placing particular lines from the *Aeneid* in incongruous passages, incorporating material that calls attention to Vergil's own problematic use of Homer, and making allusions to characters from the *Aeneid* but transferring them to other individuals.

29. Rosati 2002, 271–304, discusses implications of the prolific internal narratives: chronological vagueness undermines the notion of a guaranteed truth,

even calling into question the stability of the Augustan order, and the appropri-
ation of allusions to earlier poetry suggests Ovid's desire to establish the legiti-
macy of his own versions of received myths. Barchiesi 2002, 180–99, noting the
carefully motivated appearance of internal narrators in Homer and Vergil, dis-
cusses the problem of multiple narrators in the story of Ceres and Proserpina:
the principal narrator Calliope gives a privileged position to nymphs as narra-
tor of an inset tale (Arethusa) and as characters (Cyane, the Sirens) in the con-
text of an audience of nymphs judging the contest at hand. Ultimately, as Bar-
chiesi observes, the embedded narratives collectively reflect the difficulty of
revealing truth through storytelling and of reconciling a narrator's intentions
with his audience's comprehension of the tale.

Chapter 1. Narcissus and Elegy

   1. Gildenhard and Zissos 2000, 129–47, develop the thesis that this episode
is a substitution for the tragedy of the house of Laius. They show how the epi-
sode is linked to the tragedy of Oedipus in its incorporation of an ambiguous
prophecy made by Tiresias, a peripeteia in the form of the hero's change from
ignorance to knowledge, paradox as a master trope, and dramatic irony in the
lament of Narcissus. See also Hardie 1990, 224–35.
   2. See Bushnell 1988, esp. 1–42, on the problem of the ironic and ambiguous
nature of oracular discourse as manifested in Greek literature, especially trag-
edy, and in Athenian society, and 67–85, on Tiresias, whose ambivalent lan-
guage is contrasted to the riddling of Oedipus and ultimately validated as the
conveyer of truth essential to the survival of the city.
   3. Knox 1986a, 19–23, discusses the major elegiac topoi applied to the ele-
giac lover in this episode: the *furor*, as both passion and madness; the concept of
oneness with the beloved; the wasting away from passion. Ovid, Knox argues,
exploits potential ambiguities of the conventions of Latin elegy, especially by
playing literal against figurative meanings, as a means of exploring the pathol-
ogy of love.
   4. Knox 1986a, 21, points out that Narcissus's pride establishes a connection
between him and the unattainable mistress of elegy but goes no further.
   5. Ovid has already hinted at the elegist's self-absorption in book 1, where
Apollo's inappropriate self-flattery fails to have any effect on Daphne, the ar-
chetypal *dura puella*. Ironically, Apollo pursues the very image of his twin sister
Diana ("nuptaeque aemula Phoebes" [476]). Nicoll 1980, 174–82, discusses the
aetiology of elegy in that episode.
   6. Rosati 1983, 41–50, has suggested that this powerfully drawn character
resembles the poet himself: Ovid, much like Narcissus, marvels at his own
virtuosity and creates an art caught up in its own beauty. Picking up on Quin-
tilian's criticism of Ovid for his *lascivia* (10.1.88 and 93), a lack of poetic re-
straint, Rosati locates the poet's self-indulgence in an overflowing imagination,

clever architectonics, and obscure preciosity. He does not, however, associate Ovid with Narcissus vis-à-vis elegy in particular.

7. Commentators have glossed this echo of Catullus with references to adaptations by Ovid. Bömer 1969, on 353–55, noting the imitations of Catullus 62.42 and 44, observes that Ovid uses a gnomic aorist with *cupiere* and that he avoids the harsh elisions in Catullus's verse. Henderson 1999 [1981], on 353–55, suggests that Ovid changes the verb out of metrical considerations, since the spondaic *optavere* will not fit into the dactylic hexameter. Anderson 1997, on 353–55, indicates that Catullus seems to have invented the "anaphora formula" used here in the first and third lines. He points out, however, that Ovid in the intervening line does not provide a reasonable rejection of sexual desire, as the girls in Catullus's poem do, but rather offers an explanation of Narcissus's cold arrogance.

8. Ovid may subtly acknowledge by his change of verb that Catullus echoed his *own* lines later in the poem by referring to the fate of the vine that is not joined to the elm tree using the verb *coluere* (53 and 55). On the implications of Ovid's use of these echoing pairs, see Hinds 1998, 7–8, who points to the significance of echo as "the trope of mannered repetition," even before the character Echo comes into the poem and who suggests the possibility of a play with amoebean verse, of which Catullus 62 is a masterpiece.

9. Fränkel 1969 [1945], 213, n.3, referring to the echo of Catullus 62.42 and 44, perceives the flower to be a foreshadowing of Narcissus's metamorphosis at the end of the episode.

10. Hardie 2002, 156, discussing Ovid's episode through a focus on the theme of absent presence, views the flower as the metamorphosed Narcissus.

11. Davis 1983, 86–88, observes that whereas the flower comparison in its original context in Catullus 62 suggests a nubile state appropriate for marriage, here it implies Narcissus's anti-connubial nature. Davis analyzes verbal effects in the intervening line referring to Narcissus's *superbia*: the virtual juxtaposition of *tenera* and *dura*, separated only by the adverb *tam*, and the caesura after *tenera* help to create the impression of a vehemence similar to that of Euripides' Hippolytus.

12. Knoespel 1985, 9, notes that *argenteus* (407), the adjective describing the pool, suggests the type of silver mirror that was commonly used in antiquity.

13. Ahl 1985, 238, thus sums up the significance of the wordplay with *sitis*: "Narcissus' thirst is not quenched by the water but reflected by it."

14. As Henderson 1999 [1981], on 417, observes, *peto, accendo, ardeo*, like *uro* in line 430, are all part of the *sermo amatorius*.

15. See Nisbet and Hubbard 1970, on *Odes* 1.19.6, for ancient views on the superiority of Parian marble for sculpture.

16. For instance, Horace in *Odes* 1.19 describes the alluring Glycera as "splendentis Pario marmore purius" ("shining more radiantly than Parian marble" [6]).

17. Hardie 2002, 146–47, suggests that the simile of the statue applies to both Narcissus and his reflection, with his static position adding to the effect: the youth becomes like the viewer of illusionistic art, reading his own fantasies into the image.

18. The comparison in the *Amores* is underscored with a humorous irony, as the poet-lover playfully exaggerates Corinna's response to a mock attack on his part. Boyd 1997, 126–27, discussing this simile in relation to a second simile comparing Corinna's tears to melting snow, notes possible epic background: Homer's comparison of Penelope's tears of joy to melting snow in *Odyssey* 24 (614–17) and Vergil's comparison of the angry, motionless Dido to Marpessian stone (a learned reference to Parian marble) in *Aeneid* 6 (470–71). Mack 1988, 59–60, comments on Ovid's ironic method in this poem: the high rhetoric with epic touches is undermined by the abrupt conclusion, as the poet's lengthy apology turns out to be nothing but a pose.

19. See Boyd 1997, 44, on the Ovid's use of this framing device in *Amores* 2.16.

20. Wyke 1989, 40, for instance, argues that the women in elegy should be "read as signifiers of moral and political ideologies."

21. Kennedy 1993, 89–90, discusses Ovid's play with the reader in the *Amores* and the *Ars* about Corinna's identity and observes that in the *Amores* and the *Tristia*, the poet hints that his mistress was merely a fiction but leaves open the possibility that she was real. Sharrock 2002, 151, also discusses the problem of the fictional status of the mistress in the *Amores*, noting that as the personified Elegy and the seductive Muse in 3.1 are represented as *puellae*, it is hard not to think of the mistress, too, as a poem. On the issue of the identity of the mistress and the elegiac poet's use of pseudonyms in general, see Randall 1979, 27–35.

22. Vergil's apostrophe certainly registers sympathy for Dido. The narrator asks about her emotional state when she watched the bustle of Aeneas's men on the shore: "quis tibi tum, Dido, cernenti talia sensus, / quosve dabas gemitus" ("What feelings did you have while seeing such things, or what groans did you utter?" [408–9]). But by following this apostrophe with an invocation to *improbe Amor* that drives humans to desperation, he alludes to the consequences of Dido's inability to control her passion. See Otis 1964, 65–95, on Vergil's creation of a "subjective style" that affects the reader's response to Dido through point of view, editorial remarks, significant epithets, especially *infelix*, similes closely related to narrative content, and highly charged metaphors, such as wounds and flames of love.

23. Fränkel 1969 [1945], 83, considers the excitability of the narrator in this passage as a lapse on Ovid's part from being too caught up in his own fiction.

24. Knoespel 1985, 12–13, observes that the breakdown between fiction and reality here is particularly ironic because a quasi-scientific discourse on optics underlies this section of the text. Knoespel seems to credit Ovid with an irony

aimed at contemporary scientific views, however, by connecting the poet's analysis of vision theory in the Narcissus narrative with ancient views about falling in love: if one is drawn to an image of the self perceived in the eyes of the beloved, then Narcissus's predicament of being caught by the beauty of his self-image is an understandable phenomenon.

25. Vinge 1967, 14-15, observes that this apostrophe enforces on the reader the presence of the narrator, which is especially ironic given that it occurs at the moment of Narcissus's total fascination with the illusion. Rosati, 1983, 41-45, accepting Vinge's interpretation of Ovid's apostrophe to Narcissus, adds that apostrophes to characters are not very common in the *Metamorphoses* and that Ovid infuses much of Narcissus's speech with a highly ironic double meaning; thus, when he refers to his image as *unice*, the youth not only describes it as "exceptional" but also unwittingly alludes to its very inseparability from himself.

26. A similar example occurs later in book 1, when the *praeceptor* sharply rebukes Achilles for his feminine garb and domestic activities on Scyros (691-96). Baldo, Cristante, and Pianezzola 1991, on 691-96, observe that the rhetoric of the passage creates the effect of a brief *suasoria*, marked by three strong questions, each with its own response, and a final exhortation.

27. Barkan 1986, 47-52, discusses the significance of the mirror in this episode in the larger context of book 3 as symbolizing the extent to which the divine or sacred presence is absent and Narcissus has become his own god.

28. Allen 1992, 4-37, discusses the cynical manipulativeness of the poet's persona in the *Ars*, a treatise on love as opposed to a volume of personal love poetry: it is a literary strategy gradually inducing the reader to perceive the value of illusion, deception, and seduction as a means of understanding art more than love.

29. Pentheus, for instance, refers sarcastically to the essence of Bacchus's rituals as "magicae fraudes" ("magician's tricks" [534]) and to Acoetes' tale of Bacchus's metamorphosis of the sailors who kidnapped him as long-winded nonsense (*ambagibus* [692]). On the problematic nature of the visual in the Pentheus episode, see Feldherr 1997, 25-55. Considering Pentheus in relation to other characters in book 3, especially Actaeon, Feldherr suggests underlying implications for Ovid's own Rome, especially in the brutality of theatrical *spectacula* and the rhetoric of national identity.

30. Anderson 1997, on 346-48, indicates that although Ovid expects his reader to perceive the allusion to the Delphic oracle, he nonetheless has Tiresias refer ironically to a shallow form of self-recognition, manifested in Narcissus's understanding of his image in the pool, so as to set up a contrast with a genuine kind of Socratic wisdom that might have enabled the youth to cope with his unfortunate passion.

31. See Knox 1986a, 20.

32. Pichon 1902, 175, states of *iocus:* "simul ad hilaritatem et ad amorem pertinet" and cites several passages of the *Ars* (1.394, 2.176, 600, 3.328) which reflect a clever transferal from amatory affairs to words. Adams 1982, 161-62, focusing

on passages in the *Ars* in which *iocus* (and its cognate verb) could refer to sexual activity, suggests the possibility of verbal jesting with risqué innuendoes at *Ars* 3.716.

33. The *praeceptor* himself pronounces the same cynical doctrine of self-knowledge to women later in *Ars* 3 (771–85) so that they may likewise set their best qualities out to advantage in the game of love.

34. Sharrock 1994, 236–45, discusses the ambivalent nature of Apollo's advice: the pomposity of the god's elaboration on the lover's use of his good qualities is balanced by the genuine wisdom underlying the advice of exploiting one's strengths. Sharrock also comments on Ovid's play with the reader's expectations in the exhortation to self-knowledge: *opus*, for instance, can significantly refer both to poetry and to sex, since poets as well as lovers need to "match *materia* to *ingenium*."

35. Cairns 1969, 131–34, expands on the generally accepted view that Propertius's elegy is indebted to Callimachus's account of Acontius and Cydippe in the *Aetia* through Acontius's plea that as many words be inscribed onto trees' bark as speak the name Cydippe (frag. 73 Pf.). Examining the summary of Callimachus's myth by Aristaenetus, Cairns finds other important similarities, such as the frustrated lover evoking the pine tree because it once experienced love, speaking to the tuneful birds, and calling on the woods to echo the name of the beloved. He concludes that Propertius cleverly transferred a third-person narrative with emotional content to a first-person subjective elegy and gave it a particularly Roman dimension by structuring the elements as a legal defense, from *proemium* to *captatio benevolentiae* to *narratio* and *refutatio*.

36. See Morgan 1977 for detailed analyses, along with extensive bibliography, of the numerous allusions to Ovid's great Roman predecessor in elegy; the younger poet acknowledges his literary debt but also defines his own contribution to the genre, often by contrast and parody that reflect the light spirit of his own elegies.

37. Warden 1980, 193, noting that several images in the last four lines repeat earlier uses in the poem, compares Propertius's landscape to an echo chamber, which mocks him as it draws attention to his lonely state.

38. Hubbard 1974, 33–34, discussing 1.17 and 18 as soliloquies spoken by the poet-lover separated from his mistress, comments that although there were numerous precedents for addressing an absent beloved in Greek as well as Latin poetry, from Mimnermus in the sixth century B.C. to Catullus and probably Gallus in the first, Propertius's originality seems to lie in the "pretence that in the circumstances successful persuasion is possible."

39. Kennedy 1993, 50–51, discusses the ways by which Propertius self-consciously refers to his own poetry as well as his love affair with a woman in 1.18: choosing "Cynthia" as the title of his poetry book; invoking wandering through a deserted place as a metaphor for literary composition; using the verb *queror* ("to complain") as a metaphor for writing elegy; using the verb *scribo* ("to inscribe") as a reference to writing poetry; writing his mistress's name on

the trees, whose bark (*cortex, liber*) also implies "books" (the poet thus declares his determination to continue writing his "Cynthia").

40. Davis 1978, 339–42, perceives an allusion here to Thrasonides in Menander's *Misoumenos,* who like Narcissus, laments the uniqueness of his erotic dilemma. The Greek comic character complains bitterly about being an *exclusus amator* from his very house, with his object of desire inside but unavailable to him. As Davis observes, the parallel is appropriate to the "pathetic-comic modulations" of Ovid's Narcissus myth.

41. Rosati 1983, 22–23, reviewing the evidence for a possible Hellenistic source for the interconnection of the myths of Echo and Narcissus, concludes that there is no real basis for projecting an association prior to Ovid; Pompeian wall paintings with a female figure in the background may depict a nymph of the pool rather than Echo herself and thus cannot point to any predecessor in common with Ovid.

42. Fränkel 1969 [1945], 84–85.

43. Hardie 1988, 71–78, points to the intertwining of the phenomena of auditory and visual images in Lucretius's account of the nature and deceptiveness of physical images, especially in creating the illusion of presence; Ovid not only mythologizes Lucretian psychology as he exposes the failure of Epicurean-based knowledge to have any positive effect on erotic suffering but also assumes the role of Echo vis-à-vis his great predecessor in philosophical poetry. His analysis is incorporated in Hardie 2002, 150–63.

44. Pichon 1902, 113, defining *copia* as "facultas cum amante conversandi," cites Propertius 2.20.24, 3.8.39, and 2.33.44.

45. Henderson 1999 [1981], ad loc.

46. Haupt, Ehwald, and Von Albrecht 1966, on 466, note that the paradox is manifested through the etymological play of *inopem* and *copia.*

47. Critics are in general reticent about the cause of Narcissus's death. Vinge 1967, 17, states that the youth perishes because there is no hope left that his passion can be satisfied.

48. Maltby 1991, s.v. *elegeus,* cites Porphyry on Horace, *Odes* 1.33.2–3, on the etymology of "elegy" from *ê ê legein.* Luck 1969, 25–27, summarizing theories about the origin of elegy, notes that the word *elegos* occurs frequently in the lyrical passages of Euripides' tragedies with the meaning of "song of mourning"; as the accepted meaning of the word in fifth-century Greece, it gave rise to the grammarians' etymologizing from *ê ê legein.* See also Holzberg 2001, 4–6.

49. On the relation of *Amores* 3.9 to Tibullus's elegies, see Perkins 1993, 459–66, especially for Ovid's parodic references to Tibullus's obsession with death, to his poor health in the midst of foreign travel, and to his attitudes toward oriental religious rites; also, Cahoon 1984, 27–35.

50. Brenkman 1976, 293–327, comments on Echo's love as a thing of the past, implied by the pluperfect tense of *amaverat* (493); as Echo now represents a union of voice and consciousness rather than body, the locus of sexuality, her desire has been transformed into pity.

51. Henderson 1999 [1981], on 501, commenting on the fading effect of the final "e," observes that in shortening the final vowel of *vale* in a hiatus before *inquit*, Ovid imitated Vergil in *Eclogue* 3: "et longum 'formose, vale, vale' inquit 'Iolla'" (79). Ovid's clever allusion (the literary echo of a literal echo) would seem to evoke further the pathos of the situation for the nymph Echo here, as the original emphasizes the duration of the young Phyllis's tearful farewell to Menalcas through the adverb *longum*. Hinds 1998, 6, also referring to Ovid's echo of Vergil's line, concludes that Echo here "becomes the annotator, precisely, of an intertextual 'echo.'"

52. See Copley 1947, 285–300, for the concept of the *domina* in Latin elegy as an element of a self-consciously literary love; its development was fostered by the activity of the rhetorical schools, which favored such myths as Hercules' enslavement to Omphale. More recently, Kennedy 1993, 73, commenting on the manipulations of elegiac discourse, observes that the language of servitude to a *domina*, posited as "real" rather than metaphorical, is essentially a strategy by the lover in an erotic-rhetorical power game.

53. Hubbard 1974, 116–56, surveying the variety of poems in Propertius's last book, finds fault with the poet's pictorial imagination and with structural inconsistency in these narratives but acknowledges the brilliance of the Tarpeia poem. DeBrohun 2003, reassessing Propertius's last book, explores the elegist's complex use of the motif of the *limen*, or boundary, and of clothing to reflect on the turmoil both in the sphere of poetics and in the experiential world of Rome.

54. See Davis 1989, 70–72, on the poet-lover's servitude in 1.3 as a pose Ovid expects the reader to see through; he promises his mistress fame through his verse, but it is actually his own fame that concerns the poet. Watson 1983, 91–103, on the poet-lover's deceit in denying an affair outright to the angry Corinna in 2.7 and then demanding further assignations from the servant in 2.8, .discusses the significant difference in style between the two poems: the first, formal and legalistic, with the structure of a forensic speech, and the second, lower and more intimate, suited to the purpose of seduction.

55. Zimmerman 1994, 39–73, considers that Theocritus found the mythical Narcissus a close analogue for Daphnis and concludes that the pastoral singer's scorn for Aphrodite caused him to be inflicted with the evil eye, which, as with Narcissus, makes him turn to himself and thus to waste away. He suggests that by a pun on the word *korê*, the "girl" whom Daphnis loves is ironically his vision of himself.

56. Segal 1969, 47.

57. Hubbard 1974, 33–34, notes the likelihood of a model for Propertius 1.18 in the lost poetry of Cornelius Gallus, as depicted by Vergil in *Eclogue* 10. Gallus, then, as well as Vergil may likewise have influenced Ovid's narrative of Narcissus.

58. Conte 1986, 103–7, discusses Vergil's allusions to *Idyll* 1, turning Gallus into the shepherd Daphnis, beginning with the question "quae nemora aut qui vos saltus habuere, puellae / Naides, indigno cum Gallus amore peribat?"

("What grove, what meadows held you, Naiad girls, when Gallus was perishing in unrequited love?" [9–10]), an echo of line 66 in Theocritus. He observes that Apollo here reverses the question posed by Priapus: acceptance of separation rather than of love is now advised.

59. Conte 1986, 108–26, emphasizes that Vergil is concerned for Gallus specifically as an elegiac poet: the elegist turns away from generic conventions causing suffering, such as war separating lovers, in order to adapt erotic passion to the meter and motifs of pastoral.

60. See, for instance, Kennedy 1993, 75–76, on the poet-lover's elaborate effort to express with precision the color as well as the texture of Corinna's hair: its fineness compares to a spider's web, but its color is more elusive, neither black nor gold but with qualities of each, specifically like cedar in the valleys of Ida after its bark is removed (Amores 1.14.9–12).

61. Rhorer 1980, 79–88, discussing the significance of red and white in numerous tales in this poem, associates the reddening of Narcissus's white skin with the erotic, assuming that the image of ripening fruit is an analogue for the youth's continued blushing.

62. Segal 1969, 46, cites background for the erotic significance of apples in Sappho frag. 105a, Ibycus frag. 5, and Theocritus 7.17 and for grapes in Alcaeus frag. 119 L-P, Theocritus 11.21, and Palatine Anthology 5.203, 5.24, and 5.304.

63. Fitzgerald 1995, 192–95, shows that the image of the apple falling from the maiden's lap in Catullus 65 unites the motifs of storehouse and womb, which at the beginning of the poem serve as analogues for the poet's own mind. Barchiesi 1993, 363–65, suggests that the apple in Catullus 65 is a programmatic allusion to story of Acontius and Cydippe in Callimachus's Aetia, in which Cydippe is tricked into reading a message on an apple that says she promises to marry Acontius: Catullus thus composes his elegy from the perspective both of deep personal loss and of commitment to a particular literary tradition of elegy.

64. Nisbet and Hubbard 1978, 86, citing Ovid's passage, call it "an evident imitation" of Odes 2.5.12–15. The two passages have in common shared diction (five words) and word pairing ("purpureum . . . colorem" specifically echoing "purpureo . . . colore"), which suggest that Ovid had Horace's passage closely in mind.

65. Horace exploits a tradition associating the vine with the erotic that goes as far back as the second half of the sixth century. Ibycus, for instance, uses a garden where "vine shoots are growing under the shade of the branches" (frag. 286) as a setting for his restless, unceasing passion. Late republican and Augustan Latin poetry often emphasizes the sexual implications of the vine in contexts that associate vines with the elm on which they were trained. In Catullus 62, for instance, the chorus of young men appeals to the young women by referring to the vine that "has been joined to the elm as its husband" ("at si forte eadem est ulmo coniuncta marito" [54]).

66. Nisbet and Hubbard 1978, 77, observe that it would be odd for Horace not to name the addressee in a private paraenesis and that, if the content seemed objectionable for a prominent individual, the poet could easily have invented a suggestive name, such as Xanthias or Thaliarchus.

67. Lalage shares the name of the beloved in *Odes* 1.22: there the poet, refraining from calling her his mistress, asserts only that he has been protected from danger by singing of her (9–12) and that he will continue to love her no matter where he is (21–24).

68. Horace overtly reflects his own distance from the stance of elegiac poet-lover in *Odes* 1.33, where he admonishes Albius (presumably the elegist Tibullus) not to "continue singing his pitiful laments" ("neu miserabilis / decantes elegos" [2–3]).

69. Hunter 1999, 67, remarks on the "watery nature" of Daphnis's fate, literal and figurative, in Theocritus's poem. In Ovid's passage, a body of water is symbolically appropriate for Narcissus as a return to his origins, since he was conceived in water, when the river god Cephisus raped his mother Liriope (342–44).

70. Knoespel 1985, 18, also comments on the irony of Narcissus as an *imago* in the underworld staring at his own *imago*.

71. Substitution seems implied since Narcissus's body dissolved into the waters of the pool. Furthermore, this flower is unlike the hyacinth and the anemone, which emerge from the blood of dead youths: the former first springs up at the death of Apollo's young beloved in book 10 (208–12) and then at the suicide of Ajax in book 13 (399–402); the latter, as we observe in chapter 4, comes into being when Venus sprinkles nectar on Adonis's blood in book 10 (731–39). But scholars disagree on the significance of the narcissus. Fränkel 1969 [1945], 84, assumes that Narcissus is metamorphosed into the flower. Galinsky 1975, 60, comments on "the lack of an intrinsic relation between Narcissus' particular predicament and his metamorphosis into the flower even in Greek myth." Stirrup 1976, 97–107, indicates that Narcissus, on dissolving, is transformed into a flower. Hardie 2002, 156, as previously observed, points to the irony of Narcissus's metamorphosis into a flower that is available to any and all. However, Brenkman 1976, 326, states that the flower is "a sign, a substitution *pro corpore*" but does not discuss its significance as such. Zgoll 2004, 237 n.420, also points to the substitution.

72. Rhorer 1980, 80–81, pointing out that *croceus* (saffron yellow) falls within the general spectrum of the color red and, as such, suggestively contrasts with *albus* (white), observes: "Even as a flower, Narcissus remains an image of innocence brushed with the fire of passion." The red and white contrast here, moreover, also reflects Narcissus's self-infliction of wounds, a moment marking the beginning of his physical disintegration, as he is unable to endure the loss of his image, from its disappearance in the rippled waters and perhaps as well from its altered state.

73. Sharrock 1991, 36, noting that Narcissus is compared to a statue of Parian marble, comments on the similar symbolism of the two episodes: "ivory and marble, snowy white and red blood all feature in an opposition between purity and sex." Given her focus on "womanufacture," however, she opts not to develop the connections. Sharrock also, esp. 41–45, points to numerous elegiac elements in the Pygmalion episode, such as the comparison of the mistress to a statue, the use of blandishments, and the offer of modest gifts. Her purpose is to reveal "gendered power relations" in the ways by which both Pygmalion and the elegist are enamored with the object of art, bring inert material to life, and ultimately create the object of desire; she is, therefore, more interested in the positive rather than negative aspects of the sculptor.

74. Segal 1998, 17–18, calling attention to the role of Venus in transforming the statue into a real woman, notes that the happy ending does not resolve the ambivalence of Pygmalion's actions. As I discuss in chapter 4, Orpheus is a complex internal narrator whose views are frequently undermined by the text.

75. On Pygmalion's actions as well as their long-range consequences, see Janan 1988, 124–28.

76. See Farrell 1992, 235–68, for a discussion of this episode focusing on its generic inclusiveness, which contributes to the ludicrousness of Polyphemus's song of seduction.

77. Milowicki 1996, 155–66, also observes that Polyphemus is a parody of Narcissus but does not connect the two with Apollo's prophecy in the *Ars*. In his brief remarks on the connection between the two episodes, he notes that the shepherd has his own Tiresias in the form of Telemus (13.770–77) and comments on the echo of *noverit* with *novi* as implying "serious dementia."

78. For poetic implications of his last major inclusion of elegy in the poem, see Myers 1994a, 225–50. Myers explores the elegiac model of the story of Pomona and Vertumnus in Propertius 4.2, which was itself influenced by Callimachus: the episode points forward to the poet's aetiological emphasis in the Roman material in the last books and suggests the importance that Ovid attaches to crossing generic boundaries in the *Metamorphoses*.

Chapter 2. The Metamorphic Medea

1. See Pucci 1980, 94–96, on Medea's invocation to Hecate as her helper (*sunergos* [396]) after she reflects on killing her enemies by being clever (*sophia*), which she considers the "straight way," and using poisons (384–85). Medea's use of "straight" here is highly ambiguous since the word is normally associated with "truth, justice, and whatever is free from manipulation and trickery."

2. See Boedeker 1997, 127–48, especially on metaphors that are developed through the perspectives of various characters on Medea and that are given additional resonance through allusions to the voyage of the Argonauts.

3. For a recent discussion of the increasingly negative portrayal of Medea's connection to magic from books 3 to 4, see Clare 2002, 240–60, along with extensive bibliography. Clare reflects on the contrast developed between Orpheus and Medea. Whereas the former exerts a power to charm nature for benevolent purposes through his connection to divinities and other forces of order, the latter aggressively binds nature to her purposes, ultimately threatening the very fabric of the universe through her association with chthonic powers.

4. We have only testimonials from a few ancient authors, including Quintilian and Tacitus, that Ovid in fact wrote a *Medea*. Holzberg 2002, 34–36, pointing to the paucity of fragments of the play, believes that Quintilian, *Institutio oratia* 10.1.98, does not really make a strong case for Ovidian authorship of the *Medea*: the Roman's statement that Ovid could have accomplished so much if he had only reined in his talent suggests that the tragedy is far too different from the poet's other works. One might claim, however, that Ovid was always intent on showing his versatility.

5. Although the consensus seems to be that *Heroides* 12 is genuine, not all scholars accept its authenticity. Knox 1986b, 207–23, states the case against Ovidian authorship. Although a definitive answer may not be possible, Barchiesi 1993, 343–44, points to the highly self-conscious nature of *Heroides* 12 as a literary work; he observes that the last two lines refer to divine possession (213), suggestive of the tragedy ascribed to Ovid, and to something greater (*maius* [214]), suggestive of a tragic mode.

6. Anderson 1972, 262, for instance, considers the skilled woman who rejuvenates Jason's father Aeson too remote from the young girl who speaks her anguished soliloquy and, 275, emphasizes that Medea is motivated to kill Pelias because of her desire to indulge in trickery. Rosner-Siegel, 1982, 231–43, however, finds that the Medea narrative is sustained by a "psychological metamorphosis" in which the young woman's love for Jason is short lived and her interest in magic increases, first for beneficial and then for malicious purposes. Medea's brutal murder of her own children thus appears as a natural consequence of her progressive change in character rather than strictly as a means of punishing Jason for his betrayal of her. Binroth-Bank 1997, 17–35, comments on the psychological state of the heroine, with references to Euripides' heroine. Newlands, 1997, 178–208, on the other hand, believes that Ovid juxtaposes the love-struck young girl and the experienced witch in order to expose inconsistencies in the myths of Medea: after sympathetically portraying the young woman's struggle over her passion for Jason, the poet fills the lengthy account of the witch with humorously exhaustive details of her magic rituals. She observes that Ovid in this episode underplays issues central to Euripides' *Medea* (marriage, betrayal, and the status of women) and displaces them onto other marriage tales in the central section, such as those of Procne, Philomela, and Tereus, so as to explore a female type whose passion is so intense that she violates cultural values and asserts her independence from conventional male authority.

7. In particular, that of Scylla (8.44–80), Byblis (9.474–516), and Myrrha (10.320–55).

8. See Anderson 1972, however, for ironic resonances in Medea's speech that Ovid would expect his reader to catch without much trouble. For example, on 40, Anderson notes that Medea's hesitation seems less motivated by filial piety than by self-interest, and, on 53, he observes that she has a ready answer to what appears to be a tormented question about leaving her family and country.

9. Anderson 1972, on 59–61, not only cites the echo here of *Odes* 1.1.36 but also notes that Medea's phrase "dis cara ferar" echoes *Odes* 1.31.13 ("dis carus ipsis"), where Horace ironically describes the merchant as an antitype of the poet himself. Anderson does not, however, associate Medea's words with poetic powers but instead connects them to the heroine's psychology, regarding them as fulfilling her amorous desires.

10. Wise 1982, 16–25, also observes that the young heroine envisions a relationship with Jason based on her own fantasy, enlivening the picture of the potential dangers of a sea voyage with Jason. Wise focuses on the sections dealing with Medea's witchcraft, especially her incantations, pointing out that the more experienced witch employs not only powers of incantation but also persuasive skills with the daughters of Pelias. Noting that the poet highlights his own powers of language in his riveting description of Jason's contest with the bulls as he simultaneously exposes Medea's failure to grasp the irony of her fears since the outcome is predetermined, Wise concludes that Ovid undermines his heroine's creative powers.

11. Hinds 1993, 9–47, discusses Medea's odd mention in *Heroides* 12 of traveling past both the Symplegades and Scylla on the trip to Greece with Jason, which would not be possible from Colchis. Later, in the *Metamorphoses* passage, the poet has Medea allude to the confusion of the Symplegades with the Planctae, which Hinds notes was a common error in antiquity; through her phrase "nescioqui . . . montes" (62–63), Ovid has Medea correct the earlier passage by suggesting her fear of the Planctae rather than the Symplegades, which were already fixed permanently when Jason went through them en route to Colchis.

12. See Bömer 1977, ad loc.

13. Newlands 1997, 182–83, finding the expression here "disarming," appropriately observes that Medea's intention is to help rather than to cause harm.

14. Ovid in *Heroides* 12 clearly has Medea allude to the literal fire that will soon consume the Corinthian princess by playing on the figurative erotic meaning of the flame: "flebit et ardores vincet adusta meos!" ("She will weep, and being burned, will surpass my flames!" [180]). Ovid's reader familiar with the *Heroides* would presumably recall Medea's ominous pun there, particularly because it is followed by the manifest threat that no enemy of hers will go unpunished as long as she has a sword, fire, or poison (181–82).

15. Anderson 1972, on 32, also cites Dido's reproach to Aeneas in Vergil (4.365-66), a text that Ovid may have in the background here.

16. See Otis 1964, 72-78 and 85-90, on the influence of Apollonius's characterization of Medea on Dido, especially through epic similes and motifs of sleeplessness and in her thoughts of suicide and use of sorcery; he concludes that Vergil brings out both the emotional and the moral implications of his heroine's state of mind on her actions much more than his predecessor.

17. Apollonius's Medea, however, is not uncomplicated, even in book 3. The poet plays her against Homer's Nausikaa, for instance, through allusions to the *Odyssey*. See the commentary of Hunter 1989. On the discordant aspects of Medea in contrast to the social integration of Nausikaa, see Pavlock 1990, 51-63.

18. Anderson 1972, on 50, notes a general allusion to Apollonius here but emphasizes the source for both poets in Euripides' play; in Euripides, Jason reminds Medea that he was responsible for bringing her to Greece, where she not only experienced culture but also received honor.

19. Haupt, Ehwald, and Von Albrecht 1966, on 79-83, note that the simile refers to Apollonius 3.291-95.

20. Newlands 1997, 185, observes that the gods play no role in setting the love affair in motion and have no concern with Jason's or Medea's interests. She furthermore notes that Ovid attributes Jason's especially handsome appearance in this scene to chance, in contrast to Apollonius, who has Hera enhance Jason's looks for the meeting with Medea. In that way as well, Ovid has eliminated the divine apparatus that helps to make sense of human events.

21. Smith 1997, 99, in a discussion of shame as a moral force for Ovid's and Apollonius's heroines, notes that *aidôs* does not fail Medea in the *Argonautica* until her meeting with the hero in the grove has taken place (3.1015-21) but that *pudor* in the *Metamorphoses* has already lapsed from the beginning of the encounter. I would emphasize, however, that Apollonius's Medea undergoes a process by which the poet shows the disintegration of her *aidôs* in part through the symbolic interplay of the colors red and white. See Pavlock 1990, 56-57 and 61-62.

22. Contrast *Heroides* 12, in which Medea, reminding Jason of his promises, especially his pledge of marriage to her alone, actually quotes his words to her in the grove of Diana (73-88). She makes his flattery at that time clear: he hoped, for instance, that she would not look down on (*dedignare* [83]) a Pelasgian suitor. Medea also indicates that he in fact said much more to her than she actually records: "et quota pars haec sunt!" ("And how small a portion [of your words] are these!" [89]).

23. Hunter 1989, on 825-27, notes the etymological play and calls attention to a similar punning with the verb *mêdeto* at 3.1137, which adds a twist by making Medea the agent of Hera's designs. Hunter also observes that the punning on Medea's name goes back at least to Pindar, *Pythian* 4.27, where Medea refers to herself with the phrase "mêdesin . . . amois." The pun on Medea's name in

Pythian 4 has in fact been acknowledged for some time; Gildersleeve 1885, ad loc., observes that Medea is not averse to alluding to her own name.

24. Later, in *Tristia* 3.8, Ovid uses Medea's flight from Corinth on the dragon chariot as an image for his own release from the constraints of exile at Tomi: "nunc ego Medeae vellem frenare dracones, / quos habuit fugiens arce, Corinthe, tua" ("Now I would wish to rein Medea's serpents, which she had as she fled from your citadel, Corinth" [3–4]). The poet goes on to mention Daedalus's wings as well as Medea's chariot as a way of retrieving what matters to him most: his homeland, his friends, and especially his wife (5–8).

25. Wise 1977, 44–59, considers flight as an analogue to poetry through the vision afforded by the aerial experience and through the artistic nature of the specific means of flight, in particular the chariot of the Sun or the wings of the artisan Daedalus. Wise acknowledges, however, that the agents of flight in Ovid's epic have only limited success in their vision and art, in contrast to the poet himself.

26. Wilkinson 1955, 235, simply indicates that Ovid uses this passage to imply that he "knows many more stories than he tells." Otis 1970, 173, dismisses the section on Medea's wanderings as "quite uninspired." Hill 1992a, on 350–401, states that Ovid includes Medea's journey "to insinuate a host of obscure metamorphoses."

27. The alliterative effect of the collocations of *male* and *mater* may reinforce the more overt, though brief, criticism of Medea here. Segal 1982, 241–46, discussing similar punning on Medea's name in Seneca's tragedy on this heroine's infanticide, including *monstrum* as well as *malum*, perceives a "tension between monstrosity and maternity as the central dynamic force of Medea's tragedy." Segal observes that Seneca implicitly has Medea transform herself from *mater* to *monstrum* through language so as to secure revenge on Jason and adds a visual image of her state as she is conveyed by the chariot drawn by serpent monsters at the end.

28. In *Argonautica* 4, Medea reveals the awesome powers of her eyes in destroying the giant Talus, guardian of Crete, when he tries to prevent the Argonauts from landing (1668–72).

29. Cameron 1995, 259–60, discusses Callimachus's association of the Telchines with *baskaniê* ("envy") in the prologue of the *Aetia*, where the poet refers to them as the "baneful race of envy" (17), and compares the prologue of the *Hymn to Apollo*, where *phthonos* occurs three times, referring to the envy that plagues the poet. Noting that later sources do not account for the Telchines' connection with malignancy, Cameron cites Strabo 14.2.7; there, the Telchines are said to have been bewitched by rivals who envied them for their skill as artisans.

30. Papathomopoulos 1968, 71–72, n.11, indicates the likelihood that Nicander alluded to Callimachus's "Acontius and Cydippe" because of clear evidence of the latter's influence in the *Heteroioumena*, especially with respect to aetiology, but also acknowledges the possibility that Antoninus Liberalis as a

learned grammarian may have made the association. Forbes Irving 1992 [1990], 232–33, asserts that Nicander would have known that Callimachus's Acontius story featured not only the motif of the inscribed apple but also the father's failed effort to marry the girl to another man; he also notes that Ioulis is the home of Acontius as well as Ctesylla. Observing that the motif of the apple here becomes redundant because Alcidamas himself makes an oath that drives the plot of the story, Forbes Irving suggests that Nicander combined elements of Callimachus's episode with a local *aetion*.

31. Forbes Irving 1992 [1990], 257, notes that Lake Conope, where swans still gather, was called Kykneia in Antoninus Liberalis. Claiming that Ovid would not have had the knowledge to correct Nicander and was therefore presumably not responsible for the change in name of the woman (and the lake) from Thyrie to Hyrie, Forbes Irving suggests that the poet may have followed the account by Areus, cited by Antoninus as a source along with Nicander. In my opinion, however, Ovid's well demonstrated inclination for linguistic play could easily account for his making this alteration.

32. In *Fasti* 5, Ovid explains the origin of the constellation Orion through a pun on the verb *oureo:* when a poor old man named Hyrieus provided them hospitality, Jupiter, Neptune, and Mercury reciprocated by giving the childless widower an infant produced from the ground on which they had urinated. Hyrieus then called the boy Urion, later changed to Orion, from the circumstances of his birth (5.495–536). Ovid here may recall the two proper names, Urion and Hyrieus, attributing to both the connotation of water. Clearly, the etymologizing is not linguistically sound, but it does have an aurally suggestive value. Palmer 1988 [1954], 229–30, comments on the "inherently unstable" nature of the glottal aspirate in Latin; he notes that some Latin words related to Greek roots without aspiration acquired an "unetymological *h*" (e.g., Latin *haurio* and Greek αὐδ).

33. Strabo 10.2.22 says that this lake, situated between Pleuron and the city Arsinoe, was then known as Lysimachia but used to be called Hydra.

34. On Callimachus's use of the swan as an image for his own nature as a refined poet and the assimilation of this motif into Latin poetry, see Donohue 1993, 18–29.

35. In Antoninus Liberalis 12, Phylius appeals to Hercules for help, and in response the latter causes two bulls to appear, butting and finally thrusting each other to the ground. Phylius is thereby able to grab one by the leg and to drag it away to the altar of Jupiter. Hercules himself urges the youth not to accede to any more of Cycnus's commands.

36. Segal 1999, 312–18, has a useful discussion of the erotic elements intruded into the Meleager episode, including an amusing interplay between elegiac and epic language and style. Meleager's traditionally heroic uncles, for instance, employ erotic language ("captus amore" [435]) in reproaching their nephew, and Meleager himself is characterized by the erotic metaphor of

flames (325). But he then assumes a more heroic stance suggestive of Odysseus with Nausikaa by asserting the happy state of the man whom Atalanta chooses as her husband.

37. Anderson 1972, on 405–7, refers to Theseus's plea as "words of passionate friendship." Ovid is probably playing on the two traditions of heroic friendship and erotic attachments in the reference to the dear one as part of his own soul. Anderson notes as background two passages in Horace's *Odes* in which the lyric poet refers to dear ones: 1.3.8 ("animae dimidium meae"), addressed to Vergil and *Odes* 2.17.5 ("meae . . . partem animae"), addressed to Maecenas. The precise nature of Horace's relations to the great Latin epic poet and to his magnificent patron cannot be known for certain. But, as Putnam 1986, 141, observes on *Odes* 4.7, the situation of Theseus's imprisonment with his dear (*caro*) friend in the underworld, juxtaposed to the non-erotic relationship of Diana and Hippolytus (25–28), strongly suggests homoerotic love. Furthermore, Ovid presumably had Callimachus, *Epigram* 42.1, in mind, in which the Hellenistic poet uses similar language in an overtly erotic context.

38. Segal 1999, 336, commenting on the Meleager episode as an "elaborate cartoon" rather than the representation of the traditional epitome of heroic prowess, refers to Achilles' amazement at finding that there was no wound ("vulnus erat nullum" [12.127]) after he has thrust his spear at Cycnus. The poet's reduction of the typical Homeric contest on the battlefield creates the effect of an innocuous pleasure derived from the violence depicted in the text.

39. Zumwalt 1977, 212–13, views Achilles' contest with Cycnus as questioning traditional notions about eternal fame and about the very *virtus* by which one earns fame. Focusing on the frailty of Achilles' heroic ego as it manifests itself through the hero's boasting, amazement at the failure of his first shot, reassurance after killing Lycian Menoites, joy at wounding Cycnus, and then finally unheroic means of combat, she points out that although Cycnus actually escaped death through metamorphosis, Achilles is still credited with victory. O'Bryhim 1988, 49–53, observing that Achilles' contest with Cycnus is the subject of conversation among the Greeks that evening, discusses the poet's devious strategy of further reducing Achilles' glory. For Nestor tells a similar story about the brutish, drunken Centaurs' battle with Caeneus: the sympathy aroused for the unfortunate Caeneus is then implicitly transferred to Cycnus, and the Greeks say no more about Achilles' contest.

40. Chance is sometimes mentioned explicitly to effect a transition: in the story of Thebes in book 3, for instance, the narrative thus moves from the birth of Bacchus to the prophet Tiresias: "While these things were going on through the earth by the law of fate, and the cradle of twice-born Bacchus was safe, they say that by chance [*forte*] Jupiter, relaxed with wine, had put away his serious concerns" (316–19). More often, it is suggested obliquely: the narrator in book 15, for instance, introduces the story of the hero Cipus who refused kingship by a series of similes describing Hippolytus's response to seeing Egeria transformed

into a spring: his wonder was like the farmer's surprise at the creation of the autochthonous Tales, or Romulus's at the transformation of his spear into a tree, or Cipus's at his new horns reflected in water (552–66).

41. Anderson 1972, ad loc., also calls attention to the beginning of Horace, *Odes* 1.28. Although he does not expand on the reference, Anderson's choice of analogue is well taken, especially because Horace demeans Archytas, a philosopher and general whose grave is paltry. Like Ovid, Horace in that instance is sarcastic rather than generally philosophic about the vicissitudes of human fate. On Horace's cynicism about Archytas's fate, see Frischer 1984, 71–102.

42. Ovid does not focus on Paris as the agent of Achilles' death in the scene itself; rather, he credits Apollo with turning the bow in the right direction and guiding the weapon. In fact, he does not even mention that Paris actually shot the arrow and immediately shifts the focus to Priam's joy at Achilles' death (607–8). He then apostrophizes the dead hero with a scathingly oblique reference to the Trojan warrior: "victus es a timido Graiae raptore maritae" ("You were conquered by the timid thief of a Greek wife" [609]).

43. The story of Paris's marriage to Oenone and their child Corythus is told by Parthenius, *Erôtika pathêmata* 4 and 34, and in Conon 23; Parthenius in 34, moreover, cites verses by Nicander making Helen the mother of Corythus. Lightfoot 1999, 392–93, discussing the similarity of Parthenius's and Conon's versions, suggests a common source in Hegesianax, which Parthenius would seem to have broken up by deleting all reference to Corythus from *Erôtika pathêmata* 4, where jealousy of Helen rather than grief for her dead son induces Oenone to refuse to heal Paris's wound.

44. Lightfoot 1999, 545–46, on *Erôtika pathêmata* 34, notes that in Parthenius's version of the myth, Paris kills Corythus out of jealousy because Helen is attracted to him, although it is not clear if the Trojan was cognizant of the young man's identity. Comparing Conon's version, in which Oenone deliberately sent Corythus to cause friction between Paris and Helen, Lightfoot postulates that Parthenius chose to separate the stories of Oenone and Corythus in order to exploit the literary potential of the theme of jealousy.

45. In Hyginus, *Fabulae* 130, Icarius becomes Arcturus (a star in the constellation Boötes) and Erigone (the constellation Virgo).

46. See Liddell, Scott, Jones, s.v. *Maira*.

47. Hill 1992a, on 362, believes that the location of Hecuba's metamorphosis here in Thrace appears to rule out an identification with Maera. But Ovid would certainly have been aware of the variations on the site of the Trojan queen's transformation in the literary accounts. Forbes Irving 1992 [1990], 207–10, observes that after Euripides, later writers elaborate considerably on the myth. Nicander (frag. 62), for instance, appears to locate the incident in Troy, where the grief-stricken Hecuba is metamorphosed after jumping into the sea. After surveying the tradition on Hecuba, Forbes Irving indicates that the older version of the myth, involving a metamorphosis as the end point in a "sequence

of unbroken suffering" (not connected to the queen's revenge on Polymestor), reflected two significant aspects of her condition: her removal from human society after losing both city and family and her endurance of more than any human is able to tolerate. On the latter point, he notes that Quintus Smyrnaeus (14.282 ff.) compares Hecuba to a dog howling obsessively prior to her metamorphosis. Given the prominence of Nicander as a source for the myths in this travelogue, Ovid in line 362 might well be alluding to his version, with its Trojan setting and focus on grief rather than revenge, and be conflating it with the more traditional scene in Thrace in book 13.

48. Anderson 1972, ad loc., accepts the identification of the snake here with that in book 11 but does not discuss its import.

49. The last of Orpheus's songs, the story of Venus and Adonis, beginning at 519 and ending at 739, is only apparently longer since it is in fact interrupted by Venus's extended inset tale of Atalanta and Hippomenes (560–704), recounted as a warning to Adonis about the dangers of wild animals in the hunt.

50. Janan 1988, 126–28, shows that Orpheus even creates a linguistic counterpart to the course of Myrrha's incestuous desire and its fulfillment; in particular, the use of the possessive adjectives *meus* ("mine") and *tuus* ("yours"), which in Latin can refer to both family members and amorous objects, here erases the difference between father and lover and between daughter and mistress.

51. Hill 1992a, on 387, refers to *Metamorphoses* 10.324–29.

52. Ellsworth, 1980, 23–29, shows that while apparently ignoring the *Iliad*, Ovid cleverly makes it the organizing principle of this section by expanding on brief passages in Homer's epic, such as the battle of Lapiths and Centaurs (12.210–535), based on Nestor's mention of the exploits of an earlier generation of heroes (*Iliad* 1.260–72), and by including stories similar to those in the *Iliad*, such as Achilles' contest with Cycnus, which replaces the hero's duel with Hector in Homer. On the latter, Ellsworth observes that the death of Cycnus rather than of Hector motivates Achilles' own death, for Cycnus's father Neptune rouses Apollo, who then aids Paris against the Greek hero. He reads Ovid's version of the *Iliad* as a condemnation of war by its emphasis on the destructiveness of brute force in the war itself and in various inset tales.

Chapter 3. Daedalus and the Labyrinth of the *Metamorphoses*

1. See Williams 1964, 48–63, on aspects of the vision of the future shown to the hero in book 6, whose goal is to move the poem away from the Trojan and Homeric past and into a world reflecting the idealized values of Augustan Rome.

2. Wheeler 2000, 7–47, viewing repetition as a "generative principle" of the *Metamorphoses*, uses the creation of the world in the first part of the poem to

reveal the ways by which Ovid repeats crucial motifs such as the chaos and separation of elements, the creation of humankind, and the destruction and renewal of the world.

3. Hollis 1983 [1970], on 162, cites Propertius 2.34.35-36, Silius 7.139, and Seneca, *Hercules Furens* 683-685, as examples of literary works that include descriptions of the Maeander.

4. Hollis 1983 [1970], on 162, also notes that Seneca imitates Ovid by having the river god play in his stream: "qualis incertis vagus / Maeander undis ludit et cedit sibi, / instatque dubius litus an fontem petat." Like Ovid, Seneca extends the personification, as the god here ponders whether his stream should flow toward the coast or back to the source.

5. Butler and Barber 1933, on 29, note that, while it is clear that Lynceus wrote tragedy, details in 33-40 suggest epic, as does the mention in 45 of Homer and Antimachus, who were associated with epics on Thebes. Camps 1985, in postscript notes, on 25-54, also assumes epic as part of the poetic output of Lynceus. Most recently, Fedeli 2005, 958-70, discusses the range of possibilities associated with the figure of Lynceus as a poet-intellectual, through both the language of Propertius's poem and its intertextual allusions. It is suggestive that Propertius also refers to the Achelous in the two lines immediately before his mention of the Maeander; he sets that river in the same context as a source of high themes (33-34). Ovid may well have been influenced by Propertius's passage in the section on the river god in book 8 as well as here on Daedalus's invention.

6. On Propertius 2.34 and the possible identification of Lynceus with the poet Varius, based on Epicurean underpinnings of the poem, see Cairns 2004, 299-321. Acknowledging the attractiveness of a possible allusion to Varius, Fedeli 2005, 953-54, nonetheless cautions that it would violate the typical practice by Roman poets of employing a pseudonym with the same number of syllables and a metrical equivalence.

7. Ovid similarly observes that, in constructing the labyrinth, Daedalus "lumina flexu / ducit in errorem" ("leads the eyes into error" [160-61]). So, too, Ovid's phrase "variarum ambage viarum" (161) suggests Vergil's *ambages* (6.29), and his phrase "caecisque includere tectis" (158) echoes Vergil's use of the metaphor of blindness for the labyrinth in "caeca regens filo vestigia" ("guiding the blind footsteps with the thread" [6.30]).

8. On Vergil's etymology for the labyrinth, Fitzgerald 1984, 55 and n.13, citing Norden's commentary on *Aeneid* 6, also connects line 27 with the underworld as a maze from which it is difficult to escape and notes the Sibyl's comment on the journey: "Hoc opus, hic labor est" (6.129). The noun *labor*, of course, is not related etymologically to the verb *labor*, the quantity of the stem vowel "a" constituting a primary difference between the two. But just as Vergil had created a fanciful etymological pun, so, I believe, Ovid responded with an analogous wordplay.

9. Ahl 1985, 253–54. The prevalence of such punning would suggest that Ovid, aiming for a variation on a literary allusion or echo, might well respond to a pun on a single word that Vergil had etymologized.

10. The ekphrasis of the temple doors in the *Aeneid* is a fulfillment of the poet's prophecy that he would in the future construct a temple to honor the achievements of Augustus. See Thomas 1988, on *Georgics* 3.1–48, for a concise discussion of the temple as a metaphor for the epic.

11. Otis 1964 articulates the complex patterning of the *Aeneid* through its temporal shifts, both in narrative sequence and in the repetition of historical prophecies and of past events; its ring composition; and its interlacing of images and motifs. See esp. 217, 228, 247, and 242 for useful schematic charts.

12. Doob 1990, 229–45, discusses in particular the interrelation of *labores* and *errores* in numerous passages that contribute to the labyrinthine nature of Vergil's narrative, from Laocoön, the wooden horse, and Aeneas's return to Troy for Creusa in book 2 up to the final combat between Aeneas and Turnus in book 12.

13. See, for example, *Metamorphoses* 2.9, where *ambiguus* is applied to the sea god Proteus as represented on the doors of the palace of the Sun; 4.280, where it describes Sithon's sex change from female to male; and 7.271, where it refers to a werewolf whose innards Medea mixes into her potion to rejuvenate Aeson. This adjective thus describes much of the content of the *Metamorphoses*, from the marvelous and bizarre to the tragic.

14. Janan 1991, 240–48, discussing the problem of self-reference in the Byblis and Caunus episode, finds that Maeander, grandfather of Byblis, is the paradigm for the young woman's erotic and poetic self-referentiality: Byblis "turns back" to her own brother, making him the object of her desire at the same time that she becomes a skewed version of the poet, repeating Ovid's own earlier works, the *Amores*, the *Ars amatoria*, and the *Heroides*.

15. Furthermore, for Ovid's own retrospective views in the *Tristia* on his poetic *lusus* in the *Ars amatoria*, see Williams 1994, 204–5.

16. On Ovid's relation to Hellenistic poetics, see Lyne 1984, 9–34; Knox 1986a, 55–98; and Hofmann 1986, 223–41.

17. The word *liquidus* as a stylistic term is used, for example, by Cicero, *Brutus* 274, to describe the smooth and charming oratorical style of Marcus Callidius: "quae primum ita pura erat ut nihil liquidius, ita libere fluebat ut nusquam adhaeresceret"; cf. Horace, *Epistulae* 2.2.120.

18. Callimachus emphasizes the purity of his stream by combining with *katharê* the adjective *achraantos*. Williams 1978, on 2.111, comments on the cleverness of the latter word, conveying the meaning "unsullied," since it is a neologism formed on the model of the Homeric *akraantos*: it thus simultaneously reflects the poet's originality and his facility with Homeric scholarship.

19. See especially Bömer 1977 for echoes of Vergil in the Erysichthon episode, e.g., on 8.743–44, 758, 762, 774.

20. Morris 1992, 215–16, refers to dramas by Sophocles, Euripides, Aristophanes, Plato, and Euboulus in which Daedalus is the title character as well as to other plays related to Daedalus's adventures in Sicily and Crete.

21. See Sharrock 1994, 112–26, on the lyric poet's use of the Daedalus and Icarus myth in all three *Odes* as a reflection of the necessity of breaking boundaries in artistic creativity. Whereas Icarus is at issue in 2.20 and 4.2, Daedalus is specifically named in 1.3, on which see especially Kidd 1977, 91–103; Basto 1982, 30–43; and Clark 2004, 4–34.

22. Putnam 1987, 182, observes that in his empathetic expression of grief for Icarus, the narrator substitutes for Daedalus and assumes a Daedalian nature, as he eternalizes the father's grief in his own artwork.

23. In her wide-ranging discussion of this myth, Sharrock 1994, 168–173, points to a number of references to it in Ovid's exile poetry that associate it closely with the *Ars* as a source of the poet's downfall. That Ovid inserted or revised this episode after receiving the notice of his *relegatio* may add another level to the intertextual play involving Daedalus: book 8 of the *Metamorphoses* thus becomes the locus of both a backward and a forward form of self-reflexiveness.

24. Hollis 1983 [1970], on 211, observes that Ovid echoes Vergil's "poignant line" ("bis patriae cecidere manus" [6.33]) that describes Daedalus at the point where he could not finish his pictures because of his grief.

25. Wise 1977, 44–59, discusses the episodes of Phaethon and Daedalus and Icarus as parallel myths involving flight as a metaphor for the creative process. In her view, Phaethon is destroyed by his obsession with a material vision of reality, a way of seeing that contrasts with the metamorphic imagination implied by the designs on doors of Phoebus's palace. With Daedalus and Icarus, she finds that the wings compared to panpipes suggest the ambiguity of art imitating art and that on the one hand, Icarus lacks the self-discipline to attain a higher vision, while, on the other, Daedalus's murder of Perdix implies an inability of the artist to accept anyone else's inventiveness.

26. Davisson 1997, 263–78, comparing the versions of the Daedalus myth in the *Ars amatoria* and the *Metamorphoses*, considers the point of view of the bird Perdix as opposed to the rustics who view the flight in awe. She includes Daedalus among the artistic failures of the poem, in part because "his art can neither produce foolproof inventions nor control his son's impulses," and compares him to Orpheus, who reveals a similar pattern as he penetrates a sphere normally unavailable to humans, almost saves his wife, but finally fails in his effort.

27. Crabbe 1981, 2277–84, cites various motival links among the Scylla, Daedalus and Icarus, and Perdix episodes in an analysis of the larger structure of book 8. She notes the similarity of age between Icarus and Perdix but mainly finds differences between the two, such as the boldness of the former in his flight and the latter's fear of high places. On the other hand, she sees several close points of contact between Scylla and Perdix; both are transformed into

birds in midair, and both fall from a tower. Scylla fantasizes that she will fall into Minos's camp; the unfortunate Perdix, on the other hand, is pushed.

28. The poet, however, implies skepticism about Minerva's act of kindness: the goddess was far less generous when, as we saw in the introduction, she herself was challenged to a weaving contest by Arachne and could find no flaw in her rival's work (129–38).

29. In the *Ars*, he directly mentions that the pair took off by thrusting themselves from a cliff (2.71–72).

30. This line has continued to vex scholars. I accept the manuscript reading (which Hollis 1983 [1970] prints, though admittedly after some reluctance). But Hollis sensibly notes that Ovid implies only that this bird does not nest in the topmost branches (line 257). Hollis also dismisses the objection that the partridge generally does not perch by noting that Ovid may have in mind the red-legged partridge and was probably influenced by the Hellenistic topos of a watching bird speaking from a tree. He considers aesthetically unacceptable the image represented by the common emendation "garrula limoso prospexit ab elice perdix," printed by Anderson 1972 and 1977 and now by Tarrant 2004.

31. Calliope's tale in book 5 is another extensively labyrinthine section, but in book 8 Ovid subtly sustains the motif itself.

32. Segal 1999, 303–18, provides as background for Ovid an insightful discussion of the earlier Greek versions of the Meleager myth in Homer and Bacchylides, pointing out how each poet privileges the value of heroic fame.

33. Hollis 1983 [1970], 68, cites frag. 525 of Euripides' *Meleager* in particular for the Greek dramatist's introduction of the hero's love for Atalanta into the myth and notes the influence on Accius's play.

34. Horsfall 1979, 324–25, in a discussion of Ovid's caricature of the heroes as hunters, comments on the high-epic images, especially lightning, employed for the boar: this simile achieves a lofty effect through its "strikingly archaic" language and rhythm.

35. Doob 1990, 48, mentions the forest among other analogues for the labyrinth in literature, such as crossroads, desert, ocean, and trackless wasteland.

36. Segal 1999, 324–25, comments on the psychological nuances of this section: Althaea's use of *viscera* as a metonymy implies that she still views her grown child as part of her own body; she later implies that she had grabbed the baby itself rather than the brand from the flames by stating that she wishes that the *infans* (501) had burned in the fire.

37. See Hinds 1998, 34–47, for a fine discussion of the "many mouths" topos, first recorded in the *Iliad*. Hinds utilizes references by the ancient commentators Eustathius and Servius as well as modern scholarship in order to examine adaptations of this topos, briefly mentioning Ovid's example here for its similarity to *Tristia* 1.5.53–56). He shows that Vergil, who employed the "many mouths" topos in the *Georgics* as well as the *Aeneid*, reflects not only Homer but also intermediaries such as Ennius, Lucretius, and the late-republican epic poet

Hostius. Through contextual considerations Hinds concludes that Vergil's passage in the *Aeneid* functions as an allusion to the *Iliad*, which serves as the exemplary model as well as the code model, to use Gian Biagio Conte's terms.

38. According to Antoninus Liberalis 2, Nicander mentioned that Artemis transformed the sisters of Meleager into birds, which she placed on the island of Leros and called *meleagrides*.

39. Thompson 1936, 198–99, mentions Pollux's description of the Meleagrides' "cackle" with the onomatopoeic verb *kagchasdein* and cites Pliny's reference to the fighting of these birds (*Naturalis historia* 10.26.38). On the basis of a passage in Columella, he assumes that the red-wattled bird mentioned by Varro is probably not the same species as the Greek *meleagris*, which had a blue wattle.

40. Due 1974, 80, referring to Achelous's grotto as a *villa marina*, observes that the cups "might have interested a Verres" and generally contrasts the grotto with the humble circumstances of Philemon and Baucis.

41. Nagle 1988b, 28, commenting on these reversals of the norm, observes that the series of tales in the Achelous section have a programmatic significance in that they address the issue of the veracity of metamorphoses, offer a "typology" of metamorphosis through reversible or non-reversible forms, and display interchange between speaker and audience.

42. See Bömer 1977 for citations of parallels and allusions to Callimachus's *Hecale*, beginning with line 639, that relate both to the humble nature of the entertainment in the simple cottage and the good will with which the guests are received. Callimachus's poem may also lurk beneath the surface of Achelous's story of his contest with Hercules. Hollis 1990, 217, on frag. 69.1 (=260.1 Pf.), cites a fragment that refers to the fact that Theseus in his victory over the Marathonian bull broke the beast's horn: "oiokerôs: heteron gar apêloiêse korunê" ("single-horned, for the club crushed the other").

43. On the food served to Theseus by Hecale, see Hollis 1983 [1970], 172–75, on frags. 35–39 (=251, 334, 248–50 Pf.): light and dark olives, coarse bread, and two vegetables common in ancient Attica, samphire and sow thistle.

44. Kenney 1986, xxviii, refers to the presence of Theseus at the narration of the tale of Baucis and Philemon as a "sly reminder" of Ovid's model, Callimachus's *Hecale*, where the hero was entertained by the old woman; he notes in addition the particular relevance of Ovid's comment that the story moved Theseus especially (*praecipue* [726]). Hinds 1987b, 19, expands on Kenney's insight, observing that, while Callimachus is also the source of the tale of Erysichthon which immediately follows, Ovid's imitation is in a manner pointedly *rejected* by the Hellenistic poet.

45. Spencer 1997, 81–88, distinguishes this "fantastic story about an incomparable monster" from a "commentary on bourgeois morality and social values"; whereas in the Hellenistic poem, Erysichthon elicits sympathy through the support of his family, here no sympathy is afforded the impious man who is guilty of a hideous familial violation by selling his own daughter.

46. Barchiesi 2001, 52–53, pointing to the unusual word *inattenuata* (844), a negative formation from *tenuis*, the technical term for a "slender style," associates the river god with a turgidity in opposition to Callimachean principles; he cites Propertius 2.34, which contrasts the poetry of Philetas and Callimachus with the grand subject matter of Achelous's contest with Hercules (31–34). Otis 1970, 414–15, states that Ovid deliberately "Vergilianized" Callimachus. For one, the impious Erysichthon recalls Mezentius, Vergil's cruel Etruscan tyrant. For another, the change of tree from a poplar in Callimachus to an oak alludes to Vergil's famous oak tree simile in *Aeneid* 4, the phrase "annoso robore quercus" (734) echoing "annoso . . . robore quercum" (441), and the bleeding of the tree alludes to Polydorus in *Aeneid* 3, the phrase "cortice sanguis" (753) echoing "de cortice sanguis" (33). Hollis 1983 [1970], 132, and on 847, observes that Mestra is analogous to Lausus, the noble son of the impious character in the *Aeneid* (7.653–54), in that she was similarly "not worthy of such a parent" ("non illo digna parente" [847]).

47. Otis 1970, 414–15, does not expand on his brief reference to the allusion to Vergil. On the Polydorus episode in general, see Biow 1996, 13–35.

48. Hollis 1983 [1970], on 771, quotes the passage on the imprecise nature of the relationship of nymphs and trees in antiquity.

49. Anderson 1972, on 763, comments on the perversion of Erysichthon's act of violating the holy oak rather than honoring Ceres with a sacrificial offering.

50. Doob 1990, 232, comments on the irony of the simile comparing Laocoön to a bull near the altar when the priest himself had been in the act of sacrifice.

51. Otis 1970, 414, offers no concrete support for his insight.

52. Tissol 1997, 70–71.

53. Tissol 1997, 69.

54. Barkan 1986, 92–93, observes that Ovid's poem is replete with cannibals, including Lycaon, Tereus, the Cyclopes, the Laestrygonians, and even Narcissus, as he "tries to eat with his eyes" (51): by having Achelous offer the only example of literal self-cannibalism, the poet implicitly contrasts his own approach to imaginative fiction with that of his internal narrator.

55. See Holzberg 1998, 83–84, on the narrative function of the horn to mark a major turn of the poem's second pentad from Theseus to Hercules.

56. Anderson 1972, on 40–41, suggests that Achelous would have done better to reverse the terms of the simile, applying the analogy of the rock to Hercules and the waves to himself.

57. See Galinsky 1972, 93–116, for parody of the *Aeneid* with this simile: whereas Vergil's conflict has the momentous goal of *imperium*, here a woman (*coniunx*) is the object of contention.

58. In discussing Achelous's bull simile and his metamorphosis into a bull, Galinsky 1972, 94–98, refers to the epic background of Hercules overcoming Cacus in *Aeneid* 8 on the fourth try.

59. In his argument on these opposing models for the reader, Feeney 1991, 230–31, notes the play on *factum* and *fictum* as divergent interpretations of Achelous's aetiological story of the island Perimele.

Chapter 4. Orpheus and the Internal Narrator

1. The tragic quality of Vergil's bard in *Georgic* 4 finds subtle expression in an extended simile comparing him to the melancholy nightingale (509–15). Perkell 1989, 80–87, comments on both the power of Orpheus's singing and its ultimate limitations resulting from its exclusive focus on an irrecoverable past: the nightingale simile encapsulates both the beauty of the song and the inevitable futility of the singer's desires. Segal 1989, 45–46, discusses the simile in the context of the antithesis between Aristaeus and Orpheus: the simile represents the bird as a victim of man's harsh control exerted over nature yet also endows the creature with a voice that represents a "nature-centered" perspective. Anderson 1982, 25–50, observes that an allusion in the simile to Procne's metamorphosis into the nightingale, eternally lamenting her son's death at her own hands, adds a deep resonance to Vergil's characterization of Orpheus.

2. See Otis 1970, 184–85, on Orpheus with Pluto and Proserpina in the underworld. Otis suggests that by making the bard's speech an example of a *suasoria*, Ovid's offers a comic touch in contrast to Vergil's tragic emphasis. Anderson 1982, 36–48, comments on the bard's "overblown rhetoric" and clever but sterile forms of persuasion, such as his claim that he is not a "tourist" or a predator like Hercules. Spencer 1997, 99–127, emphasizing Ovid's parody of Vergil, suggests that Ovid may be criticizing rhetoric and the practice of rhetoricians, amusing his readers by showing the effect of a poor speech and wryly commenting on the low standards of the infernal gods.

3. Hill 1992b, 124–37, emphasizes the immaturity of Ovid's Orpheus in contrast to the dignity of Vergil's bard. Although not totally unsympathetic to Ovid's character, he points out that Eurydice's forgiveness of her husband reflects her understanding of his sincere but callow love and that Orpheus himself is naively overconfident in the power of his singing to induce acceptance of his loss.

4. Pöschl 1960, 13–21, connects the trees in the catalogue with refined kinds of poetry, including pastoral and elegy, the genre with which Ovid displayed such ease. However, Ovid may distance himself from Orpheus by having him turn to young boys in contrast to Vergil's bard, who simply rejects women and lives alone in the forest. Makowski 1996, 25–38, finds that Ovid undercuts Vergil's portrayal of Orpheus "by satirizing him as an effeminate, gynophobic pederast"; he emphasizes the exaggerated physical details of his audience of trees, such as the elaborate hairdo of the pine tree and the grotesquely large antlers and jewelry of Cyparissus's beloved deer.

5. In the brief tale of Jupiter's rape of Ganymede (155–61), the king of the gods sets aside his majesty and assumes a disguise as his own bird. In Homer's and Vergil's version of this myth, by contrast, Jupiter's eagle swoops down to carry the young Trojan boy off to Olympus. Homer merely states that "the gods" took up the beautiful Ganymede to be Zeus's cupbearer so that he might live with them (*Iliad* 20.232–35), thereby suggesting no lust on the part of the king of the gods. Vergil says nothing about Jupiter's passion but describes the eagle with the verb *rapuit* (*Aeneid* 5.255), suggestive of rape.

6. Knox 1986a, 47–64, discusses aspects of Alexandrian poetics in Orpheus's tales: by employing the discourse and motifs of elegy, such as the lover's simple gifts to an unfeeling mistress in the tale of Pygmalion, and by alluding to earlier literary versions of the myths of Myrrha, Orpheus offers a consummate example of the light and learned poetry espoused by Ovid himself.

7. Describing the song of Orpheus as one of two *carmina perpetua* in the *Metamorphoses*, Nagle 1988a, 111–13, provides an overview of the numerous links between the bard's song and Ovid's poem: the erotic subject matter, location and lineage as structural principles, and the obvious similarity of stories with similar themes (Orpheus's tale of Myrrha and Ovid's of Byblis and the closely paired tales of Cyparissus and Hyacinthus, for example). Hardie 2002, 66, adds that the repetitive nature of Orpheus's song, manifested in the function of the individual tales as substitutes for the bard's dead wife, provides another analogue to the *Metamorphoses*.

8. See Janan 1991, 245–56, on this tale, with its numerous allusions to the *Amores* and *Ars amatoria* in Byblis's letter to Caunus, by which Ovid implies the potential danger of repeating his past career in elegy.

9. Although focusing on Ovid's control as poet in Orpheus's song, Galinsky 1975, 86–92, examines thematic links within the tale that highlight the bard's virtues; he observes, for instance, that Myrrha's "ghastly" passion for Cinyras is opposed to Orpheus's "pure" love for Eurydice. Solodow 1988, 215–19, finds it fitting that Orpheus, having possessed the ability to bring his own wife back to life, recounts the story of the supreme artist Pygmalion. Perceiving no real difference between Orpheus and Ovid as narrators, Solodow fully accepts the bard's idealization of the sculptor, emphasizing the creative powers that seem to animate the statue even independently of Venus. Janan 1988, 110–37, argues that Orpheus deeply explores the nature of love as he progresses through his song, examining in the course of it the themes of identity, *auctoritas* (as both authorship and authority), and language. Commenting on the theme of the lover's gain at the expense of the lost beloved, first suggested in the tale of Apollo and Hyacinthus, she finds that when it recurs with Venus and Adonis, the bard abruptly leaves off his song in a profound gesture of self-awareness.

10. Leach 1974, 122–25, observes that Orpheus's idealization of Pygmalion is a form of wish fulfillment, a result of his own failure with Eurydice, and that the sculptor's involvement with the statue is analogous to Myrrha's incest with

her father. Leach points to textual details that undermine the positive surface of this narrative. For instance, the very material with which Pygmalion creates his dream woman recalls the literary association of ivory with false dreams; the echoes of pastoral and elegiac poetry in the sculptor's courtship of the statue draw attention to his object's inanimate nature; and the ivory woman's identification of her husband with heaven, after she is brought to life by Venus, reaffirms how distant this narcissistic love story is from reality. Anderson 1989, 1–11, stressing Orpheus's misogyny, observes that Pygmalion embodies the bard's extreme views when he rejects women in general and resorts to art as a remedy. He also points out that, in his desire to animate the statue and to marry the woman, the sculptor ironically reverses the pattern of Orpheus's own life: nature in this case ultimately wins out over art. Barchiesi 2001, 55–62, comments on the irony of Orpheus's address warning his audience that he is about to refer to incest (300–303), given that his audience consists in part of the very beasts whom Myrrha herself points to as justification for engaging in sexual relations with her father (10.324–29).

11. Anderson 1972, on 543, citing a parallel in Theseus's advice to Pirithous at 8.405–7, notes Venus's use of paradox, along with the alliteration of "f" and the brief suspense created by the *que*, calling attention to the anticlimax. It might also be noted that Venus effectively postpones the anticlimactic word *tuta* to the very end of the aphoristic expression in line 544.

12. The spirit of Venus's command here, however, is ambivalent: the emphasis may be more strongly on the word *meo*, primarily reflecting self-concern. Nagle 1988a, 99–125, comments on Venus's self-interest here, noting that her creation of the anemone "will memorialize *her* grief and cause annual reenactments of *her* lamentation" (115).

13. Apollodorus 3.9.2 says that Atalanta, the daughter of Iasus and Clymene, exposed at birth but raised by hunters, later discovered her parents; she herself devised the strategy of the race, which she ran bearing arms, to avoid marriage urged by her father. Calling the successful suitor Melanion, the mythographer simply states that he obtained Atalanta through the device of Aphrodite's golden apples. Hyginus, *Fabulae* 185, indicates that Atalanta was defeated by Hippomenes after she picked up the apples and marveled at the gold. Schoeneus then was pleased to give his daughter in marriage to the man because of his cleverness. In a brief reference to the myth in Theocritus, *Idyll* 3 (40–42), however, a shepherd courting a girl named Amaryllis mentions that Atalanta upon seeing the apples thrown by Hippomenes "grew mad" (*emanê*) and was thrust into a deep love. Hunter 1999, on 40–42, compares Aphrodite's gift of the *zonê*, a kind of belt, to Hera at *Iliad* 14.214–17 as an analogue for the magical properties of the apples and cites a verse from the Augustan period involving an apple intended to drive a certain girl mad for the writer of the inscription.

14. In the next line, Atalanta continues to employ elegiac conventions when she uses the interjection *a!* and calls Hippomenes *miser*. Kershaw 1980, 71–72,

demonstrates that the major Latin elegists preferred the first position in the line for the interjection *a!,* which generally implies pathos.

15. Nagle 1988a, 115-16, considers the problem of the dissolution of personal identity through love not only here but more broadly in this embedded story as implied by the oracle warning Atalanta to avoid marriage, which would cause her to "lack herself" (566).

16. Janan 1988, 129, in commenting on the implication of narcissism in this passage, connects it to Orpheus's transferal of love from the female to males who reflect himself.

17. Detienne 1979, 30-31, notes that in myth running and hunting for women are not necessarily separated and that in *Metamorphoses* 10 the runner Atalanta is implicitly a huntress by her recourse to the forests after she decides to avoid marriage (567-68). Forbes Irving 1992 [1990], 74-75, n.44, rejects the view that there were two separate characters named Atalanta in myth (the Arcadian huntress won over by Melanion and the Boeotian runner defeated by Hippomenes) but instead assumes the two activities refer to chronological developments in the career of a female characterized by a rejection of sex and wildness in general. Referring to the tradition of the transformation of Atalanta and Hippomenes into the lions of Cybele's chariot (76), he thus defines her situation: "She is now permanently wild, and yet paradoxically not free but yoked or tamed as if she were married." Ovid is unclear about the relationship of the two Atalantas, perhaps deliberately so: in his own narrative about Atalanta in the Calydonian boar hunt in book 8, he emphasizes that her beauty would seem to be girlish for a boy or vice versa (322-23), shows Meleager responding to her with instant passion (324-28), much like Hippomenes here, and makes her outstrip all the men except Meleager in the hunt by having her wound the boar first (380-83). Although Ovid refers to her tersely as Arcadian (*Tegeaea* [317]), he does not clearly distinguish the huntress, who simply disappears from the Calydonian boar narrative when Meleager kills his uncles, from the runner whom Venus simply calls *Schoeneia,* the daughter of Schoeneus (609, 660), a king in Boeotia.

18. It is perhaps relevant in this regard that Atalanta's name itself implies "equivalence." See Liddell, Scott, Jones, s.v. *atalantos:* "equal in weight, equivalent to, like." Ovid may be playing with the etymology here since even outside of the sphere of beauty Atalanta is, with different emphases, equivalent to Hippomenes, Adonis, and Venus and is even relevant to Orpheus's own story.

19. See, for instance, Horace, *Odes* 3.8, an invitation to Maecenas reminding the poet's patron of the present state of tranquility in the empire. Horace caps his list of tribes no longer a threat to the Romans with a reference to the Scythians, citing both their reputation as archers and their nomadic lifestyle: "iam Scythae laxo meditantur arcu / cedere campis" ("now the Scythians with their bows unstrung plan to move to the plains" [23-24]).

20. Anderson 1972, on 654-55, notes the effect of the second-person verb form *putes* ("you would think").

21. Nagle 1988a, 115, citing Orpheus's statement, assumes that Adonis's "courageous nature" causes him to ignore the goddess's warnings. Leach 1974, 122–23, points to Venus's "maternal" attitude and concludes that her admonitions against the hunt in themselves cause Adonis to do the opposite.

22. Davis 1983, 106–9, comments on Venus's adoption of the role of huntress vis-à-vis the literary convention of the woman who chooses to be a companion to the lover-hunter: the goddess becomes merely an ordinary *amator* from the elegiac and pastoral tradition.

23. In the *Hippolytus*, Artemis does not specifically mention Adonis but rather refers cryptically to avenging her protégé by destroying the "next mortal" whom Aphrodite will love. The playwright's contemporary audience presumably would not have needed to be told the particular name of the youth well known to them not only in myth but also through the popular cult of the Adonia. Barrett 1964, 412, assuming that Euripides is alluding to Adonis here, cites Apollodorus 3.14.4.1 for a version of the myth in which Artemis in her anger sends the boar to kill Adonis while he is hunting.

24. Thomas 1998, 99–109, discusses the similarities between Myrrha and Phaedra and between the nurses in *Metamorphoses* 10 and the *Hippolytus*, including the heroine's initial resistance to her incestuous feelings, the attempts at suicide, a recourse to silence, and a reluctance to accept the nurse's interference. He observes that Artemis (whose own favorite was the victim of his amorous stepmother) accomplishes her plan through the offspring of Myrrha's incestuous relations with her father and that Ovid makes Adonis a substitute for Cupid, thus adding another suggestion of incest. However, I find that Ovid invests Venus's guise as Diana with more deeply negative implications for the goddess and therefore disagree with Thomas's optimistic interpretation of Ovid's stories of Orpheus, Adonis, and Hippolytus in which he draws on the interconnected motifs of rebirth, resurrection, and immortality.

25. Hardie 2002, 187–88.

26. Hardie 2002, 188, also comments on the suggestion of incest in *Aeneid* 1: Venus's approach to Aeneas in disguise as a huntress (314–20) alludes to the meeting of Aphrodite and Anchises in the *Homeric Hymn to Aphrodite*, which resulted in the birth of Aeneas; in addition, Dido's first appearance to Aeneas, figuratively as Diana (498–502), recalls the scene with Venus, thus adding another ominous suggestion to their union.

27. In the first line, the vocabulary defining their kinship (*puer, matri*) creates a verbal frame around the word for "kisses" (*oscula*). In the second, the description of the wound itself is a "golden line," the formal patterning of two nouns and two adjectives separated by a verb, privileged by Augustan poets, who tended to restrict their use to important moments in a poem. Ovid as controlling poet may suggest that the act described here is less frivolous than it may appear on the surface.

28. Zissos 1999, 97–113, observes that Venus's scheming in contrast with

Jupiter's subordination in Calliope's narrative of the rape of Proserpina in book 5 reverses their roles in the Homeric *Hymn to Demeter*. Cahoon 1996, 51, notes that Venus even embarks on her own epic by echoing the opening of the *Aeneid* with the words "arma manusque meae" (5.365) when she arrogantly tells Cupid of her intention to expand her "empire" by adding Hades to her domain. See also Johnson 1996, 125–49, for an overview of Venus's sense of entitlement in book 5.

29. In book 5, urging Cupid to shoot Pluto with his arrow, Venus instructs him specifically to unite the goddess with her uncle: "iunge deam patruo" (379). The Greeks in their myths did not conceive of the gods as subject to the same social restraints as humans, and in their own society did under certain circumstances permit the marriage of a young woman with her uncle. But Venus's command here might register differently with Ovid's Roman audience. Crook 1967, 100, notes that the Romans prohibited unions among those who were nearer than first cousins; the marriage of an uncle with his brother's daughter was allowed only after the precedent of Claudius and Agrippina.

30. Orpheus apostrophizes Myrrha here, using strong language to convey Cupid's denial: "ipse negat nocuisse tibi sua tela Cupido, / Myrrha, facesque suas a crimine vindicat isto: / stipite te Stygio tumidisque adflavit echnidis / e tribus una soror" ("Cupid himself denies that his weapons harmed you, Myrrha, and defends his torches from such a crime; one of the three sisters scorched you with her Stygian firebrands and vipers" [311–14]). Hardie 2002, 188, expressing skepticism about Cupid's credibility here, refers to the problem of differentiating between the activities of Cupid and Allecto in the *Aeneid*.

31. Coleman 1971, 468, notes that the characterization of Myrrha is indebted to Euripides' Phaedra, especially in the young woman's struggle with her passion and her awareness of its hideous nature. The nurse's role as a go-between in Ovid also recalls Euripides' play. Thomas 1998, 99–105, develops the parallels more fully.

32. For the story of Venus here, there is a keen irony in the fact that Aphrodite in the *Hippolytus* caused Phaedra's passion in the first place to punish the youth for scorning her divinity. Michelini 1987, 288–90, concisely discusses the complex factors motivating Phaedra's behavior in Euripides' tragedy, in particular, the queen's laudable concern for the social values of modesty (*aidôs*) and reputation (*kleos*); her incomplete understanding of the nurse's intentions in approaching Hippolytus; and the young man's own excessively violent reaction to the nurse and his retraction of his oath of silence.

33. One textual detail in particular suggests Venus's concern with luxury: Orpheus characterizes her city of Amathus on Cyprus as "gravidamve Amathunta metallis" ("or Amathus, rich in metals" [531]).

34. The mention of Persephone in the context of Adonis's death may in addition recall an alternate version of the myth involving rivalry between the two goddesses. According to Apollodorus 3.14.4, Aphrodite entrusted Persephone

with a chest containing the beautiful infant Adonis; when the goddess later opened it, she became so enamored of the beautiful boy that she refused to give him up. Zeus then allotted to Adonis a third of the year for himself but gave Aphrodite and Persephone each possession of Adonis for a third of the year. Hyginus, *Poetica astronomica* 2.7, records that Calliope, assigned by Jupiter the duty of judging, determined that Venus and Proserpina should each have Adonis for half the year. Hyginus then connects the story of Adonis with that of Orpheus, for Venus, who wanted the youth for the whole year, stirred up the Thracian women against the bard and thus brought about his death.

35. Detienne 1994, 70–98, discusses the extant sources of the myth of Mintha, including Oppian, *Halieutica* 3.486–97, and Strabo 8.3.14, from a structuralist point of view relating to relationships based on seduction in opposition to the legitimate institution of marriage. He contrasts the myth of Persephone as the mistress of Adonis with her role as the legitimate wife threatened by the powers of her husband's former concubine, citing Oppian's account in which Mintha asserted her superiority over Persephone in beauty and claimed that she would regain Hades' love and drive her rival out of Hades' palace.

36. In Oppian, *Halieutica* 3.486–97, Demeter is enraged at Mintha's boasts and stomps on the nymph; the mint plant then springs up from the ground. Strabo 8.3.14 says that Kore trampled upon this concubine of Hades, who was then metamorphosed into garden mint.

37. Solodow 1988, 206, observes that the words *monimentum, imago,* and *simulamen* are a regular part of the vocabulary of art. *Simulamen,* however, is a rare word, used in place of *simulacrum,* which often denotes artistic images, especially statues of the gods. In the episode of Pygmalion, Orpheus uses *simulacrum* to refer to the ivory statue, which the sculptor again kisses just before it becomes alive ("simulacra suae petit ille puellae" [280]).

38. Detienne 1994, esp. 64–66, 79–81, 99–101, and 108–9, discusses aspects of the Adonia in Athens, such as the sexual freedom associated with it and the planting of quickly withering spices and cereals, in antithesis to the festivals in honor of Demeter, especially the Thesmophoria, promoting serious cultivation of crops: sterility rather than fertility is the distinguishing characteristic of the ritual for Aphrodite's young lover. By contrast, the festival for Aphrodite's victim Hippolytus in Troezen was integrated into a context promoting fertility, through honors paid to the young man by girls entering into marriage. In Euripides' *Hippolytus,* Artemis herself assures her dying protégé that prior to their wedding girls in Troezen would cut their hair in his memory and lament him in hymns (1423–30; cf. Pausanias 2.32.1).

39. Anderson 1972, on 731–35, defends the reading *caelo,* found in most of the manuscripts, over Merkel's emendation *caeno* ("mud") on the basis that the image accurately reflects the yellowish appearance of the Italian sky created by the bright sunlight. Bömer 1980, on 733–34, accepts the conjecture of *caeno* for *caelo;* he dismisses possible aesthetic objections to the image as

irrelevant to Ovid's poem, noting a passage in the very next episode where the poet describes the grotesque reaction of the trees to Orpheus's death (11.46–47). Myers 1994b, 47, defends the reading *caeno* on the grounds that Ovid's simile inverts scientific theory found in Aristotle, *De generatione animalium* 762a–63f, and Diodorus 1.7.3. Tarrant 2004 prints *caeno*. I follow Anderson in keeping with the manuscript tradition but concede that this particular instance is hard to determine. In any case, the potential allusiveness of the word *bulla* remains unaffected.

40. Cowell 1980 [1961], 36, notes that the material for the *bulla* varied: leather or bronze for the lower and gold for the upper classes. For the wealthy, the amulet could thus be described with the epithet *perlucida*, like the *bulla* in this passage.

41. Ovid's version of the rape of Proserpina in book 5 differs in major details from its model, the Homeric *Hymn to Demeter*, where it is by Zeus's will that Persephone is carried off by Hades in the first place (30–32). In Calliope's song, Jupiter tells Ceres that, by the decree of the three Fates, Proserpina may return to Olympus only if she has eaten nothing in Hades. But the young goddess herself picked a pomegranate from an orchard there and, after peeling the rind, ate seven seeds, which Asculaphus observed and reported (512–42). In the Greek poem, when Hermes by Zeus's order arrives to convey Persephone to Olympus, Hades, affirming that he will be a worthy spouse as he sends her off, surreptitiously gives her a pomegranate (359–74). When Demeter tells her daughter that if she has eaten anything while in the underworld, she will spend a third of the year there and two-thirds with the Olympian gods, Persephone admits to consuming the fruit, which she claims was forced on her by Hades (390–413). Hinds 1987a, 87–90, has some insightful remarks on structural and verbal parallels between Persephone's abduction and her actions in the underworld in *Metamorphoses* 5; he compares the account not only in the Homeric *Hymn* but also in *Fasti* 4, where Ovid again connects Persephone's abduction with her consumption of food in Hades.

42. See Foley 1993, 56–57, with bibliography, on the association of pomegranates in ancient Greece with both sexuality and death, owing to their blood-red color and abundant seeds. She points to the importance of eating in the Greek marriage ritual: by consuming food in her husband's home, the bride "accepts her transition to a new life under her husband's authority."

43. Janan 1988, 131–33, comments on the oxymoronic nature of the flower, a memorial that eternalizes by its fragility. In addition, she discusses the linguistic paradox by which the text points beyond the referent-sign (flower, anemone) to the signifier (the name "anemone") and simultaneously erases both. Tissol 1997, 175–76, also points to the paradox here as an example of a "stylistic enactment of metamorphosis."

44. Hardie 2002, 68–70, calls attention to this similarity between the two stories.

45. Noting the pre-Hellenic nature of Hyacinthus, Rose 1991 [1959], 142, states that the festival was clearly held in honor of a vegetation god, thus connecting it to fertility.

46. Ovid thus describes Orpheus's rejection of love for women: "omnemque refugerat Orpheus / femineam Venerem" (79–80). The metonymy of Venus for *amor* calls attention to the bard's lack of respect for the goddess of love herself.

47. Coleman 1971, 469, suggests a similarity between the bard and the protagonist of the inset story in that Hippomenes is brought to ruin because he ignores his debt to Venus for her help.

48. Anderson 1972, ad loc.

49. Coleman 1971, 461–77, finds that by adopting the permanent condition of an *innuba* in an attempt to circumvent the oracle about "losing herself" if she married, Atalanta has shown a lack of piety to Venus. Otis 1970, 192, also considers her punishment justifiable because of her neglect of Venus and her desecration of the sacred precinct. Unlike her counterpart in Apollodorus, Atalanta has not willfully rejected love. She is not a version of Euripides' Hippolytus, whose loathing of sexuality offends Aphrodite, nor is she like Ovid's Propoetides, who denied Venus's divinity (10.238–39). On the sacrilege in the temple, Venus herself acknowledges that she caused it to happen in order to see Hippomenes punished for his lack of gratitude ("nec grates immemor egit / nec mihi tura dedit" [681–82]).

50. Michalopoulos 2001, 42, notes Ovid's etymological gloss in the phrase "avidus videndi" when Orpheus looks back at Eurydice, for the adjective was thought to be derived from "non videre," indicating excessive eagerness (Festus 23).

51. Although Ovid compares the bard to the husband here on the basis of his immobility after losing Eurydice, he may also imply that Orpheus is similar to the arrogant Lethaea. Heath 1996, 364–66, observes that the cause of the metamorphosis in the simile, Lethaea's overweening confidence in her own good looks ("confisa figurae" [69]), may suggest that the bard's own extreme trust in the powers of his art is the real cause of his failure to rescue Eurydice. As he observes, the bard, like Olenos, could have remained with his wife, but, opting to try to succeed through his poetry, he is now rebuffed at the gate of the underworld.

52. Leach 1974, 123, connects the metamorphosis of Pygmalion's statue into a real woman with Orpheus's need for a satisfying love. Rosati 1983, esp. 58–67, discusses narcissistic qualities of Pygmalion through analogies with Narcissus in book 3. Sharrock 1991, 36–49, considers Pygmalion to be a type of elegist in his manner of bestowing gifts, caresses, and kisses on his creation. She suggests that the sculptor in love with his own creation has an analogue in Ovid, who is described by Quintilian as "nimium amator ingenii sui" ["too much a lover of his own talent"]).

53. Orpheus in the underworld, by contrast, assumed the role of advocate

attentive to his audience. Smith 1997, 158, comments on Orpheus's masterful manipulation of his audience by alluding to Pluto and Proserpina's "romance" in Calliope's song in book 5; the bard can "create the role of focalizer" for the king and queen of the underworld but also keep others there interested.

54. For ironic aspects of the narrative of Orpheus's death, see Miller 1990, 140–47, focusing on the double simile that compares Orpheus to day-blind owl and to a stag in the arena: the bard who previously held the stage with his rapt audience of trees and beasts is now symbolically an ineffective predator out of its element in the wild and a pitiful victim in the amphitheater.

55. Knox 1986a, 58, observes that the analogy of a good-looking boy to Cupid is common in Hellenistic epigrams, citing Asclepiades, *Palatine Anthology* 12.75, in which the epigrammist may be using verb *graphô* ("to write" or "to paint") to refer to a painting of the boy.

56. Anderson 1972, on 654–55, notes the similarity, observing that Ovid might have recalled it because Atalanta, like Camilla, is "a virgin competing with men." But Ovid's passage is a very close paraphrase of Vergil's, and it is followed by an echo of another passage in the *Aeneid*. Vergil himself had a model for the analogy of skimming over grainfields or the sea in *Iliad* 20.226–29. But he turned a literal description into an analogy, for Homer's passage depicts the marvelous horses of Erichthonius sired by Boreas running through grainfields without snapping off the tassels and dashing through breaking waves of the seashore.

57. Vergil's powerful warrior-maiden also enters into Ovid's representation of his other Atalanta in the story of Meleager. Just as Camilla with her Volscians concludes the catalogue of Latin troops (7.1055–71), so Atalanta ends the catalogue of hunters (8.317–23); both poets refer to the maiden warrior's simple hairstyle and to the quiver holding the arrows for her bow.

Chapter 5. Ulysses and the Arms of Achilles

1. The contest was recounted in the epic cycle, both in the *Aethiopis* and in the *Little Iliad*. It was also the subject of a tragedy by Aeschylus and, much later in Rome, by Pacuvius and by Accius. See Hopkinson 2000, 10–16, for a convenient summary of the background, with scholarship. Wilkinson 1955, 229–30, commenting on Odysseus as an analogue for ambitious politicians in fifth-century Athens, notes that the sophist Antisthenes in his *Ajax and Odysseus* took the side of the clever rather than the brave Greek.

2. Wilkinson 1955, 230, observes that Ovid's Roman audience would probably have been attuned to Vergil's negative portrayal of the cunning Greek in the *Aeneid* and would thus not have been prepared for a sympathetic approach.

3. The phrase "hortator scelerum" is used by the spirit of the hero Deiphobus while recounting his disgraceful death at the hands of Menelaus with Ulysses as companion (*Aeneid* 6.528–29).

4. The debt to Latro is discussed by Wilkinson 1955, 230, and Kennedy 1972, 406, citing Seneca, *Controversiae* 2.2.8.

5. We know from the elder Seneca that Ovid especially admired the *sententiae* of Latro, whose declamations Augustus, Maecenas, and Agrippa are also said to have attended. Higham 1958, 34–35, commenting on the attendance of the princeps and his close circle at Latro's speeches, suggests that Latro's facility with *sententiae* may have earned him his high reputation.

6. Ajax's exhortation in Ovid's version lacks the punch of Latro's pithy statement "mittamus arma in hostis, et petamus" ("Let us send the arms into the enemy, and let us seek them"). In the phrase from Latro's *Armorum iudicium*, the words for "arms" and "enemy" are neatly caught between the two strong verbs of action. Furthermore, the rhetorical device of *homoeoteleuton*, or rhyming of the verb endings, makes the last word echo the first and thus shapes a tight unit. Ajax, by contrast, uses weaker, passive verb forms and loses the aural effect by retaining the subjunctive form of *mittantur* but following it with the blunt imperative phrase "iubete peti."

7. Earlier in the *Metamorphoses*, the god Apollo describes Ajax himself with the superlative form of the same adjective when he promises to memorialize the dead Hyacinthus: a new flower will be created, with markings that will inscribe the god's cry of grief and in the future will also record the name of a *fortissimus heros* (10.206–8). Through Apollo's prophecy, then, this flower metamorphosis gives Ajax a status secondary to Hyacinthus and reduces the dignity of the warrior by association with an erotic object of desire.

8. Otis 1970, 284–85, stresses the humorous wit which Ulysses employs against Ajax, for instance, by treating his opponent's presumed obtuseness about the meaning of Achilles' shield as an insult to the artist. The hero also utilizes pathos effectively. Twice, Ulysses in plangent tones evokes the owner of the arms: he apostrophizes the dead hero as the true possessor of the arms (130) and recalls his grief in elegiac language at seeing Achilles dead (280). By contrast, Ajax never employs such expressions of pathos for Achilles. Although he movingly apostrophizes Philoctetes, left alone on Lemnos at Ulysses' suggestion (46–49), the abandonment of the hero is a potential source of embarrassment to all the major Greek leaders, not just to Ulysses. Responding to the criticism, the latter reminds the leaders that they agreed with his decision ("factum defendite vestrum, / consensistis enim" [314–15]). He also apostrophizes Philoctetes ("dure Philoctète" [329]) in a clever move by which he assures his audience that although the wounded man curses Agamemnon and the allies as well as Ulysses, he himself will bring Philoctetes back, along with his arrows (329–34).

9. Duc 1994, 126–31, suggests that Ovid has the two speakers represent opposing types of oratory in order to set up a kind of competition between the classical oratory and the Hellenistic: in opposition to Ajax's linear, structured argument is Ulysses' flexible and free-flowing speech, which incorporates numerous digressions and transitional elements within a complex, basically

chronological, framework. He suggests that, with its rather loosely connected threads and circular composition, Ulysses' speech reflects the form of the *Metamorphoses* itself. He points to a specific analogue in Calliope's tale in book 5, which has a similar form of introduction and asymmetric structure. In contrast, he notes that the linear structure of Ajax's speech follows the precepts of the rhetorical manuals and contains a considerable number of *sententiae* in the manner of the *rhetor* Latro, consonant with its relative tightness and brevity.

10. In *Epistulae ex ponto* 2.5.65–70, Ovid uses the terms *nervi* and *nitor* to distinguish the two spheres, which he himself skillfully combines in his own pleas for recall to Rome. Discussing the passage, an address to a teacher of rhetoric named Salanus, Kennedy 1972, 418–19, observes that the "muscle" of rhetoric would likely include "'proper' diction, pointed *sententiae*, ethos, pathos, argumentation" while the "brilliance" of poetry would result especially from poetic diction, rhythmic units, poetic figures, and amplification.

11. Otis 1970, 284–85, finds that Ulysses' intelligence and resourcefulness are ultimately close to Ovid's own, especially as they share an ironic distance from the traditional heroic code. He observes that the poet of the *Metamorphoses* rejects the "traditional respect for brawn," citing Ovid's deflation of the battle of the Lapiths and Centaurs. Otis, however, does not elaborate on the similarities between the clever Greek and the Roman poet.

12. Hopkinson 2000, on 22, points out that such patronymic phrases often occur at the end of the hexameter in epic.

13. Ovid, however, has already undercut Ajax's position here. In referring to the first exploit, he focused on Hercules and only mentioned the fact that Telamon was rewarded with Hesione as a prize for his efforts (11.216–17). More significantly, Telamon is shown to be especially inept in the Calydonian boar hunt, during which, in his eagerness to hit the boar, he trips on a root and falls flat on his face just before the heroine Atalanta makes a successful shot (8.378–83).

14. The post-Homeric tradition of Sisyphus as the father of Odysseus is preserved by Hyginus, *Fabulae* 201. Sisyphus foiled Autolycus's attempt to steal his cattle by branding the undersides of their hooves; when Sisyphus remained with Autolycus, he slept with his host's daughter Anticleia shortly before her marriage to Laertes. Odysseus was said to have been the product of that illicit union.

15. Hopkinson 2000, on 33, considers *inseris* (or *inserit*) here to be from the verb "to graft on," citing the *Oxford Latin Dictionary*, s.v. 2b, for the related adjective form *insitivus* "applied to children introduced into a family tree under false pretences." Lewis and Short cite the example of *inserit* here (s.v. *insero* [2], B.II): "to bring into, introduce, mix, mingle with," noting a similarly pejorative use of the word in Tacitus with the direct object "ignobilitatem suam magnis nominibus" (*Annales* 6.2).

16. Citing Ennius (quoted by Varro, *De lingua Latina*. 5.65) and Cicero, *De natura deorum* 2.64, Michalopoulos 2001, 102–4, discusses Ovid's use of the

etymology of Jupiter from the verb *iuvo* ("to help") and the noun *pater;* he contrasts Ulysses' clever play with Ajax's reference to Jupiter, in which the god's name occurs only once (28), far removed from the word *pater* (25) so as to preclude any reinforcement of the relationship through etymology.

17. Gross 2000, 57, in a brief discussion of Ulysses as a speaker in the contest over the arms, also notes that the hero avoids mentioning Autolycus because of the "dubious connotations" associated with that grandparent. Gross takes a quite different position from mine about Ovid's Ulysses; contrasting him with the Homeric Odysseus, he finds his rhetorical skill undermined by his prolixity and by his inclusion of inappropriate material, such as his discovery of Achilles on Scyros and his participation in the sacrifice of Iphigenia.

18. See Peradotto 1990, 114–16, for insightful remarks on the significance of the word *polutropos* in the prologue of the *Odyssey*, where it describes the hero well before his name is mentioned and substitutes for the anticipated proper name. Peradotto comments on the instability and ambiguity of this epithet, whose range of meanings, both active and passive, includes "infinitely clever," "versatile," "shifty," "of many guises/disguises," and "of changeable/ exchangeable character." It thus serves a function much the opposite of a name by connoting mutability, the transgression of boundaries, and the adoption of multiple roles.

19. Pucci 1987, 23–25, reveals some specific textual connections between Homer's Odysseus and Hermes in the god's two appearances in the *Odyssey*. In book 10, Circe suggests that Odysseus is another Hermes when she describes him at his arrival as *polutropos* (10.330); besides the hero, the epithet is applied only to Hermes in the *Odyssey*. In book 5, after Hermes is sent by Zeus to have Calypso release the hero, the nymph seats Odysseus in the chair which Hermes has just vacated and describes him as *theios,* "godlike" (5.195–96). Pucci also points out other ways by which Homer links the hero and the messenger god; in the Circe episode, for example, Hermes deceptively warns the goddess about the failure of her magic against the hero but then supplies Odysseus with the *môlu* to ward off her potential danger.

20. Warmington 1979 [1935], 24, cites this line from Gellius 18.9.5, who commented on the form *insece* in place of *inseque.* Hinds 1998, 61–62, observes that Livius's use of *versutus* also cleverly suggests the "turn" from Greek to Latin since the verb *verto* regularly means "to translate" in archaic Latin.

21. Much more so than his predecessors in epic, Ovid stresses the verbal cunning of the messenger god as he depicts him operating largely outside of the ethical sphere. Mercury's function in the *Metamorphoses* as the intermediary of the king of the gods on earth lacks the sharply ideological underpinning of his role in the *Aeneid.* On the divine messenger in Vergil, see Feeney 1998, 105–27.

22. Enchanting Argus with the dulcet tones of the panpipes, he arouses Argus's interest and then responds to his question about the origin of the instrument ("quaerit quoque . . . qua sit ratione reperta" [687–88]). Mercury is

thus able to take a racy erotic story and turn it into a sleep-inducing drug. Konstan 1991, 18–19, supplies some perceptive remarks about the point at which Argus falls asleep, just when Pan is about to make his case to Syrinx. Rightly emphasizing the reader's interest in the story in contrast to the boredom experienced by the fictional audience, who falls asleep in the middle of the tale, Konstan categorizes Argus as a "detached, rather than involved, narratee." On the status of the story of Syrinx as narrative, see Nagle 1988c, 33–34.

23. Because Argus falls asleep, the god breaks off his song just as Pan is about to address Syrinx with words of seduction ("talia verba refert" [700]). Ovid himself picks up the story in a virtually seamless flow with Mercury's narrative (700–712). Although recounting the remainder of the story in indirect discourse, he concludes by quoting Pan's expression of joy that his new instrument will provide a form of union with the object of his desire ("'hoc mihi conloquium tecum' dixisse 'manebit'" [710]).

24. In an amusing twist, he has made Mercury the singer of a tale that attributes the invention of the pipes to Pan instead of himself. Like Mercury, Ovid is a devious narrator: here, he manages to "trick" even this most savvy divinity. Myers 1994b, 77–78, elaborates on Bömer's observation that Ovid makes Mercury the narrator of the aetiological tale of the *syrinx* in order to "correct" the tradition, mentioned in the Homeric *Hymn to Hermes* (511–12) and in Euphorion (frag. 182 Gröningen), that Mercury rather than Pan was the inventor of the pipes.

25. Gaunt 1971, 191–98, discusses the problem of the unity of the night raid in *Iliad* 10, suggesting that the story of a spying expedition and the tale of Rhesus's murder may have had the character of Dolon in common.

26. Hopkinson 2000, on 251–52, observes that a Roman general celebrating a triumph would ride in a chariot pulled by a team of white horses, like those of Rhesus. He assumes, however, that the hero did ride in the elaborate chariot of his victim, which also contained the dead man's precious armor.

27. Leaf 1900, on 513, commenting on *hippôn*, notes that Homer elsewhere uses that word for "chariot" as well as for "horses." But he concludes that the passage overall suggests that Odysseus and Diomedes "actually ride on the horses bare-backed." He points out that otherwise one must assume that Diomedes reacts to Athena's warning by picking up the chariot and, along with Odysseus, harnessing the horses, which the text does not indicate. He adds that the phrase "lashes with the bow" indicates that the whip has been left behind in the chariot. Hainsworth 1993 is silent about the problem of whether Odysseus and Diomedes ride on the horses or in the chariot.

28. Smith 1997, 43–53, comments on the self-consciousness of Ulysses in line 258 toward Vergil as well as Homer. He finds that Ovid's hero "corrects" the *Aeneid*, which assigns the line to Turnus's exploits against the Trojans (9.767); by adding a translation of two lines from *Iliad* 5 (677–78), Ulysses here restores these acts of martial prowess to the Homeric hero. Although I do not disagree with

Smith's conclusions in general, I find his view that Ovid thereby returns Ulysses "to his proper place in the heroic tradition" does not do justice to the complexity of the poet's manipulation of Homer's texts in the contest over the arms.

29. See Pucci 1987, 145–47, on *Iliad* 11.473–88, a simile in which Odysseus is compared to a deer eaten by a lion, which represents Aias; the deer has in fact been attacked by several predators: the hunter who shoots it and a pack of jackals. The simile thus implies that Aias figuratively devours Odysseus by replacing him on the battlefield, from which he virtually disappears for the rest of the poem.

30. See Hopkinson 2000, on 255–62, for the ironic interpretation that it is difficult to conceive of warriors less famous than those mentioned just before.

31. Hopkinson 2000, on 260, suggests that Ovid may have transferred the description of another Ennomus in Homer; though a seer, that man "was not able to keep off dark fate by means of his omens, but he was killed by Achilles" (*Iliad* 2.859–60, Hopkinson's translation). Ovid may thus suggest that his Ennomus also had foreknowledge of his own death.

32. See Hopkinson 2000, on 262. Citing Petronius 1.1, Valerius Maximus 7.7.1, and Livy 6.20.8, he observes on 262–65 that displaying one's scars from battle was a ploy used in Roman courts to win over the jury.

33. Ajax insists, for instance, that the Greeks have seen his deeds: "vidistis enim" (14).

34. Leigh 1995, 195–216, discusses numerous instances of Romans publicizing their battle scars to gain an advantage in running for public office and cites cases of ambitious *novi homines*, such as Cato the Elder and Marius, and more radical types, such as L. Sicinius Dentatus, boasting of their wounds as signs of their success in public life that men of high status fail to respect. The scar for Romans thus served as a "mark of authentication," which seems to have been especially exploited in the late republic.

35. See Michalopoulos 2001, 140, citing Isidore, *De differentiis verborum* 2.64, on the origin of the word for chest (*pectus*) from the root for vision (the noun *aspectus*, related to the verb *aspicio*): "pectus hominis ab aspectu vocatum."

36. Hopkinson 2000, on 265, also attributing mental as well as physical implications to Ulysses' words here, cites the hero's later contrast between *pectora* and *manus* (369).

37. Of course, the lack of any mention of scars from wounds in the *Odyssey* may reflect the difference in the ethos of that poem and in the role of Odysseus as the central hero. Homer, furthermore, may have eliminated references to other wounds of the hero so as to privilege the thigh wound that the boar inflicted on the young Odysseus in his first hunt, by which his old nurse Eurykleia recognizes him in book 19.

38. Bömer 1987, on 266, cites Pindar, *Isthmian* 6.45–46, and Aeschylus, frag. 292b Mette, as the earliest extant references to the tradition of Ajax's invulnerability, which was presumably unknown to Homer.

39. See, for example, Schein 1984, 68, on the importance of Homeric heroes winning *kleos* on the battlefield through "the brilliance and efficiency with which they kill."

40. See Dimock 1962, 106–21, on the twofold meaning of Odysseus's name as one who both receives and inflicts pain, emblematized by the scar. More recent studies have emphasized a greater degree of complexity, a destabilizing significance, in Odysseus's scar, which Ovid himself may have perceived. Peradotto 1990, esp. 156–58, discusses the difference between Eurykleia's acceptance of the scar as an "unequivocal sign" (23.77) and Penelope's resistance to such a superficial and untrustworthy physical token as inferior to "unapparent signs" (23.110). The term "unequivocal sign," as earlier used in Tiresias's prophecy of the journey in which Odysseus will have to plant an oar that will be mistaken for a winnowing fan, reflects "the sign's unstable relation with what it signifies." Pucci 1987, esp. 88–89, discusses the narrative function of the scar in revealing the relation of Odysseus to Autolycus and, figuratively, to Hermes. Pucci notes the hero's odd forgetfulness of the scar when his old nurse bathes him and suggests an inevitable loss incurred by disguise.

41. On Ovid's clever reworking of Homeric material in books 12 and 13, see Ellsworth 1980, 23–29, stressing Ovid's rejection of the senseless destruction of warfare.

42. As a suitor for Helen, Odysseus had sworn to support the man who became her husband if she were ever carried off. Achilles, by contrast, had not been one of her suitors and therefore was under no personal obligation to aid in retrieving her from Paris. That contrast goes back to the earliest tradition on the competition for Helen, recorded in Hesiod's *Catalogue of Women*, which mentions Odysseus's suit (21–27) but states that Achilles was still a child cared for by Chiron (100–105).

43. I owe the observation of wordplay between *maturior* and *mater* to Dr. Andreas Michalopoulos. Maltby 1991, s.v. *maturus*, cites Festus 125, which connects *mater matuta* and *maturus:* "mana bona dicitur, unde et mater matuta et poma matura." For other similar punning language by which Ulysses suggestively connects himself to Achilles, see Pavlock 2003, 147–49.

44. See Simmons 1920 [1899] on 285.

45. Proclus in *Chrestomathy* ii states that in the *Aethiopis* Ajax carried Achilles' body to the ships while Ulysses fended off the assault of the Trojans.

46. In line 294, I diverge from Anderson's text: instead of "diversasque urbes," I read "diversosque orbes," which Tarrant 2004 prints, though bracketing both 294–95. On the variant readings and the substantive issues involved, see note 52 below.

47. Michalopoulos 2001, 57, noting on *clipeus* that the custom of engraving on ancient shields was so common that it influenced etymological theorizing on the word itself, cites Pliny, *Naturalis historia* 35.13, on the connection.

48. Michalopoulos 2001, 57, points out that Ulysses places the words "clipei caelamina" together right after the caesura of the line.

49. Hardie 1985, 15–17, briefly discusses Ajax's and Ulysses' references to the shield in the *Metamorphoses* in the context of the Hellenistic allegorical inter-pretations of Homer's shield ekphrasis by Eustathius and Crates, emphasizing cosmology, especially the four elements, the tripartite division of the universe, the heavenly bodies, the fixed stars, and the zodiac.

50. See Varro, *De lingua Latina*, on this reverse, but acceptable, etymology: "non male, quod (im)positor multo potius (caelare) a caelo quam caelum a caelando."

51. The power of Ulysses' etymological play with *caelo* and *caelum* may be reinforced in light of similar punning at the beginning of book 2, where Ovid as narrator describes the doors of the palace of the Sun engraved (*caelarat* [6]) with elements of the universe, including the sky (*caelumque* [7]). The poet alludes to the etymology of *caelum* from *caelo* but adds a new twist. Michalopoulos 2001, 45, observes that "the sky and the stars themselves are now merely part of a larger engraving." Here, in book 13, Ovid allows Ulysses to have the last word about this linguistic issue.

52. Although most editors print "diversas urbes," which of course would refer to the two cities on the Iliadic shield, one in peace and the other at war (*Iliad* 18.490–540), objections to this reading were raised long ago. Simmons 1920 [1899], 294, cites the following readings of his predecessors: "diversas ursas" (the conjecture of Schenkl, followed by Zingerle) and "diversos orbes" (interpreted by Korn as a reference to the polar circles and by Ehwald as a refer-ence to the sun and the moon, both of which occur at the beginning of Homer's shield ekphrasis).

53. On Eudoxus, see Dicks 1970, 155–60, where the polar theories are briefly discussed.

54. Hopkinson 2000, on 368–69, suggests that by privileging the power of the mind over that of the hand and by affirming it as the seat of human energy, Ovid may have Ulysses allude to physiological theories about the mind as ex-plained by Lucretius in *De rerum natura* 3.136–60. That view would make sense as Ulysses' theoretical culmination to his more concrete, even poetic, line of ar-gumentation immediately preceding in which he contrasts himself with Ajax through the distinction between *animus* and *corpus* and through comparisons to captain versus oarsman and general versus soldier (365–68).

55. Ovid's own interest in scientific speculation as an underpinning for his broader vision of metamorphosis emerges most prominently in the cosmogony passage at the very beginning of book 1. See in general Myers 1994b, 27–60. Wheeler 1995, 95–121, discusses Ovid's literary allusiveness to earlier poetry with cosmological implications, such as to the song of Orpheus in Apollonius's *Argonautica* and to Vergil's song of Iopas in *Aeneid* 1, which are indebted to

Homer's shield ekphrasis. He notes references to Homer's shield ekphrasis, some mediated through Lucretius and Vergil, in Ovid's account of the creation, including the sun and the "waxing" moon, though not the other heavenly bodies, and the river Ocean. The poet implies that the creation is a work of art and that he is ultimately a legitimate successor in epic to Homer and Hesiod.

56. His competitor, by contrast, reflects a far more rigid view of language. For instance, Ajax perceives Ulysses' fleeing from the battle without stopping to help Nestor as a willful betrayal rather than as a result of ignorance of the situation (63–69) because he adopts one specific interpretation of the verb used by Homer in the relevant passage in *Iliad* 8 (66–129). See Hopkinson 2000, on 63–81, for a discussion of the ambiguous language in the scene in which Nestor is pressed by Hector and would have been killed if Diomedes had not rescued the old man. Although his comrade tried unsuccessfully to enlist Odysseus's help, it is unclear in particular whether Odysseus in flight did not "listen" to Diomedes or simply did not "hear" him.

57. On Ovid's use of Homer's Trojan War material, see Ellsworth 1980 and O'Bryhim 1988. We have already seen in chapter 3 how extensively the poet undermines traditional heroism in the Meleager episode.

Bibliography

Adams, J. N. 1982. *The Latin Sexual Vocabulary*. Baltimore: Johns Hopkins University Press.

Ahl, Frederick. 1985. *Soundplay and Wordplay in Ovid and Other Classical Poets*. Ithaca: Cornell University Press.

Allen, Peter L. 1992. *The Art of Love: Amatory Fiction from Ovid to the* Romance of the Rose. Philadelphia: University of Pennsylvania Press.

Anderson, William S., ed. 1972. *Ovid's* Metamorphoses. Bks. 6-10. Norman: University of Oklahoma Press.

———, ed. 1977. *P. Ovidii Nasonis:* Metamorphoses. Leipzig: Teubner.

———. 1982. "The Orpheus of Virgil and Ovid: *Flebile Nescio Quid.*" In *Orpheus: The Metamorphoses of a Myth*, ed. John Warden, 25-50. Toronto: University of Toronto Press.

———. 1989. "The Artist's Limits in Ovid: Orpheus, Pygmalion, and Daedalus." *Syllecta Classica* 1: 1-11.

———, ed. 1997. *Ovid's* Metamorphoses. Bks. 1-5. Norman: University of Oklahoma Press.

Bakhtin, M. M. 1981. *The Dialogic Imagination: Four Essays*. Ed. Michael Holquist. Trans. Caryl Emerson and Michael Holquist. Austin: University of Texas Press.

Baldo, Gianluigi, Lucio Cristante, and Emilio Pianezzola, eds. 1991. *Ovidio: L'Arte di amare*. Milan: Mondadori.

Barchiesi, Alessandro. 1993. "Future Reflexive: Two Modes of Allusion and Ovid's *Heroides*." *Harvard Studies in Classical Philology* 95: 333-65.

———. 2001. *Speaking Volumes: Narrative and Intertext in Ovid and Other Latin Poets*. Ed. and trans. Matt Fox and Simone Marchiesi. London: Duckworth.

———. 2002. "Narrative Technique and Narratology in the *Metamorphoses*." In *The Cambridge Companion to Ovid*, ed. Philip Hardie, 180-99. Cambridge: Cambridge University Press.

Barkan, Leonard. 1986. *The Gods Made Flesh: Metamorphosis and the Pursuit of Paganism in the Renaissance*. New Haven: Yale University Press.

Barrett, W. S., ed. 1964. *Euripides:* Hippolytos. Oxford: Clarendon Press.

Basto, Ronald. 1982. "Horace's Propempticon to Vergil: A Re-examination." *Vergilius* 28: 30–43.

Binroth-Bank, Christine. 1997. "Der Monolog der Medea in Ovids *Metamorphosen*." *Der Altsprachliche Unterricht* 40 (4–5): 17–35.

Biow, Douglas. 1996. *Mirabile Dictu: Representations of the Marvelous in Medieval and Renaissance Epic*. Ann Arbor: University of Michigan Press.

Boedeker, Deborah. 1997. "Becoming Medea: Assimilation in Euripides." In *Medea: Essays on Medea in Myth, Literature, Philosophy, and Art*, ed. James J. Clauss and Sarah Iles Johnston, 127–48. Princeton: Princeton University Press.

Bömer, Franz, ed. 1969. *P. Ovidius Naso:* Metamorphosen. Bks. 1–3. Heidelberg: Carl Winter.

———, ed. 1977. *P. Ovidius Naso:* Metamorphosen. Bks. 6–7. Heidelberg: Carl Winter.

———, ed. 1980. *P. Ovidius Naso:* Metamorphosen. Bks. 10–11. Heidelberg: Carl Winter.

———, ed. 1987. *P. Ovidius Naso:* Metamorphosen. Bks. 12–13. Heidelberg: Carl Winter.

Bonner, Stanley F. 1977. *Education in Ancient Rome from the Elder Cato to the Younger Pliny*. Berkeley: University of California Press.

Boyd, Barbara Weiden. 1997. *Ovid's Literary Loves: Influence and Innovation in the Amores*. Ann Arbor: University of Michigan Press.

Brenkman, John. 1976. "Narcissus in the Text." *Georgia Review* 30 (2): 293–327.

Bushnell, Rebecca W. 1988. *Prophesying Tragedy: Sign and Voice in Sophocles' Theban Plays*. Ithaca: Cornell University Press.

Butler, H. E., and E. A. Barber, eds. 1933. *The Elegies of Propertius*. Oxford: Clarendon Press.

Cahoon, Leslie. 1984. "The Parrot and the Poet: The Function of Ovid's Funeral Elegies." *Classical Journal* 80 (1): 27–35.

———. 1996. "Calliope's Song: Shifting Narrators in Ovid, *Metamorphoses* 5." *Helios* 23 (1): 43–66.

Cairns, Francis. 1969. "Propertius i.18 and Callimachus, *Acontius and Cydippe*." *Classical Review* n.s. 19 (2): 131–34.

———. 2004. "Varius and Vergil: Two Pupils of Philodemus in Propertius 2.34?" In *Vergil, Philodemus, and the Augustans*, ed. David Armstrong, Jeffrey Fish, Patricia A. Johnston, and Marilyn Skinner, 299–321. Austin: University of Texas Press.

Cameron, Alan. 1995. *Callimachus and His Critics*. Princeton: Princeton University Press.

Camps, W. A., ed. 1985. *Propertius: Elegies*. Bk. 2. Bristol: Bristol Classical Press.

Clare, R. J. 2002. *The Path of the Argo*. Cambridge: Cambridge University Press.

Clark, Raymond J. 2004. "Horace on Vergil's Sea-crossing in *Ode* 1.3." *Vergilius* 50: 4–34.

Cohon, Robert. 1991. "Vergil and Pheidias: The Shield of Aeneas and of Athena Parthenos." *Vergilius* 37: 22–30.

Coleman, Robert. 1971. "Structure and Intention in the *Metamorphoses*." *Classical Quarterly* n.s. 21 (2): 461–77.

Conte, Gian Biagio. 1986. *The Rhetoric of Imitation: Genre and Poetic Memory in Vergil and Other Latin Poets*. Trans. Charles Segal. Ithaca: Cornell University Press.

Copley, F. O. 1947. "*Servitium Amoris* in the Roman Elegists." *Transactions and Proceedings of the American Philological Association* 78: 285–300.

Cowell, F. R. 1980 [1961]. *Life in Ancient Rome*. New York: Putnam.

Crabbe, Anna. 1981. "Structure and Content in Ovid's *Metamorphoses*." In *Aufstieg und Niedergang der Römische Welt* 2.31.4: 2274–327.

Crook, J. A. 1967. *Law and Life in Rome, 90 B.C. to A.D. 212*. Ithaca: Cornell University Press.

Dällenbach, Lucien. 1989. *The Mirror in the Text*. Trans. J. Whiteley with Emma Hughes. Chicago: University of Chicago Press.

Davies, Malcolm. 2001 [1989]. *The Greek Epic Cycle*. London: Duckworth.

Davis, Gregson. 1978. "Ovid's *Metamorphoses* 3.442 ff. and the Prologue to Menander's *Misoumenos*." *Phoenix* 32 (4): 339–42.

———. 1983. *The Death of Procris: Amor and the Hunt in Ovid's Metamorphoses*. Rome: Ateneo.

Davis, John T. 1989. *Fictus Adulter: Poet as Actor in the Amores*. Amsterdam: Gieben.

Davisson, Mary H. T. 1997. "The Observers of Daedalus and Icarus in Ovid." *Classical World* 90 (4): 263–78.

DeBrohun, Jeri B. 2003. *Roman Propertius and the Reinvention of Elegy*. Ann Arbor: University of Michigan Press.

Detienne, Marcel. 1979. *Dionysus Slain*. Trans. Mireille Muellner and Leonard Muellner. Baltimore: Johns Hopkins University Press.

———. 1994. *The Gardens of Adonis: Spices in Greek Mythology*. Trans. Janet Lloyd. Princeton: Princeton University Press.

Dicks, D. R. 1970. *Early Greek Astronomy to Aristotle*. London: Thames and Hudson.

Dimock, George. 1962. "The Name of Odysseus." In *Homer: A Collection of Critical Essays*, ed. George Steiner and Robert Fagles, 106–21. Englewood Cliffs, N. J.: Prentice Hall.

Donohue, Harold. 1993. *The Song of the Swan: Lucretius and the Influence of Callimachus*. Lanham, Md.: University Press of America.

Doob, Penelope R. 1990. *The Idea of the Labyrinth from Classical Antiquity through the Middle Ages*. Ithaca: Cornell University Press.

Duc, Thierry. 1994. "'Postulat, et capiat, quae non intellegit, arma' (Ov., *Met.* XIII, 295): Un discours programmatique?" *Latomus* 53 (1): 126–31.

Due, Otto Steen. 1974. *Changing Forms: Studies in the* Metamorphoses *of Ovid*. Copenhagen: Gyldendal.

Duff, J. D. 1966 [1898]. *D. Iunii Iuvenalis: Saturae*. Bk. 14. Cambridge: Cambridge University Press.

Ellsworth, James D. 1980. "Ovid's *Iliad* (*Metamorphoses* 12.1–13.622)." *Prudentia* 12 (1): 23–29.

Farrell, Joseph. 1992. "Dialogue of Genres in Ovid's 'Lovesong of Polyphemus' (*Metamorphoses* 13.719–897)." *American Journal of Philology* 113 (2): 235–68.

Fedeli, Paolo, ed. 2005. *Properzio: Elegie*. Bk. 2. Cambridge, England: Francis Cairns.

Feeney, Denis. 1991. *The Gods in Epic: Poets and Critics of the Classical Tradition*. Oxford: Oxford University Press.

———. 1998. "Leaving Dido: The Appearance(s) of Mercury and the Motivations of Aeneas." In *A Woman Scorn'd: Responses to the Dido Myth*, ed. Michael Burden, 105–27. London: Faber and Faber.

Feldherr, Andrew. 1997. "Metamorphosis and Sacrifice in Ovid's Theban Narrative." *Materiali e Discussioni per l'Analisi dei Testi Classici* 38 (1): 25–55.

Fitzgerald, William. 1984. "Aeneas, Daedalus, and the Labyrinth." *Arethusa* 17 (1): 51–65.

———. 1995. *Catullan Provocations: Lyric Poetry and the Drama of Position*. Berkeley: University of California Press.

Foley, Helene P., ed. 1993. *The Homeric Hymn to Demeter: Translation, Commentary, and Interpretive Essays*. Princeton: Princeton University Press.

Forbes Irving, P. C. M. 1992 [1990]. *Metamorphosis in Greek Myths*. Oxford: Clarendon Press.

Fränkel, Hermann. 1969 [1945]. *Ovid: A Poet between Two Worlds*. Berkeley: University of California Press.

Frischer, Bernard. 1984. "Horace and the Monuments: A New Interpretation of the Archytas *Ode*." *Harvard Studies in Classical Philology* 88: 71–102.

Galinsky, G. Karl. 1972. "Hercules *Ovidianus* (*Metamorphoses* 9, 1–272)." *Wiener Studien* n.s. 6: 93–116.

———. 1975. *Ovid's* Metamorphoses: *An Introduction to the Basic Aspects*. Berkeley: University of California Press.

Gamel, Mary-Kay. 1984. "Baucis and Philemon: Paradigm or Paradox?" *Helios* 11 (2): 117–31.

Gaunt, D. M. 1971. "The Change of Plan in the *Doloneia*." *Greece and Rome*, 2nd ser., 18 (2): 191–98.

Gentilcore, Roxanne. 1995. "The Landscape of Desire: The Tale of Pomona and Vertumnus in Ovid's *Metamorphoses*." *Phoenix* 49 (2): 110–20.

Gildenhard, Ingo, and Andrew Zissos. 2000. "Ovid's Narcissus (*Met.* 3.339–510): Echoes of Oedipus." *American Journal of Philology* 121 (1): 129–47.

Gildersleeve, Basil L., ed. 1885. *Pindar: Olympian and Pythian Odes.* New York: Harper.

Gross, Nicolas P. 2000. "Allusion and Rhetorical Wit in Ovid, *Metamorphoses* 13." *Scholia* n.s. 9: 54–65.

Hainsworth, Bryan. 1993. *The Iliad: A Commentary.* Cambridge: Cambridge University Press.

Hardie, Philip. 1985. "*Imago Mundi:* Cosmological and Ideological Aspects of the Shield of Achilles." *Journal of Hellenic Studies* 105: 11–31.

———. 1988. "Lucretius and the Delusions of Narcissus." *Materiali e Discussioni per l'Analisi dei Testi Classici* 20–21: 71–89.

———. 1990. "Ovid's Theban History: The First 'Anti-*Aeneid*'?" *Classical Quarterly* n.s. 40 (1): 224–35.

———. 1995. "The Speech of Pythagoras in Ovid, *Metamorphoses* 15: Empedoclean Epos." *Classical Quarterly* n.s. 45 (1): 204–14.

———. 1997. "Questions of Authority: The Invention of Tradition in Ovid *Metamorphoses* 15." In *The Roman Cultural Revolution,* ed. Thomas Habinek and Alessandro Schiesaro, 182–98. Cambridge: Cambridge University Press.

———. 2002. *Ovid's Poetics of Illusion.* Cambridge: Cambridge University Press.

Hardy, Clara Shaw. 1995. "Ecphrasis and the Male Narrator in Ovid's Arachne." *Helios* 22 (2): 140–48.

Harries, Byron. 1990. "The Spinner and the Poet: Arachne in Ovid's *Metamorphoses.*" *Proceedings of the Cambridge Philological Society* n.s. 36: 64–82.

Harrison, Stephen. 2002. "Ovid and Genre: Evolutions of an Elegist." In *The Cambridge Companion to Ovid,* ed. Philip Hardie, 79–94. Cambridge: Cambridge University Press.

Haupt, Moriz, Rudolf Ehwald, and Michael Von Albrecht, eds. 1966. *P. Ovidius Naso:* Metamorphosen. Bks. 1–7. Zurich: Weidmann.

Heath, John. 1996. "The *Stupor* of Orpheus: Ovid's *Metamorphoses* 10.64-71." *Classical Journal* 91 (4): 353–70.

Heinze, Richard. 1919. *Ovids elegische Erzählung.* Leipzig: Teubner.

Henderson, A. A. R., ed. 1999 [1981]. *Ovid:* Metamorphoses. Bk. 3. London: Bristol Classical Press.

Higham, T. F. 1958. "Ovid and Rhetoric." In *Ovidiana: Recherches sur Ovide,* ed. N. I. Herescu, 32–48. Paris: Les Belles Lettres.

Hill, D. E., ed. 1992a. *Ovid:* Metamorphoses. Bks. 5–8. Warminster: Aris and Phillips.

———. 1992b. "From Orpheus to Ass's Ears: Ovid, *Metamorphoses* 10.1-11.193." In *Author and Audience in Latin Literature,* ed. Tony Woodman and Jonathan Powell, 124–37. Cambridge: Cambridge University Press.

Hinds, Stephen. 1987a. *The Metamorphosis of Persephone: Ovid and the Self-conscious Muse.* Cambridge: Cambridge University Press.

——. 1987b. "Generalizing about Ovid." *Ramus* 16 (1): 4–31.

——. 1993. "Medea in Ovid: Scenes from the Life of an Intertextual Heroine." *Materiali e Discussioni per l'Analisi dei Testi Classici* 30: 9–47.

——. 1998. *Allusion and Intertext: The Dynamics of Appropriation in Roman Poetry*. Cambridge: Cambridge University Press.

Hoefmans, Marjorie. 1994. "Myth into Reality: The Metamorphosis of Daedalus and Icarus (Ovid, *Metamorphoses*, VIII, 183–235)." *L'Antiquité Classique* 63: 137–60.

Hofmann, Heinz. 1986. "Ovid's *Metamorphoses: Carmen Perpetuum, Carmen Deductum*." In *Papers of the Liverpool Latin Seminar*, vol. 5, ed. Francis Cairns, 223–41. Leeds: Francis Cairns.

Hollis, A. S., ed. 1983 [1970]. *Ovid's* Metamorphoses. Bk. VIII. Oxford: Clarendon Press.

——, ed. 1990. *Callimachus:* Hecale. Oxford: Clarendon Press.

Holzberg, Niklas. 1998. "*Ter Quinque Volumina* as *Carmen Perpetuum:* The Division into Books in Ovid's *Metamorphoses*." *Materiali e Discussioni per l'Analisi dei Testi Classici* 40 (1): 77–98.

——. 2001. *Die römische Liebeselegie: Eine Einführung*. Darmstadt: Wissenschaftliche Buchgesselschaft.

——. 2002. *Ovid the Poet and His Work*. Trans. T. R. Goshgarian. Ithaca: Cornell University Press.

Hopkinson, Neil, ed. 2000. *Ovid:* Metamorphoses. Bk. 13. Cambridge: Cambridge University Press.

Horsfall, Nicholas. 1979. "Epic and Burlesque in Ovid, *Met.* viii.260 ff." *Classical Journal* 74 (4): 319–32.

Hubbard, Margaret. 1974. *Propertius*. London: Duckworth.

Hunter, Richard, ed. 1989. *Apollonius of Rhodes:* Argonautica. Bk. 3. Cambridge: Cambridge University Press.

——, ed. 1999. *Theocritus: A Selection*. Cambridge: Cambridge University Press.

Janan, Micaela. 1988. "The Book of Good Love? Design versus Desire in *Metamorphoses* 10." *Ramus* 17 (2): 110–37.

——. 1991. "The Labyrinth and the Mirror: Incest and Influence in *Metamorphoses* 9." *Arethusa* 24 (2): 239–56.

——. 1994. "'There beneath the Roman ruins where the purple flowers grow': Ovid's Minyeides and the Feminine Imagination." *American Journal of Philology* 115: 427–48.

Johnson, Patricia J. 1996. "Constructions of Venus in Ovid's *Metamorphoses* V." *Arethusa* 29 (1): 125–49.

Keith, Alison. 1992. *The Play of Fictions: Studies in Ovid's* Metamorphoses. Ann Arbor: University of Michigan Press.

Kennedy, Duncan F. 1993. *The Arts of Love: Five Studies in the Discourse of Roman Love Elegy*. Cambridge: Cambridge University Press.

Kennedy, George. 1972. *The Art of Persuasion in the Roman World, 300 B.C. to A.D. 300*. Princeton: Princeton University Press.

Kenney, E. J. 1986. Introduction. *Ovid: Metamorphoses*. Trans. A. D. Melville. Oxford: Oxford University Press.

———. 2002. "Ovid's Language and Style." In *Brill's Companion to Ovid*, ed. Barbara Weiden Boyd, 27–89. Leiden: Brill.

Kershaw, Allan. 1980. "Emendation and Usage: Two Readings of Propertius." *Classical Philology* 75 (1): 71–72.

Kidd, D. A. 1977. "Virgil's Voyage." *Prudentia* 9 (2): 91–103.

Knoespel, Kenneth. 1985. *Narcissus and the Invention of Personal History*. New York: Garland.

Knox, Peter E. 1986a. *Ovid's* Metamorphoses *and the Traditions of Augustan Poetry*. Cambridge: Cambridge University Press.

———. 1986b. "Ovid's Medea and the Authenticity of *Heroides* 12." *Harvard Studies in Classical Philology* 90: 207–23.

Konstan, David. 1991. "The Death of Argus, or What Stories Do: Audience Response in Ancient Fiction and Theory." *Helios* 18 (1): 15–30.

Lateiner, Donald. 1984. "Mythic and Non-mythic Artists in Ovid's *Metamorphoses*." *Ramus* 13 (1): 1–30.

Leach, Eleanor Winsor. 1974. "Ekphrasis and the Theme of Artistic Failure in Ovid's *Metamorphoses*." *Ramus* 3 (1): 102–42.

Leaf, Walter, ed. 1900. *The* Iliad. Vol. 1. London: Macmillan.

Leigh, Matthew. 1995. "Wounding and Popular Rhetoric at Rome." *Bulletin of the Institute of Classical Studies* 40: 195–216.

Lightfoot, J. L., ed. 1999. *Parthenius of Nicaea: The Poetical Fragments and the* Ἐρωτικὰ Παθήματα. Oxford: Clarendon Press.

Luck, Georg. 1969. *The Latin Love Elegy*. 2nd ed. London: Methuen.

Lyne, R. O. A. M. 1984. "Ovid's *Metamorphoses*, Callimachus, and l'Art pour l'Art." *Materiali e Discussioni per l'Analisi dei Testi Classici* 12: 9–34.

Mack, Sara. 1988. *Ovid*. New Haven: Yale University Press.

Makowski, John F. 1996. "Bisexual Orpheus: Pederasty and Parody in Ovid." *Classical Journal* 92 (1): 25–38.

Maltby, Robert. 1991. *A Lexicon of Ancient Latin Etymologies*. Leeds: Francis Cairns.

McKay, Alexander G. 1998. "*Non Enarrabile Textum*? The Shield of Aeneas and the Triple Triumph in 29 BC (*Aen.* 8.630–728)." In *Vergil's Aeneid: Augustan Epic and Political Context*, ed. Hans-Peter Stahl, 199–221. London: Duckworth.

Michalopoulos, Andreas. 2001. *Ancient Etymologies in Ovid's* Metamorphoses. Leeds: Francis Cairns.

Michelini, Ann Norris. 1987. *Euripides and the Tragic Tradition*. Madison: University of Wisconsin Press.

Miller, John F. 1990. "Orpheus as Owl and Stag: Ovid *Met.* 11.24–27." *Phoenix* 44 (2): 140–47.

Milowicki, Edward J. 1996. "Reflections on a Symbolic Heritage: Ovid's Narcissus." *Syllecta Classica* 7: 155–66.

Morgan, Kathleen. 1977. *Ovid's Art of Imitation: Propertius in the* Amores. Leiden: Brill.

Morris, Sarah P. 1992. *Daidalos and the Origins of Greek Art.* Princeton: Princeton University Press.

Myers, K. Sara. 1994a. "*Ultimus Ardor*: Pomona and Vertumnus in Ovid's *Met.* 14.623–771." *Classical Journal* 89 (3): 225–50.

———. 1994b. *Ovid's Causes: Cosmogony and Aetiology in the* Metamorphoses. Ann Arbor: University of Michigan Press.

Mynors, R. A. B., ed. 1985 [1969]. *P. Vergili Maronis Opera.* Oxford: Clarendon Press.

Nagle, Betty Rose. 1988a. "Two Miniature *Carmina Perpetua* in the *Metamorphoses:* Calliope and Orpheus." *Grazer Beiträge* 15: 99–125.

———. 1988b. "Ovid's 'Reticent' Heroes." *Helios* 5 (1): 23–39.

———. 1988c. "Erotic Pursuit and Narrative Seduction in Ovid's *Metamorphoses.*" *Ramus* 17 (1): 32–51.

Newlands, Carole E. 1997. "The Metamorphosis of Ovid's Medea." In *Medea: Essays on Medea in Myth, Literature, Philosophy, and Art,* ed. James J. Clauss and Sarah Iles Johnston, 178–208. Princeton: Princeton University Press.

Nicoll, W. S. M. 1980. "Cupid, Apollo, and Daphne (Ovid, *Met.* 1.452 ff.)." *Classical Quarterly* n.s. 30 (2): 174–82.

Nisbet, R. G. M., and Margaret Hubbard. 1970. *A Commentary on Horace:* Odes, *Book I.* Oxford: Clarendon.

———. 1978. *A Commentary on Horace:* Odes, *Book II.* Oxford: Clarendon.

O'Bryhim, Shawn. 1988. "Nestor: Wit or Windbag at *Metamorphoses* 12." *Augustan Age* 8: 49–53.

Otis, Brooks. 1964. *Virgil: A Study in Civilized Poetry.* Oxford: Clarendon Press.

———. 1970. *Ovid as an Epic Poet.* 2nd ed. Cambridge: Cambridge University Press.

Palmer, L. R. 1988 [1954]. *The Latin Language.* Norman: University of Oklahoma Press.

Papathomopoulos, Manolis, ed. 1968. *Antoninus Liberalis: Les* Metamorphoses. Paris: Les Belles Lettres.

Pavlock, Barbara. 1990. *Eros, Imitation, and the Epic Tradition.* Ithaca: Cornell University Press.

———. 2003. "Ulysses' Exploitation of Etymological Puns in *Metamorphoses* 13." In *Etymologia: Studies in Ancient Etymology,* ed. Christos Nifadopoulos, 143–51. Münster: Nodus.

Peradotto, John. 1990. *Man in the Middle Voice: Name and Narration in the* Odyssey. Princeton: Princeton University Press.

Perkell, Christine. 1989. *The Poet's Truth: A Study of the Poet in Virgil's* Georgics. Berkeley: University of California Press.

Perkins, Caroline A. 1993. "Love's Arrows Lost: Tibullan Parody in *Amores* 3.9." *Classical World* 86 (6): 459–66.

Pichon, René. 1902. *De sermone amatorio apud Latinos elegiarum scriptores.* Paris: Hachette.

Pöschl, Viktor. 1960. "Der Katalog der Bäume in Ovids Metamorphosen." In *Medium aevum vivum: Festschrift für Walter Bulst,* ed. Hans Robert Jauss and Dieter Schaller, 13–21. Heidelberg: Carl Winter. Reprinted in *Ovid,* ed. Michael von Albrecht and Ernst Zinn. Darmstadt: Wissenschaftliche Buchgesellschaft, 1968.

Pucci, Pietro. 1980. *The Violence of Pity in Euripides' Medea.* Ithaca: Cornell University Press.

———. 1987. *Odysseus Polutropos: Intertextual Readings in the* Odyssey *and the* Iliad. Ithaca: Cornell University Press.

Putnam, Michael C. J. 1986. *Artifices of Eternity: Horace's Fourth Book of* Odes. Ithaca: Cornell University Press.

———. 1987. "Daedalus, Virgil, and the End of Art." *American Journal of Philology* 108 (2): 173–98.

Quint, David. 1989. "Repetition and Ideology in the *Aeneid.*" *Materiali e Discussioni per l'Analisi dei Testi Classici* 23: 9–54. Reprinted in *Epic and Empire: Politics and Generic Form from Virgil to Milton,* 50–96. Princeton: Princeton University Press, 1993.

Randall, J. G. 1979. "Mistresses' Pseudonyms in Latin Elegy." *Liverpool Classical Monthly* 4 (2): 27–35.

Rhorer, Catherine C. 1980. "Red and White in Ovid's *Metamorphoses:* The Mulberry Tree in the Tale of Pyramus and Thisbe." *Ramus* 9 (1): 79–88.

Rosati, Gianpiero. 1983. *Narciso e Pigmalione: Illusione e spettacolo nelle* Metamorfosi di Ovidio. Florence: Sansoni.

———. 1999. "Form in Motion: Weaving the Text in the *Metamorphoses.*" In *Ovidian Transformations: Essays on the* Metamorphoses *and Its Reception,* ed. Philip Hardie, Alessandro Barchiesi, and Stephen Hinds, 240–53. Cambridge: Cambridge University Press.

———. 2002. "Narrative Techniques and Narrative Structures in the *Metamorphoses.*" In *Brill's Companion to Ovid,* ed. Barbara Weiden Boyd, 271–304. Leiden: Brill.

Rose, H. J. 1991 [1959]. *A Handbook of Greek Mythology.* New York: Penguin.

Rosner-Siegel, Judith. 1982. "*Amor,* Metamorphosis and Magic: Ovid's Medea (*Met.* 7.1–424)." *Classical Journal* 77 (3): 231–43.

Schein, Seth. 1984. *The Mortal Hero: An Introduction to Homer's* Iliad. Berkeley: University of California Press.

Segal, Charles. 1969. *Landscape in Ovid's* Metamorphoses: *A Study in the Transformation of a Literary Symbol.* Wiesbaden: Franz Steiner.

———. 1982. "*Nomen Sacrum:* Medea and Other Names in Senecan Tragedy." *Maia* 34 (2): 241–46.

————. 1989. *Orpheus: The Myth of the Poet*. Baltimore: Johns Hopkins University Press.

————. 1998. "Ovid's Metamorphic Bodies: Art, Gender, and Violence in the *Metamorphoses*." *Arion* n.s. 5 (3): 9–41.

————. 1999. "Ovid's Meleager and the Greeks: Trials of Gender and Genre." *Harvard Studies in Classical Philology* 99: 301–40.

Sharrock, Alison. 1991. "Womanufacture." *Journal of Roman Studies* 81: 36–49.

————. 1994. *Seduction and Repetition in Ovid's* Ars Amatoria *II*. Oxford: Clarendon Press.

————. 2002. "Ovid and the Discourses of Love: The Amatory Works." In *The Cambridge Companion to Ovid*, ed. Philip Hardie, 150–62. Cambridge: Cambridge University Press.

Simmons, Charles, ed. 1920 [1899]. *P. Ovidii Nasonis:* Metamorphoseon. Bks. 13 and 14. 2nd ed. London: Macmillan.

Smith, R. A. 1997. *Poetic Allusion and Poetic Embrace in Ovid and Virgil*. Ann Arbor: University of Michigan Press.

Solodow, Joseph B. 1988. *The World of Ovid's* Metamorphoses. Chapel Hill: University of North Carolina Press.

Spencer, Richard A. 1997. *Contrast as Narrative Technique in Ovid's* Metamorphoses. Lewiston, N.Y.: Edwin Mellen Press.

Stirrup, Barbara E. 1976. "Ovid's Narrative Technique: A Study in Duality." *Latomus* 35 (1): 97–107.

Tarrant, R. J. 2002. "Ovid and Ancient Literary Theory." In *The Cambridge Companion to Ovid*, ed. Philip Hardie, 13–33. Cambridge: Cambridge University Press.

————, ed. 2004. *P. Ovidi Nasonis:* Metamorphoses. Oxford: Clarendon Press.

Thomas, M. D. 1998. "Ovid's Orpheus: Immoral Lovers, Immortal Poets." *Materiali e Discussioni per l'Analisi dei Testi Classici* 40 (1): 99–109.

Thomas, Richard F., ed. 1988. *Virgil:* Georgics. Vol. 2, bks. 3 and 4. Cambridge: Cambridge University Press.

Thompson, D'Arcy W. 1936. *A Glossary of Greek Birds*. Oxford: Oxford University Press.

Tissol, Garth. 1997. *The Face of Nature: Wit, Narrative, and Cosmic Origins in Ovid's* Metamorphoses. Princeton: Princeton University Press.

Vincent, Michael. 1994. "Between Ovid and Barthes: *Ekphrasis*, Orality, Textuality in Ovid's 'Arachne.'" *Arethusa* 27: 361–86.

Vinge, Louise. 1967. *The Narcissus Theme in Western Literature up to the Early 19th Century*. Lund, Sweden: Gleerups.

Warden, John. 1980. *Fallax Opus: Poet and Reader in the Elegies of Propertius*. Toronto: University of Toronto Press.

Warmington, E. H., ed. and trans. 1979 [1935]. *Remains of Old Latin*. Vol. 2. Cambridge, Mass.: Harvard University Press.

Watson, Patricia. 1983. "Ovid *Amores* 2, 7 and 8: The Disingenuous Defense." *Wiener Studien* n.s. 17: 91–103.

Wheeler, Stephen M. 1995. "*Imago Mundi:* Another View of the Creation in Ovid's *Metamorphoses.*" *American Journal of Philology* 116 (1): 95–121.

———. 1999. *A Discourse of Wonders: Audience and Performance in Ovid's* Metamorphoses. Philadelphia: University of Pennsylvania Press.

———. 2000. *Narrative Dynamics in Ovid's* Metamorphoses. Tübingen: Gunter Narr Verlag.

Wilkinson, L. P. 1955. *Ovid Recalled.* Cambridge: Cambridge University Press.

Williams, Frederick, ed. 1978. *Callimachus,* Hymn to Apollo: *A Commentary.* Oxford: Clarendon Press.

Williams, Gordon. 1994. *Banished Voices: Readings in Ovid's Exile Poetry.* Cambridge: Cambridge University Press.

Williams, R. D. 1964. "The Sixth Book of the *Aeneid.*" *Greece and Rome* n.s. 11 (1): 48–63.

Wills, Jeffrey. 1989. "Callimachean Models for Ovid's Apollo-Daphne." *Materiali e Discussioni per l'Analisi dei Testi Classici* 24: 143–56.

Wise, Valerie. 1977. "Flight Myths in Ovid's *Metamorphoses:* An Interpretation of Phaethon and Daedalus." *Ramus* 6 (1): 44–59.

———. 1982. "Ovid's Medea and the Magic of Language." *Ramus* 11 (1): 16–25.

Wyke, Maria. 1989. "Mistress and Metaphor in Augustan Elegy." *Helios* 16 (1): 25–47. Reprinted in *The Roman Mistress: Ancient and Modern Representations,* 11–45. Oxford: Clarendon Press, 2002.

Zgoll, Christian. 2004. *Phänomenologie der Metamorphose: Verwandlung und Verwandtes in der Augusteischen Dichtung.* Tübingen: Gunter Narr Verlag.

Zimmerman, Clayton. 1994. *The Pastoral Narcissus: A Study of the First Idyll of Theocritus.* Lanham, Md: Rowman and Littlefield.

Zissos, Andrew. 1999. "The Rape of Proserpina in Ovid *Met.* 5.341–661: Internal Audience and Narrative Distortion." *Phoenix* 53 (1–2): 97–113.

Zumwalt, Nancy. 1977. "*Fama Subversa:* Theme and Structure in Ovid *Metamorphoses* 12." *California Studies in Classical Antiquity* 10: 209–22.

Index

Achaemenides, 134–35

Achelous: and contest with Hercules, 83–86; double nature as river god and swollen stream, 66, 76; as host of Theseus, 76–77, 87–88; as narrator of the tale of Erysichthon, 78–83; and shame over his broken horn, 86–87

Adonia, 100–103, 171n38. *See also* Adonis; Hyacinthia

Adonis: as audience of Venus's tale of Atalanta and Hippomenes, 92–96; and interchangeability with Venus, Atalanta, and Hippomenes, 92; metamorphosis of, 99–102, 172n43; promise of ritual for, as substitute for Cupid, 96–98

Ajax: as hero of traditional values, 110–12; hubris of, 111–12. *See also* Porcius Latro

Alcidamas, 50–51

Alexandrianism. *See* Hellenistic poetics

Althaea, torment of, 73–74, 162n36

Antoninus Liberalis, 50, 52, 53, 154n30, 155nn 31, 35

Apollo, 17–18, 23, 102–3, 140n27, 141n5, 145n34, 175n7

Apollonius, *Argonautica*, 39–40, 45–48, 79, 153nn 16–21, 23, 154n28

Arachne, as complex artist and surrogate for the poet, 3–6, 138nn 7–10, 139nn 16–18. *See also* paradox

Atalanta: as fleet maiden and object of desire by Hippomenes, 91–94, 167nn 13, 14, 168n15, 174n56; as participant in the Calydonian boar hunt and object of desire by Meleager, 72–73, 174n57; and relationship of the two Atalantas, 168n17

Autolycus, cunning of, 114–15, 176n14, 177n17. *See also* Ulysses

Callimachus, 4, 154n30, 155n34, 164n46; *Aetia*, 51–52, 138n13, 145n35, 154n29; *Epigrams*, 156n37; *Hecale*, 77–79, 163nn 42–44; *Hymn to Apollo*, 66, 154n29, 160n18; *Hymn to Delos*, 79; *Hymn to Demeter*, 63, 163n45, 164n46

Calliope, as poet figure, 7–8, 139n23

Catullus, 16, 33, 142nn 7, 8, 9, 11, 148n63

centrifugal, 4, 6, 7, 129, 137–38n6

centripetal, 4, 7, 111, 137–38n6

Cinyras, 36, 58, 90. *See also* Myrrha

WISCONSIN STUDIES IN CLASSICS

General Editors
William Aylward, Nicholas D. Cahill, and Patricia A. Rosenmeyer

---

E. A. THOMPSON
Romans and Barbarians: The Decline of the Western Empire

JENNIFER TOLBERT ROBERTS
Accountability in Athenian Government

H. I. MARROU
A History of Education in Antiquity
Histoire de l'Education dans l'Antiquité, translated by George Lamb

ERIKA SIMON
Festivals of Attica: An Archaeological Commentary

G. MICHAEL WOLOCH
Roman Cities: Les villes romaines by Pierre Grimal, translated and edited by G. Michael Woloch, together with A Descriptive Catalogue of Roman Cities by G. Michael Woloch

WARREN G. MOON, editor
Ancient Greek Art and Iconography

KATHERINE DOHAN MORROW
Greek Footwear and the Dating of Sculpture

JOHN KEVIN NEWMAN
The Classical Epic Tradition

JEANNY VORYS CANBY, EDITH PORADA, BRUNILDE SISMONDO RIDGWAY, and TAMARA STECH, editors
Ancient Anatolia: Aspects of Change and Cultural Development

ANN NORRIS MICHELINI
Euripides and the Tragic Tradition

JUDITH LYNN SEBESTA and LARISSA BONFANTE, editors
The World of Roman Costume

JENNIFER LARSON
Greek Heroine Cults

WARREN G. MOON, editor
Polykleitos, the Doryphoros, and Tradition

PAUL PLASS
The Game of Death in Ancient Rome: Arena Sport and Political Suicide

MARGARET S. DROWER
Flinders Petrie: A Life in Archaeology

SUSAN B. MATHESON
Polygnotos and Vase Painting in Classical Athens

JENIFER NEILS, editor
Worshipping Athena: Panathenaia and Parthenon

PAMELA A. WEBB
Hellenistic Architectural Sculpture: Figural Motifs in Western Anatolia and the Aegean Islands

BRUNILDE SISMONDO RIDGWAY
Fourth-Century Styles in Greek Sculpture

LUCY GOODISON and CHRISTINE MORRIS, editors
Ancient Goddesses: The Myths and the Evidence

JO-MARIE CLAASSEN
Displaced Persons: The Literature of Exile from Cicero to Boethius

BRUNILDE SISMONDO RIDGWAY
Hellenistic Sculpture II: The Styles of ca. 200–100 B.C.

PAT GETZ-GENTLE
Personal Styles in Early Cycladic Sculpture

CATULLUS
DAVID MULROY, translator and commentator
The Complete Poetry of Catullus

BRUNILDE SISMONDO RIDGWAY
Hellenistic Sculpture III: The Styles of ca. 100–31 B.C.

ANGELIKI KOSMOPOULOU
The Iconography of Sculptured Statue Bases in the Archaic and Classical Periods

SARA H. LINDHEIM
Mail and Female: Epistolary Narrative and Desire in Ovid's Heroides

GRAHAM ZANKER
Modes of Viewing in Hellenistic Poetry and Art

ALEXANDRA ANN CARPINO
Discs of Splendor: The Relief Mirrors of the Etruscans

TIMOTHY S. JOHNSON
A Symposion of Praise: Horace Returns to Lyric in Odes IV

JEAN-RENÉ JANNOT
Religion in Ancient Etruria
Devins, Dieux et Démons: Regards sur la religion de l'Etrurie antique,
translated by Jane K. Whitehead

CATHERINE SCHLEGEL
Satire and the Threat of Speech: Horace's Satires, Book 1

CHRISTOPHER A. FARAONE and LAURA K. MCCLURE, editors
Prostitutes and Courtesans in the Ancient World

PLAUTUS
JOHN HENDERSON, translator and commentator
Asinaria: The One about the Asses

PATRICE D. RANKINE
Ulysses in Black: Ralph Ellison, Classicism, and African American Literature

PAUL REHAK
JOHN G. YOUNGER, editor
Imperium and Cosmos: Augustus and the Northern Campus Martius

PATRICIA J. JOHNSON
Ovid before Exile: Art and Punishment in the Metamorphoses

www.ingramcontent.com/pod-product-compliance
Lightning Source LLC
Chambersburg PA
CBHW060837100426
42814CB00016B/405/J